Hilary T. Hudson

The Methodist Armor

A Popular Exposition of the Doctrines, Peculiar Usages and Ecclesiastical Machinery

of the Methodist Episcopal Church, South

Hilary T. Hudson

The Methodist Armor
A Popular Exposition of the Doctrines, Peculiar Usages and Ecclesiastical Machinery of the Methodist Episcopal Church, South

ISBN/EAN: 9783337812560

Printed in Europe, USA, Canada, Australia, Japan

Cover: Foto ©Lupo / pixelio.de

More available books at **www.hansebooks.com**

THE
METHODIST ARMOR;

OR,

A POPULAR EXPOSITION

OF THE

Doctrines, Peculiar Usages, and Ecclesiastical Machinery of the Methodist Episcopal Church, South.

By HILARY T HUDSON., DD.,

North Carolina Conference.

Revised and Enlarged.

NASHVILLE, TENN.:
SOUTHERN METHODIST PUBLISHING HOUSE.
PRINTED FOR THE AUTHOR.
1884.

TO THE

METHODISTS OF NORTH CAROLINA,

THIS VOLUME IS

Most Respectfully and Affectionately Inscribed

BY

H. T. HUDSON.

PREFACE.

THE design of this little book is to give a condensed view of the prominent doctrines, peculiar usages, and polity of the Methodist Episcopal Church, South. The Articles of Faith and the General Rules are given also, with Scripture quotations and explanatory notes. The book, putting into a small compass what lies scattered in many volumes of Methodist authors, is especially intended to meet the wants of the popular masses adhering to Methodism.

THE AUTHOR.

SHELBY, N. C., April, 1882.

CONTENTS.

CHAPTER		PAGE
	Introduction...	7, 8
I.	Origin of Methodism in England—The First Methodist Society—Rev. John Wesley, the Founder.	9–12
II.	Origin of Methodism in America—The First Methodist Society—The First Annual Conference—The Organization of the Church—Historical Statement—Validity of Methodist Ordination	12–21
III.	Articles of Religion (with Scripture Quotations and Notes)	21–54
IV.	The General Rules (with Scripture Quotations and Notes)	54–90
V.	Prominent Doctrines of Methodism—Universal Redemption — Repentance — Justification Through Faith — Regeneration — Witness of the Spirit—Holiness, or Sanctification—The Possibility of Final Apostasy....	90–116
VI.	Orders in the Methodist Ministry—Deacons—Elders—Bishops	116–118
VII.	The Mode of Baptism—Baptism of Paul—Baptism of the Jailer—Baptism of Cornelius—Baptism of the Three Thousand	118–126
VIII.	Objections Answered—Buried with Him in Baptism—The Baptism of Christ—John Baptizing in Jordan—Bapto and Baptidzo	126–134
IX.	Infant Baptism—As Taught in the Old Testament—Christ's Recognition of Infant Membership—The Apostles Preached the Doctrine of Infant Church-membership— Family Baptisms — The Jailer's Family—Historical Statement—Objections.	135–142
X.	Government of the Church—General, Annual, District, Quarterly, and Church Conferences	143–148
XI.	Church Officers—In the Ministry: Bishops, Presiding Elders, Pastors, Local Preachers—Lay Officers of the Church: Exhorters, Class-leaders, Stewards, Trustees, Superintendents of Sunday-schools	148–156

CHAPTER		PAGE
XII.	Peculiar Usages of Methodism—Class-meetings—The Itinerancy—Love-feast	156–162
XIII.	Ministerial Support—The Divine Law on the Support of the Ministry—The Immense Benefits Arising from the Diffusion of the Gospel—The Cheapness of Preaching—The Ability of the People to Pay—The Amount to be Given, etc.	162–199
XIV.	Church-membership—Who are Admitted into the Methodist Church?—Penitent Seekers—The Introduction of Baptized Children into the Church—The Duty of Joining the Church	199–223
XV.	Methodism and Sunday-schools—Origin—Eminent Usefulness of these Schools—Statistics	223–227
XVI.	Methodism and Revivals—What is a Revival?—Benefits of Revivals—The Agencies to be Used in Securing a Revival—The Coöperation of the People with the Preachers—The Transcendent Importance of Revivals—Hinderances to a Revival	227–246
XVII.	Methodism and Missions—The Genius of Methodism is Missionary—Facts that should Stir our Missionary Zeal—Statistics	246–252
XVIII.	Methodism and Education—Statistics	252–255
XIX.	Acts of the General Conference to 1844—Organization of the Methodist Episcopal Church, South—Bishops—Deceased Bishops—Statistics, 1882.	255–275
XX.	General Summary of Methodists	276–281
XXI.	The Apostolic Features of the Methodist Church	281–294
XXII.	The Training of Children in Christian Homes—The Religion of Methodists Ought to be Transmitted to and Reproduced in their Children—The Family Life and Habits of Methodists	294–311
XXIII.	A Model Christian and a Loyal Methodist	311–319
XXIV.	Loyalty to Your Own Church—The Glory of Methodism	319–329
	APPENDIX: World-wide View of Methodism	330–342

INTRODUCTION
BY REV. L. L. HENDREN, D.D.

METHODISM had its birth in an age of sharp and searching controversy, and, in reaching its present distinguished position among the Protestant denominations, every inch of ground was fiercely contested. Its prominent doctrines, peculiar usages, and polity, were frequently and publicly discussed; therefore, the multitudes had better and more clearly defined views of the distinctive features of Methodism than in this age of tacit fraternity, the tendency of which is to conventionalism. These subjects being now less frequently discussed in a controversial way, there exists a lamentable ignorance on these points. Many otherwise intelligent persons have not the inclination, or, having that, have not the patience, to persevere in such a research as would be necessary to gain the proper information. The necessity for a book containing this in a comprehensive and condensed form has been long and painfully felt, resulting often in a loss of members to our Church. Other denominations have their distinctive dogmas clearly expressed and formulated, while ours are found only in our scholastic and theological works. The author of the book which we now introduce to the reader, feeling this absolute necessity, has most opportunely and successfully met this great need of the Church and the people. He gives us a concise history of the rise and progress of Methodism in England and America, and also of its chief instruments. This puts the reader in possession of the proper historical information at the very outset, enabling him to appreciate more fully the subjects discussed. The "validity of Methodist ordination" is stated in the simplest, clearest, and most conclusive manner, adducing facts and testimonials which refute unanswerably the assumptions of Highchurchism. The Articles of Religion, General Rules, and prominent doctrines are presented in a most convenient and scriptural way for the general reader. The brief, striking manner of bringing out the fact that there are but two orders of the ministry by divine right will be highly interesting and instructive. The arguments on the mode and fit subjects of baptism are so scriptural, simple, and conclusive as to satisfy and convince all who are not blinded by prejudice. On the subject of Church government, and peculiar usages of Methodism, the author is unusually happy, clear, and forcible in his explanation of the powers and functions of the several Conferences, and the peculiar advantages of the itinerant ministry. On the support of the ministry he takes the ground that the tenth of the income is still required. He gives cogent arguments and reasons in regard to the obligation of sustaining the gospel, supported by many strong and striking facts and illustrations. He shows the great blessings and benefits accruing to those who devise liberal things for the temporal comfort of those who minister in holy things, which, at the same time, contribute largely to the efficiency and usefulness of the ministry. He especially shows the great intellectual and spiritual benefits of a well-supported and efficient clergy. The chapter on Church-membership is a clear, sound, and scriptural statement of this important subject. If carefully studied, it will certainly remove a great deal of error prevalent with the masses on this question. The people will read with pleasure and profit the Methodistic origin of Sunday-schools and revivals, as integral parts of our Church, their missionary spirit, and their power for good. Missions and education, as essential elements of Methodism, have been succinctly and satisfactorily discussed. The treatment of the apostolic features of Methodism—the thorough training of children, and attaching them more firmly to our Church—is comprehensive and conclusive. The reader will find in this book *multum in parvo*—"the sincere milk," "the living bread," and "strong meat" of Methodist doctrine and polity.

We honestly advise every Methodist to buy, carefully read, and study the "Methodist Armor," for its intrinsic merit, its necessity, its compactness and cheapness. Dr. Hudson was peculiarly fortunate in the suggestive name of his admirable little book. Incased in this armor, with a thorough knowledge and skillful use of the weapons furnished, the young as well as the old Methodist soldier can meet and defeat on every field any human or Satanic foe.

L. L. HENDREN.

STATESVILLE, N. C., January, 1883.

THE METHODIST ARMOR.

CHAPTER I.

ORIGIN OF METHODISM IN ENGLAND.

The History of Methodism began in the year 1729. It was born in the University of Oxford, England. While at college, John Wesley, Charles Wesley, and George Whitefield, and a few others, banded themselves together for the purpose of intellectual and spiritual improvement. So systematic were these young men in their habits of religious duty that the gayer students in derision called them

METHODISTS.

So the disciples of Christ were first called "Christians" at Antioch by a deriding world; yet the name was so appropriate that they gloried in it. And since Methodism has wrought out such a glorious history, none of her followers are ashamed of her name.

1739. THE FIRST METHODIST SOCIETY

was organized in London by Mr. Wesley. It began with about ten persons, and soon swelled up to hundreds. A great revival soon began to spread over the British realm. It was a work of great depth and duration.

"It came sweeping along like the winds which God had let loose from his fists, swaying devout souls, breaking down stubborn sinners, overturning hopes built on false foundations, but quenching not the smoking flax, nor breaking the bruised reed. It was Heaven's bountiful gift to the silent prayer of the world's sorrow by reason of its great sin. In the midst of this spiritual darkness, God raised up a bishop, a preacher, a poet: three men the equals of whom have probably never been seen in the world at once since the apostolic days. The bishop was John Wesley, the preacher was George Whitefield, the poet was Charles Wesley. To these three men, and those whom they gathered to their standard, did the Lord commit the precious work of awaking the British kingdom to a sense of God and duty, and by them he wrought a reformation which stands alone as a spiritual revival without admixture of State-craft or patronage of parliament or king."

Methodism began with experimental religion in the heart, and by spontaneous energies from within projected itself out into organic forms of life, such as class-meetings, love-feasts, Conferences, the itinerancy, and Church polity. This is the philosophy of the Methodist economy. It is the power of divine life clothing itself with such organic functions as are necessary to perpetuate and spread itself through the world. In ten years the outlines of the coming Church were already prepared. Societies were formed, quarterly-meetings held, Annual Conferences assembled, and preachers exchanged, and Methodism began her glorious career.

REV. JOHN WESLEY, THE FOUNDER.

The illustrious Founder of Methodism was born June 14, 1703, in the parish of Epworth, Lincolnshire. He was descended from a long line of able ministers. "When God sets out to make a great man, he first makes a great woman." This is eminently true in the case of John Wesley. His mother, Susannah Wesley, was a woman of strong intellect, fine culture, deep piety, and rare domestic qualities. John Wesley came of good stock. His father was a preacher before him. He entered college at the age of seventeen, and came out a distinguished graduate of one of the most famous universities of the world. His intellectual training was of the highest order. *A happy and thorough conversion* marked his religious experience. He says: "*I felt my heart strangely warmed. I felt I did trust in Christ alone for salvation; an assurance was given me that he had taken away my sins, even mine, and saved me from the law of sin and death.*" Before he knew what religion was theologically, now he knows what it is *experimentally*. From this time on he is a new man full of power and the Holy Ghost. His intellectual faculties kindled up into a luminous condition, and his spiritual vision was clear and comprehensive. The enthusiasm growing out of his experience went with him, and caught material everywhere for new flame and fervor. The torch of Mr. Wesley's experience set the world on fire, which has glowed and spread from that day till now. The celestial fire which warmed his heart is the light of the world.

John Wesley died in 1791, exclaiming, "*The best of all is—God is with us!*"

As beautiful as the summer sunset in a cloudless sky was the death of Mr. Wesley. The sun of his long life, beautiful in the morning of youth, radiant at the noon of manhood, after shining almost a century to enlighten and make fruitful the earth, went down in full-orbed glory, gilding the world left behind with the reflected splendor of its departing rays.

"I consider him as the most influential mind of the last century, the man who will have produced the greatest results centuries hence," said Southey. "No man has risen in the Methodist Society equal to their founder, John Wesley," said Dean Stanley. "A greater poet may arise than Homer or Milton, a greater theologian than Calvin, a greater philosopher than Bacon, a greater dramatist than any of ancient or modern fame, *a greater revivalist of the Churches than John Wesley—never!*" said Dr. Dobbins of the Church of England. "As Mount Everest lifts its tall head not only above every other peak of the Himalayas, but above the tallest peak of every other mountain in the wide world, so John Wesley, as a revivalist and reformer, towers not only above the other great men of Methodism, but above the greatest in all other Churches of Christendom," said Dr. J. O. A. Clark. Though not a century and a half have elapsed since he founded the Methodist Church, yet no less than *fifteen millions* of persons, including communicants and adherents to his systems, are his followers.

CHAPTER II.

ORIGIN OF METHODISM IN AMERICA.

THE Methodism which swept through England as a spreading fire over a field of dry stubble soon crossed the Atlantic and began to glow and burn in America.

1766. THE FIRST METHODIST SOCIETY.

It was organized by Philip Embury, a local preacher, in the city of New York. Barbara Heck, a Christian woman, has the honor of being the prime mover in the work. Embury and Barbara Heck were emigrants from Ireland—originally of German stock. Robert Strawbridge, from Ireland also, organized a Methodist society in Maryland about the same time. These two local preachers were greatly assisted in their work by a British officer named Captain Webb. The first Methodist church was built in John street, New York, 1768. The society consisted of but five members. As green forests sleep in the tiny cup of acorns, so grand possibilities slumbered in this mustard-seed of vital religion.

1769. Richard Boardman and Joseph Pilmore, the first itinerant preachers sent out by Mr. Wesley, arrived in America; the former was stationed at John Street Church, New York, and the latter as pastor in Philadelphia.

1771. Francis Asbury and Richard Wright came. The latter soon returned to England, but Mr. Asbury remained, and became the most memorable and influential man in American Methodism.

1773. THE FIRST ANNUAL CONFERENCE
was held in Philadelphia. The roll of names: Thos. Rankin, R. Boardman, J. Pilmore, Francis Asbury, R. Wright, George Shadford, Thomas Webb, John King, A. Whitworth, Joseph Yearby. Thomas Rankin presided. The business was simple and brief. It consisted mainly in the agreement of the preachers to abide by the doctrines and discipline of Mr. Wesley. There were then but ten traveling preachers, six circuits, and eleven hundred and sixty members.

1774. Robert Williams began to form societies in Virginia.

1776. The first circuit was organized in North Carolina, and called the "Carolina" Circuit.

Robert Williams came from England; landed in America, 1769. To him belongs the honor of introducing Methodism into Virginia and North Carolina. He was a rousing preacher, and instrumental in the salvation of many souls.

1777-78. The whole country was seething and boiling over with the war-spirit of the Revolution, yet great revivals prevailed in the south-eastern part of Virginia and in the counties of Halifax and Warren in North Carolina. Eighteen hundred souls were added to the societies in one year.

1784. THE ORGANIZATION OF THE CHURCH.

The "Methodist Episcopal Church" was formally organized at a conference of Methodist ministers called by Thomas Coke, LL.D., an assistant of Mr. Wesley in England, and sent over by the latter for the purpose of consummating such organization. The first bishops, Coke and Asbury, were elected by the Conference (called the Christmas Conference) which met in Baltimore, Dec. 25, 1784, and continued its session until Jan. 2, 1785.

HISTORICAL STATEMENT

The organization constituted it a valid Christian Church. The associations formed by Mr. Wesley and his preachers were originally called societies. They were voluntary associations of persons for mutual improvement in experimental and vital piety. They were still members of the Church of England; they attended its regular services and received the sacraments at its altars. Mr. Wesley himself continued during life a regular presbyter in that Church. The same state of things arose in America, and continued during the existence of the colonial government. Soon after the close of the Revolution most of the clergymen of the English Church, many of whom were Tories, returned to England. This left the Methodist people without sacraments. The preachers did not think themselves authorized to administer them, and appealed to Mr. Wesley for relief. He regarded the societies as sheep in a wilderness without a shepherd, and felt himself providentially called upon to provide for them proper pastoral care. Accordingly he ordained Dr. Coke, a presbyter of the Church of England, giving him authority to exercise the office of a bishop, calling him a superintendent, which is only another name for the same thing. Mr. Wesley sent Dr. Coke to America, directing him to ordain Francis Asbury to the same episcopal office. These two were to have a general superintendency of all the Methodist societies in America; they were to travel at large through the length and breadth of the land, and were to ordain elders, whose services were required by the exigences of the people.

Mr. Wesley prepared a form of Discipline for the use of the Methodists, which contained the Articles of Religion, the General Rules, a Ritual for ordination and other services of the Church. As already stated, the preachers assembled in General Conference, received Dr. Coke in his office as bishop, and elected Francis Asbury to the same office, in accordance with Mr. Wesley's direction. The Conference adopted the Discipline as their ecclesiastical constitution, and thus became a *regularly and a fully organized Christian Church*.

The Methodists of America were no longer mere societies within the pale of the English Church, but were themselves a properly constituted gospel Church of God. They are now "a congregation of faithful men in which the pure word of God is preached and the sacraments are duly administered according to Christ's ordinance, in all those things that of necessity are requisite to the same."

It is a Methodist *Episcopal* Church, not a Congregational nor a Presbyterian Church. It is a Church governed and superintended by bishops, who are elected and ordained to the work of the episcopacy.

It is sometimes said that Mr. Wesley did not intend to authorize the establishment of a Methodist *Episcopal* Church, and the proof alleged is that he called Dr. Coke and Asbury superintendents, and rebuked them for allowing themselves to be called bishops. The facts are, Mr. Wesley, in the beginning of his ministry, was a High-churchman, but the reading of Stillingfleet's "Irenicum" cured him of that belief. He entirely changed his views on this subject. He said: "I still believe the episcopal form of Church-government to agree with the practice and writings of the apostles, but that it is prescribed in Scripture I do not believe." He intended to give, and did give, the episcopal form of Church-government to the Methodist Church in America.

Mr. Wesley shunned the term bishop, and rebuked Mr. Asbury for wearing it, because of the worldly pride, pomp, and ostentation with which that word was connected in the English Church. But the thing intended by the term when properly applied he approved by giving the same when he ordained Coke and sent him to ordain Asbury and organize the Methodist Church under the government of the episcopacy.

VALIDITY OF METHODIST ORDINATION.

1. The presbyters, or elders, of the New Testament exercised the power of ordination. Timothy was ordained by "the *laying on of the hands of the presbytery*," or body of elders. (1 Tim. iv. 14.) To deny that elders have the right to ordain is to run directly against the expressed declaration of the Bible. Of his power to ordain Mr. Wesley had no doubt. He says: "Lord King's account of the primitive Church convinced me, many years ago, that bishops and presbyters are the same order, and consequently have the same right to ordain. I have accordingly appointed Dr. Coke and Francis Asbury to be joint superintendents; as also Richard Whatcoat and Thomas Vasey to act as elders among them in North America, by baptizing and administering the Lord's Supper." In 1780, he said: "I verily believe I have as good a right to ordain as to administer the Lord's Supper." Luther, Calvin, Melanchthon, as well as Mr. Wesley, believed in the validity of presbyterial ordination.

2. There are two ordinations, a divine and a human. The divine is the call of God to preach the gospel. The Saviour called and sent the apostles out to preach. "Go ye into all the world and preach the gospel." Their ordination was the unction of the Holy Ghost. Human ordination recognizes the essential one of the Holy Ghost. When you can get the two, well and good; but if not, give us the divine, let who will have the human. The Churches, properly enough for the sake of order, license and ordain men to the work of the ministry, but no ecclesiastical authority can make

ministers. They only recognize the call of God. The chief and essential ordination then is of God; and wherever this exists it matters but little what the human ordination is. Mr. Wesley, called of God, and eminently qualified by intellectual and spiritual endowment, had, by reason of these endowments, and as being a founder of a great Church, as much right to ordain a ministry as any pope, patriarch, bishop, or archbishop, that ever performed that function. The true validity of the Methodist ministry is derived from Mr. Wesley, who was not only a presbyter in the English Church, but under God became an illustrious founder of a great evangelical Church of Christ. Richard Watson says: "The Reformed Churches held the call of the people the only essential thing to the validity of the ministry; and teach that ordination is only a ceremony which renders the call the more august and authentic. Accordingly, the Protestant Churches of Scotland, France, Holland, Switzerland, Germany, Poland, Hungary, Denmark, etc., have no episcopal ordination; for Luther, Calvin, Bucer, Melanchthon, and all the first reformers and founders of these Churches, who ordained ministers among them, *were themselves presbyters*, and no other." Thus it appears that all these Churches had no other ministry than such as was ordained by the *presbytery*. Mr. Watson goes on to say: "In opposition to episcopal ordination, they (Protestants) urge that Timothy was ordained 'by the laying on of the hands of the presbytery;' that Paul and Barnabas were ordained by certain prophets and teachers in the Church of Antioch, and not by bishops presiding in that city. (Acts xiii. 1–3.) Furthermore, it is a well-known fact that *presbyters* in the Church of Alexandria ordained even their own bishops for more than two hundred years in the earliest ages of Christianity. They further argue that bishops and presbyters are in Scripture the *same*," and therefore episcopal ordination means nothing more than presbyterial ordination. They are but two names for one and the same thing.

3. The theory of High-churchism affirms that the right of ordination is derived from an episcopal ordination transmitted in an unbroken succession from the apostles, and that without this so-called apostolic succession there can be no Church or lawful ministry. Consequently the Episcopalians claim to be the only true Church.

The alleged succession is not historically true. I mean that there has been no such unbroken succession of ordinations in the past. Such a succession cannot be proved; and it is morally certain that such an unbroken chain never existed. The world recently saw that the champions of popery could not even prove that St. Peter was ever at Rome, to say nothing of his ordinations. The facts already mentioned, that in the primitive Church several pastors took part in each ordination, and that the modern popish view of ordination was unknown, would naturally render it impossible to trace each ordination to any one bishop or presbyter. The Church-curate who comes with a printed list of his ecclesiastical pedigree up to the apostles must have wonderful confidence in the ignorance of those whom he expects to accept his list with unquestioning faith. Many eminent ministers and laymen of the English Church, who have made this subject a special study, have confessed that the historical succession is utterly untenable. Chillingworth said: "I am fully persuaded that there hath been no such succession." Lord Macaulay says: "Even if it were possible, which assuredly it is not, to prove that the Church had the apostolical orders in the third century, it would be impossible to prove that those orders were not in the twelfth century so far lost that no ecclesiastic could be certain of the legitimate descent of his own spiritual character. We see no satisfactory proof that the Church of England possesses apostolical succession."

Bishop Hoadly says: "It hath not pleased God in his providence to keep up any proof of the least probability, or moral possibility, of a regular uninterrupted succession; but there is a great appearance, and, humanly speaking, a certainty, to the contrary, that the succession hath often been interrupted." Dr. Comber, as quoted by Mr. Bleby, says: "There is neither truth nor certainty in the pretended succession of the first popes." Bishop Stillingfleet says: "Come we, therefore, to Rome, and here the succession is as muddy as the Tiber itself. . . . The succession so much pleaded by the writers of the primitive Church was not a succession of persons in apostolic power, but a succession of persons in apostolic doctrine." Archbishop Whately says: "There is not a minister in all Christendom who is able to trace up, with approach to certainty, his spiritual pedigree." John Wesley, whom Churchmen are so fond of quoting for the benefit of Methodists, says: "The uninterrupted succession I know to be a fable, which no man ever did or can prove." Let it be remembered that all these testimonies are from Churchmen, whom it would naturally gratify to find evidence of an unbroken succession, whatever might be their estimate of its value. Yet this is the dogma on the strength of which High-churchmen disfranchise non-episcopal Churches of their Christian birthrights.

CHAPTER III.
ARTICLES OF RELIGION.

THE Church being regularly organized and officered, the Articles of Religion were adopted as her standard of faith. The Twenty-five Articles of Religion were extracted by Mr. Wesley from the Thirty-nine Articles of the Church of England. We give these Articles, with Scripture quotations and such notes as tend to explain the meaning and importance of them.

I. OF FAITH IN THE HOLY TRINITY.

There is but one living and true God, everlasting, without body or parts; of infinite power, wisdom, and goodness; the maker and preserver of all things, both visible and invisible. And in unity of this Godhead, there are three persons of one substance, power, and eternity—the Father, the Son, and the Holy Ghost.

PROOFS.—"Hear, O Israel: The Lord our God is *one* Lord." (Deut. vi. 4.) "*One* God and Father of all." (Eph. iv. 6.) "But the Lord is the *true* God. He is the *living* God." (Jer. x. 10.) "From *everlasting to everlasting* thou art God." (Ps. xc. 2.) "God is a *Spirit*." (John iv. 24.) "The Lord God *omnipotent* reigneth." (Rev. xix. 6.) "To God only *wise*, be glory." (Rom. xvi. 27.) "The Lord is *good* to all; and his tender mercies are over all his works." (Ps. cxlv. 9.) "There are *three* that bear record in heaven, the Father, the Word, and the Holy Ghost." (1 John v. 7.)

NOTE.

The Creative Power of God.—"In the beginning

God created the heaven and the earth." The Bible assumes the existence of God. "The architect is simply named in the description of the building." It is left to the reader to see the eternal cause in the stupendous effect before him. There can be no effect without an adequate cause. This is a self-evident truth. Common sense leads men to believe that the existence of a house implies a builder; the picture implies a painter; a watch implies a watch-maker. So the existence of the world, the earth, sun, moon, and stars, implies an eternal Creator. This universe could not have built itself; such a supposition is a bold contradiction, because it implies the existence of a thing possessed of creative powers before it did exist.

II. OF THE WORD, OR SON OF GOD, WHO WAS MADE VERY MAN.

The Son, who is the Word of the Father, the very and eternal God, of one substance with the Father, took man's nature in the womb of the blessed Virgin; so that two whole and perfect natures—that is to say, the Godhead and manhood—were joined together in one person, never to be divided, whereof is one Christ, very God and very man, who truly suffered, was crucified, dead and buried, to reconcile his Father to us, and to be a sacrifice, not only for original guilt, but also for actual sins of men.

PROOFS.—"There is one God, and one Mediator between God and man, the man Christ Jesus." (1 Tim. ii. 5.) "In the beginning was the Word, and the Word was with God, and the Word was God." (John i. 1.) "The Word was made flesh, and dwelt among us, and we beheld his glory, the glory as of the only-begotten of the Father, full of grace and truth." (John i. 14.) "Forasmuch then as the children are partakers of flesh and blood, he also himself likewise took part of the same." (Heb. ii. 14.) "The Holy

Ghost shall come upon thee, and the power of the Highest shall overshadow thee." (Luke i. 35.)

NOTE.

Jesus Christ is God, being the Word, or Logos.—" In the beginning was the Word." "For in him dwelleth all the fullness of the Godhead, bodily." "For by him were all things created that are in heaven, and that are in earth, visible and invisible, whether they be thrones, or dominions, or principalities, or powers: all things were created by him, and for him. He is before all things, and by him all things consist:
For it pleased the Father that in him should all fullness dwell." (Col. i. 16–19.) If Christ created the world, then it follows necessarily that he is *older* than the world. The builder of a house must be *older* than the house. His *preëxistence* is thus established. *Christ is greater than the universe.* The maker is necessarily grander than the thing made. He is greater in extent, greater in power. His omnipresence stretches out far beyond the outskirts of this almost immeasurable universe. His omnipotence is greater than all the forces of nature. He calmed the winds that sweep in the wild rush of the tornado; he controls the lightning that shivers in splinters the sturdy oak. The earthquake, lifting a continent on its gigantic shoulders, he wielded to liberate Paul and Silas from imprisonment. *He is owner of all things.* Creation gives the most valid title to all things made. "For him all things were created." All temporal things are but as a scaffold used to build up the great temple of salvation among men.

III. OF THE RESURRECTION OF CHRIST.

Christ did truly rise again from the dead, and took

again his body, with all things appertaining to the perfection of man's nature, wherewith he ascended into heaven, and there sitteth until he return to judge all men at the last day.

PROOFS.—"Go quickly and tell his disciples that he is risen from the dead." (Matt. xxviii. 7.) "But he, whom God raised again, saw no corruption." (Acts xiii. 37.) "To this end Christ both died, and rose, and revived, that he might be Lord both of the dead and living; for we shall all stand before the judgment-seat of Christ." (Rom. xiv. 9, 10.) "But now is Christ risen from the dead, and become the first-fruits of them that slept." (1 Cor. xv. 20.)

NOTES.

1. *The resurrection of Christ was his glorification and the seal of his atoning work.*—It demonstrated his divinity. It established the truth of his own prediction, "Destroy this temple, and in three days I will raise it again." I lay down my life, that I may take it again. I have power to lay it down, and I have power to take it again." The resurrection was the infallible proof of his true Messiahship. For either he arose by his own power, and if he did then he was divine, or he was raised up by the power of the Father, and if this be so, then God sets his seal to his work, for God would not raise from the dead an impostor.

2. *His resurrection is a pledge of the future life of his people.*—On it depended the gift of the Spirit of life, the fruit of the ascension. The Lord rose again as the first-fruits of them that slept. "If we be dead with him, we shall also live with him." "Because I live, ye shall live also."

3. *The proofs of Christ's resurrection are abundant.*—Five times he showed himself alive on the day of his resurrection—to Mary Magdalene, to another company

of women, to Peter, to two disciples on their way to Emmaus, to the eleven; to St. Thomas in the prayer-meeting; then in Galilee; to seven, and to five hundred. They knew him by many infallible proofs. He showed them the marks of his hands and feet, even eating and drinking with his disciples, thus proving the verity of his body. The Holy Spirit confirmed their faith, for while Peter preached the risen Christ, "the Holy Ghost fell on all them that heard the word."

IV Of the Holy Ghost.

The Holy Ghost, proceeding from the Father and the Son, is of one substance, majesty, and glory, with the Father and the Son, very and eternal God.

PROOFS.—"Baptizing them in the name of the Father, and of the Son, and of the Holy Ghost." (Matt. xxviii. 19.) "When he, the Spirit of truth, is come, he will guide you into all truth." (John xvi. 13.) "The Spirit itself beareth witness with our spirit, that we are the children of God." (Rom. viii. 16.) "The *eternal* Spirit." (Heb. ix. 14.) "Holy men of God spake as they were moved by the Holy Ghost." (2 Pet. i. 21.)

Notes.

1. "The Christian creed receives and adores the mystery that one essence exists in a trinity of coëqual personal subsistences, related as the Father, the Eternal Son of the Father, and the Holy Ghost eternally proceeding from the Father and Son."

2. The personality and divinity of the Holy Spirit are set forth in the Old Testament Scriptures. As, "Let us make man in our image;" "And the Spirit of God moved upon the face of the waters." The Spirit of God is creative: "The Spirit of God hath made me, and the breath of the Almighty hath given me

life." He is no less active in providence: "My Spirit shall not always strive with man." He is omnipresent: "Whither shall I go from thy Spirit?"

3. The Holy Ghost is a divine person, distinct from the Father and the Son. He proceeds from the Father and the Son, and therefore can be neither; yet he is associated with the Father and the Son in the divine work of creating and preserving all things. The personal pronoun *he* is applied to one who is *another Comforter*: "When the Comforter is come, *whom* I will send unto you from the Father, even the Spirit of truth, who proceedeth from the Father, *he* shall testify of me."

V The Sufficiency of the Holy Scriptures for Salvation.

The Holy Scriptures contain all things necessary to salvation; so that whatsoever is not read therein, nor may be proved thereby, is not to be required of any man, that it should be believed as an article of faith, or be thought requisite or necessary to salvation. In the name of the Holy Scripture, we do understand those canonical books of the Old and New Testament, of whose authority was never any doubt in the Church. The names of the canonical books are Genesis, Exodus, Leviticus, Numbers, Deuteronomy, Joshua, Judges, Ruth, The First Book of Samuel, The Second Book of Samuel, The First Book of Kings, The Second Book of Kings, The First Book of Chronicles, The Second Book of Chronicles, The Book of Ezra, The Book of Nehemiah, The Book of Esther, The Book of Job, The Psalms, The Proverbs, Ecclesiastes, or the Preacher, Cantica, or Songs of Solomon, Four Prophets the greater, Twelve Prophets the less

All the books of the New Testament, as they are commonly received, we do receive and account canonical.

Proofs.—"The law of the Lord is perfect, converting the soul; the testimony of the Lord is sure, making wise the simple." (Ps. xix. 7.) "Search the Scriptures: *for in them ye think ye have eternal life;* and they are they which which testify of me." (John v. 39.) "From a child thou hast known the Holy Scriptures, *which are able to make thee wise unto salvation.*" (2 Tim. iii. 15.) "All Scripture is given by inspiration of God, and is profitable for doctrine, for reproof, for correction, for instruction in righteousness." (2 Tim. iii. 16.) "And receive with meekness the ingrafted word, which is able to save your souls." (James i. 21.)

Notes.

1. This Article teaches that the Bible is to be appealed to in the *final settlement of all questions of faith and practice.* It is the rule of faith and practice. "The Bible, the Bible is the religion of Protestants." But the Catholic Church teaches that "Scripture *and tradition,* and these explained by the Catholic clergy, are the rule of faith." The bulls of popes, filling eight volumes; the decretals, acts of councils, the acts sanctum, making *ninety* volumes; an unlimited mass of unwritten traditions, which have been accumulating, like drift-wood on a river, from the commencement of the Christian era up to the present time—all these cumbrous human inventions, added to the Bible, constitute the Catholic rule of faith. The Council of Trent decreed that these traditions, both written and unwritten, are of equal authority with the Bible, and he that denies this shall be accursed. But Methodism, in common with all Protestants, teaches that "the *Holy Scriptures contain all things necessary to salvation.*"

2. The Romanists oppose the *private reading* of the Bible as a sin. But we hold the truths of the Bible *are addressed to all*, and are comprehensible by all, and therefore the command "Search the Scriptures" is equally binding upon all. "The Word of God is the book of the common people; it is the workingman's book; it is the child's book; it is the slave's book; it is the book of every creature that is downtrodden; it is a book that carries with it the leaven of God's soul; it is a book that tends to make men larger, and better, and sweeter, and that succors them all through life. And do you suppose it is going to be lost out of the world? When the Bible is lost out of the world, it will be because there are no men in it who are in trouble and need succoring, no men who are oppressed and need release, no men who are in darkness and need light, no men who are hungry and need food, no men who are sinning and need mercy, no men who are lost and need the salvation of God. Let us therefore take the Word of God as our friend, and hold it to our heart, and make it the man of our counsel, our guide, the lamp to our feet, the light to our path. Use it, as God meant it to be used, as the soul's food and the soul's joy, and it shall be your life's rest."

VI. Of the Old Testament.

The Old Testament is not contrary to the New; for both in the Old and New Testament everlasting life is offered to mankind by Christ, who is the only Mediator between God and man, being God and man. Wherefore they are not to be heard who feign that the old fathers did look only for transitory promises. Although the law given from God by Moses, as touching ceremonies and rites, doth not bind Christians, nor ought the civil precepts thereof of necessity to be received in any Commonwealth, yet, notwithstanding, no Christian whatsoever is free from the obedience of the commandments which are called moral.

PROOFS.—"Beginning at Moses and all the prophets, he expounded unto them in *all* the Scriptures the things concerning himself. And he said unto them, These are the words which I spake unto you, while I was yet with you, that all things must be fulfilled, which were written in the *law of Moses*, and in the *prophets*, and in the *Psalms*, concerning me." (Luke xxiv. 27, 44–45.) "Think not that I am come to destroy the law, or the prophets; I am not come to destroy, but to fulfill." (Matt. v. 17.)

NOTE.

The *harmony* of the Old and New Testament is clearly seen in the fact that Christ and the apostles made frequent quotations from the former. Some writer has shown that about *ninety* quotations from the Old Testament are found in the teaching of Christ. To establish the resurrection against the Sadducees, Christ quotes from Ex. iii. 6; to establish the primitive institution of marriage, quotes from Gen. i. 27; to answer the question as to the great commandment, quotes from Deut. vi. 5; to show that David's Son was David's Lord, from Ps. cx. 1; to preach a sermon, from Isa. lxi. 1. Besides these, and many more, there are references in our Lord's discourses to Jonah as a type of the resurrection, to the brazen serpent, to the living water and manna in the desert, to Abel, Noah, Abraham, Lot, Solomon, Moses, Elijah, and Daniel. When tempted by the devil, his great weapon of defense was, "It is written." It is clear that Christ studied the Old Scriptures with devoted care, and made constant use of their truths in his teachings. "The two Testaments, Old and New, like two breasts of the same person, give the same milk." The river of salvation took its rise in the mountains of Judea, and descended into the plain of the gospel, and, like the Nile, spread beauty and fertility along its deepening and widening course.

VII. OF ORIGINAL OR BIRTH SIN.

Original sin standeth not in the following of Adam (as the Pelagians do vainly talk), but it is the corruption of the nature of every man that naturally is engendered of the offspring of Adam, whereby man is very far gone from original righteousness, and of his own nature inclined to evil, and that continually.

PROOFS.—"By one man sin entered into the world, and death by sin; and so death passed upon all men, for that all have sinned." (Rom. v. 12.) "By one man's disobedience many were made sinners." (Rom. v. 19.) "Behold, I was shapen in iniquity, and in sin did my mother conceive me." (Ps. li. 5.) "And were by nature the children of wrath, even as others." (Eph. ii. 3.)

NOTES.

1. The doctrine of the Pelagians was that children are born pure and innocent, and that they become corrupt by *outside* influences, by imitating or following evil examples, by vicious education and society.

2. "The orthodox view is that this native corruption is *derived from a sinful ancestry*, in whose loss of purity their whole posterity is involved. This view represents the depravity of human nature as coming from the laws of natural descent, the child inheriting from the parent a corrupt nature, prone to evil, in consequence of which he runs easily into open sin. 'Adam begat a son in his own likeness.' (Gen. v. 3.) 'Be-

hold, I was shapen in iniquity, and in sin did my mother conceive me.' (Ps. li. 5.) 'From *within*, out of the heart of men, proceed evil thoughts.' (Mark vii. 21.) On these passages, and others, the doctrine of original sin is based. There is nothing unreasonable in this doctrine. For it is well known that men *do* transmit bodily ailments and mental peculiarities to their children. Dishonest men tend to have dishonest children; thieves tend to breed thieves; murderers, murderers; drunkards, drunkards; insane men propagate insanity. 'He that soweth to the flesh shall of the flesh reap corruption.' Man, when he comes into the world, has seeds in his very nature—tendencies to act, and this in a particular way. Some of these are for good; some are decidedly toward evil. There is certainly an original sin—otherwise there would not be universal actual sin—among children as soon as they begin to act for themselves, and among men of all ages and countries. My view of this original sin is that it is very much like that tendency toward evil which is produced by a course of wickedness. Let a man go on in intemperance for a length of time, and this creates a craving for drink. It is said that when the father has been an habitual drunkard the son is apt to have an inclination toward bodily stimulants. This tendency of evil to propagate itself is inherited from the first transgressors, and has become hereditary."—*Dr. McCosh.*

3. *The moral status of children.*—"The benefits of Christ's death are coëxtensive with the sin of Adam (Rom. v. 18), hence all children dying in infancy partake of the free gift." "Infants are not indeed born justified; nor are they capable of that voluntary ac-

ceptance of the benefits of the free gift which is necessary in the case of adults; but, on the other hand, they cannot *reject* it, and it is by the rejection of it that adults perish. The *process* by which grace is communicated to infants is not revealed; the manner doubtless differs from that employed toward adults."
—*Watson.*

"Children are born into the world sustaining, through the atonement, such a relation to the moral kingdom of God as that they are proper subjects of God's regenerating grace, and those dying in infancy come into actual possession of all these blessings. They may now be prepared for and admitted into the kingdom by the grace of God. This is sufficiently evident from our Lord's words, 'Suffer the little children to come unto me, and forbid them not, for of such is the kingdom of heaven.'"—*Dr. Raymond.*

4. *How soon can we look for the conversion of our children?*—"There is absolutely no authority whatever in Scripture for the popular notion that a certain degree of mental and moral development is necessary before this gift of divine life can be imparted. We should pray for our children that, like John the Baptist, they may be filled with the Holy Ghost from their mother's womb. We should expect that, like Isaiah and Jeremiah, they will be sanctified from the cradle. How old must a rosebud be before it receives that life that enables it to blossom? It may be stunted, and dwarf and die—the blossom may never come. But the normal law of God is rosebud and blossom on every bush. Converted! Christ says, 'Except ye be converted, and become as little children, ye shall not enter the kingdom of heaven.' We reverse his saying. Our

reading to the children is, Except ye become as grown men, and be converted. The vine need not trail on the ground till it is ten years old, and then be trained on the trellis. The only way to insure a good peach is to cut back the stick that grows from the stone, and put on a new graft. In God's kingdom the best fruit grows from the stone. The son need not wander off from his father's home, spend his substance in riotous living, and eat the husks that the swine do feed on, in order to be acceptable to his father, and have the best robe, and the ring, and the fatted calf. The immeasurable love of God gives us this infinite grace, not because of our wanderings, but in spite of them. The Church will never make its best progress until it gets rid of this unscriptural idea—that the child must grow up recreant and be converted in maturity, that it must grow up outside the kingdom of God and be brought in late in life. What progress should we make in the common virtues if we were to proceed in the same philosophy?"

VIII. Of Free-will.

The condition of man after the fall of Adam is such, that he cannot turn and prepare himself, by his own natural strength and works, to faith, and calling upon God; wherefore we have no power to do good works, pleasant and acceptable to God, without the grace of God by Christ preventing us, that we may have a good will, and working with us, when we have that good will.

Proofs.—"I am the vine, ye are the branches. He that abideth in me, and I in him, the same bringeth forth much fruit; for without me ye can do nothing." (John xv. 5.) "For when ye were yet without strength, in due time Christ died for the ungodly."

(Rom. v. 6.) "You hath he quickened, who were dead in trespasses and sins." (Eph. ii. 1.)

Notes.

1. The term "preventing" has here the old English meaning of "going before and helping."

2. Man is convicted and converted by the power of the Holy Ghost, but the will of man must coöperate in the work. "Work out your own salvation with fear and trembling, for it is God which worketh in you both to will and to do of his good pleasure."

"The Divine Spirit is atmospheric, and it becomes personal whenever any person appropriates it. The sunlight has in it all harvests; but we do not reap a single thing until that sunlight is appropriated by some root, or some leaf, or some blossom, or something in the ground. The sunlight on the Sahara has neither wheat nor corn. These are only to be had in the field where seeds are planted, where the nature of the seeds works with the sunlight, and where the soil is quickened and stimulated by the heat and moisture that go with them. The divine influence works in men to will and to do by their nature, by their very law of organization; and when a man becomes converted, it is by both the divine influence and the exercise of his own energies; that is to say, they coöperate. It is a unitary, although a complex work.

"Some say that you must wait for the Spirit. Wait for the Spirit! How long must a man lie in bed waiting for the sunrise? The sun is up, and has been up an hour, two hours, five hours. It is noonday, it is afternoon, and the sluggard lies waiting for the sun to bring him out! How foolish it is when you apply it to any thing except a technically religious matter!

The Divine Spirit is like the mother's heart. It is universal and infinite. It is the mother-soul of the universe, with infinite power, and sweetness, and beauty, and glory, shining down upon all men, good and bad, high and low, ignorant and educated, and stimulating them to be better, to be nobler, to be higher; and what time any man accepts the influence of the Divine Spirit, and coöperates with it, that moment the work is done by the *stimulus* of God acting with the practical energy and will of the human soul."

IX. OF THE JUSTIFICATION OF MAN.

We are accounted righteous before God only for the merit of our Lord and Saviour Jesus Christ, by faith, and not for our own works or deservings: wherefore, that we are justified by faith only, is a most wholesome doctrine, and very full of comfort.

PROOFS.—{"For by grace are ye saved through faith; and that not of yourselves: it is the gift of God; not of works, lest any man should boast." }(Eph. ii. 8, 9.) "Therefore we conclude that a man is justified by faith without the deeds of the law." (Rom. iii. 28.) "Being justified by faith, we have peace with God through our Lord Jesus Christ." (Rom. v. 1.)

NOTES.

1. *Doctrine.*—The *originating cause* of justification is the free, spontaneous love of God. "God so loved the world that he gave his only-begotten Son, that whosoever believeth in him should not perish, but have everlasting life."

2. The *meritorious ground* of pardon is the atonement of Jesus Christ. It is *through Jesus Christ*. We are "justified by his blood." "Reconciled to God by the *death* of his Son." "Christ once suffered for sins."

3. *Personal faith is the instrumental cause* of justification. It is *through faith.* "Being justified by faith." Saving faith *excludes works* as a ground of justification. It is not by the *merit* of faith itself, but only by faith, as that which *embraces* and *appropriates* the merit of Christ. Faith is the *hand receiving* the gift of salvation.

Results: First, restoration to Divine favor. "We have peace with God." Second, *adoption* into the family of God. "If children, then heirs, heirs of God." "Whom he justifies, them he also glorifies."

X. Of Good Works.

Although good works, which are the fruits of faith, and follow after justification, cannot put away our sins and endure the severity of God's judgment; yet are they pleasing and acceptable to God in Christ, and spring out of a true and lively faith, insomuch that by them a lively faith may be as evidently known as a tree is discerned by its fruit.

Proofs.—"By the deeds of the law there shall no flesh be justified in his sight." (Rom. iii. 20.) "Not by works of righteousness which we have done, but according to his mercy he saved us." (Titus iii. 5.)

Notes.

1. The Bible clearly teaches that *faith in Christ* is the ground of salvation, but that good works are the measure of our reward. *Saved* by faith, but *preserved* by good works, is the true doctrine.

2. The above Article also levels its force against the Catholic doctrine of good works as having an atoning merit in them. Thus it was taught that when men made pilgrimages, went through a course of fasting, gave donations, repeated the *Credo,* the *Ave,* the *Pater*

Noster, these were set down to their credit as so much over against wrong-doing. They falsely assumed religion to be a mere business, conducted as the transactions of a man's store where books of debit and credit were kept.

3. While the Article cautions us as to the two particulars mentioned, it at the same time, in harmony with the teaching of the Scriptures, urges the necessity of maintaining good works as the evidence and fruits of regeneration. Good works may be defined to be *right motives flowing out into right actions*. Good works are the outward expression of good feelings. Grace in the heart is the fountain, the good works are the streams flowing from it. Love and good works are fountain and stream. And in proportion to the fullness of the lake of grace in the heart will be the greatness, beauty, and fertility of the rivers of good works flowing from it. A feeble fountain will produce a feeble stream.

XI. OF WORKS OF SUPEREROGATION.

Voluntary works, besides over and above God's commandments, which are called works of supererogation, cannot be taught without arrogancy and impiety. For by them men do declare that they do not only render unto God as much as they are bound to do, but that they do more for his sake than of bounden duty is required: whereas Christ saith plainly, When ye have done all that is commanded you, say, We are unprofitable servants.

PROOFS.—" Is it any pleasure to the Almighty, that thou art righteous? or is it gain to him, that thou makest thy ways perfect?" (Job xxii. 3.) "So likewise ye, when ye shall have done all those things which are commanded you, say, We are unprofitable servants: we have done that which was our duty to do." (Luke xvii. 10.)

NOTE.

The error of the Catholic Church against which this Article is directed teaches that "there is an immense treasure of merit, composed of the pious deeds of the saints, which they have performed beyond what was necessary for their own salvation, and which were applicable to the benefit of others." But the Bible teaches that the circle of *duty* takes in the entire ability of man, and therefore leaves no room for the works of supererogation. Out of the doctrine of supererogation came the wicked system of selling indulgences to commit sin, which so shocked Luther as moved him to begin and carry on the great work of the German Reformation.

XII. OF SIN AFTER JUSTIFICATION.

Not every sin willingly committed after justification is the sin against the Holy Ghost, and unpardonable. Wherefore, the grant of repentance is not to be denied to such as fall into sin after justification: after we have received the Holy Ghost, we may depart from grace given, and fall into sin, and, by the grace of God, rise again and amend our lives. And, therefore, they are to be condemned who say they can no more sin as long as they live here, or deny the place of forgiveness to such as truly repent.

PROOFS.—"Return, ye backsliding children, and I will heal your backslidings." (Jer. iii. 22.) "If any man sin, we have an advocate with the Father, Jesus Christ the righteous." (1 John ii. 1.) "If we confess our sins, he is faithful and just to forgive us our sins." (1 John i. 9.) "Remember therefore from whence thou art fallen, and repent, and do the first works." (Rev. ii. 5.)

NOTE.

This Article denies the dogma anciently taught by some, that every sin committed after justification is the sin against the Holy Ghost. The sin against the Holy Ghost is ascribing the miraculous works of Christ to the *agency* of the devil. The scribes said, "He (Christ) hath Beelzebub, and by the prince of devils casteth he out devils." And Christ, commenting on this charge, says: "But he that shall blaspheme against the Holy Ghost hath never forgiveness. *Because they* said, *He hath an unclean spirit.*" This unpardonable sin is that grade of wickedness and settled malignity, that hardening of the heart, which is not the result of ignorance, but of a deliberate, systematic, and persevering opposition to clearly demonstrated and unmistakable truth. It is not a state arrived at all at once, but is approached by a long series of willful resistances to the known truth, and is unpardonable, not because God withholds mercy to any truly penitent, but because all such have reached such a state of moral desperation *that they will not ask or receive pardon* on the conditions of the gospel. The unpardonable state is *in the man*, not in the unwillingness of God to forgive. The sign of this condition is utter moral insensibility. Wherever there is spiritual *sensibility* enough to make a man fear he has committed it, it is certain proof that he has not.

XIII. OF THE CHURCH.

The visible Church of Christ is a congregation of faithful men, in which the pure word of God is preached, and the sacraments duly administered, according to Christ's ordinance, in all those things that of necessity are requisite to the same.

PROOFS.—" Unto the Church of God   to them that are sanctified in Christ Jesus, called to be saints, with all that in every place call upon the name of Jesus Christ our Lord, both theirs and ours." (1 Cor. i. 2.) "And he gave some, apostles; and some, prophets; and some, evangelists; and some, pastors and teachers; for the perfecting of the saints, for the work of the ministry, for the edifying of the body of Christ." (Eph. iv. 11, 12.)

NOTES.

1. The definition of a Church given in the above Article is broad and comprehensive. In the analysis we have: (1) A congregation of *faithful men*. (2) The recognition of the *Bible*, or the pure Word of God, as the rule of faith and practice. (3) The recognition of the *living ministry* to preach and expound this word. (4) The *sacraments* (Baptism and the Lord's Supper) properly administered. These are the *four* corner-stones of the Church which Christ founded on the rock—his own divine character. The definition harmonizes perfectly with the elements found in the apostolic Church as described in the Acts of the Apostles; and allows all Methodists to recognize all other denominations as being gospel Churches that come in the scope of the above definition.

2. Denominational exclusiveness grows out of a *false* definition of what a gospel Church is. To illustrate, the Romish authority defines a Church thus: "The company of Christians knit together by the profession of the same faith, and communion of the same sacraments, under the government of lawful pastors, and especially of the Roman bishop as the only vicar of Christ on earth." Thus it makes the supremacy of the Pope an essential element of a gospel Church. Consequently, it would logically follow that the Cath-

olic is the only true Church. Hence Romish bigotry. The Baptists define: "A visible Church of Christ is a congregation of *baptized* (immersed) believers," etc. This definition cuts off all Churches whose members are not immersed. Hence their exclusiveness.

XIV OF PURGATORY.

The Romish doctrine concerning purgatory, pardon, worshiping and adoration, as well of images as of relics, and also invocation of saints, is a fond thing, vainly invented, and grounded upon no warrant of Scripture, but repugnant to the word of God.

PROOFS.—"Who can forgive sins but God only?" (Mark ii. 7.) "Thou shalt not make unto thee any graven image." (Ex. xx. 4.) "Thou shalt worship the Lord thy God, and him only shalt thou serve." (Matt. iv. 10.)

NOTE.

This Article condemns a cluster of Romish errors. The first is that of *purgatory*. The doctrine of the Romish purgatory implies a *second* probation for certain men. But the Bible teaches that there is no second probation after death. "In the place where the tree falleth, there it shall be." (Eccl. xi. 3.) "He that is unjust, let him be unjust still; and he which is filthy, let him be filthy still." (Rev. xxii. 11.) "Whatsoever a man soweth, that shall he also reap." We are cleansed from sin, not by purgatorial fires, but by *the blood of Christ*. There is not a single passage of Scripture, properly expounded, favoring this doctrine.

The second error is *priestly absolution*. God alone exercises the right to pardon sin. "Who can forgive sins but God only?" (Mark ii. 7.)

The third error is *image-worship*, which is positively forbidden. "Thou shalt not make unto thee any graven image," etc. "I fell down to worship before the feet of the *angel* which shewed me these things. Then saith he unto me, See thou do it not, for I am thy fellow-servant: *worship God.*" (Rev. xxii. 8, 9.)

The fourth error is *praying to departed saints* to intercede in behalf of men on earth. This doctrine makes saints *sub-mediators* between God and men, whereas the Word teaches, "There is one God, and *one* Mediator between God and men, the man Christ Jesus." (1 Tim. ii. 5.)

XV Of Speaking in the Congregation in Such a Tongue as the People Understand.

It is a thing plainly repugnant to the Word of God, and the custom of the primitive Church, to have public prayer in the church, or to minister the sacraments, in a tongue not understood by the people.

PROOFS.—"He that speaketh in an unknown tongue, speaketh not unto men, but unto God: for no man understandeth him. In the church I had rather speak *five* words with my understanding than *ten thousand* words in an unknown tongue." (1 Cor. xiv. 2, 19.)

NOTE.

This Article justly condemns the Roman Catholic practice of reading the service in the Latin language to English congregations. It is "plainly repugnant to the word of God." To conduct the public prayers of the Church in an unknown tongue is not only contrary to common sense, but to the custom of the primitive Church. In 202 A.D., Origen says: "The Grecians pray to God in the Greek, the Romans in the Roman, and every one in his own tongue." "The modern practice of intoning prayers and other parts of religious worship is also unintelligible, and opposed to reasonable service."

XVI. OF THE SACRAMENTS.

Sacraments, ordained of Christ, are not only badges or tokens of Christian men's profession, but rather they are certain signs of grace, and God's good-will toward us, by the which he doth work invisibly in us, and doth not only quicken, but also strengthen and confirm our faith in him.

There are two sacraments ordained of Christ our Lord in the gospel; that is to say, Baptism and the Supper of the Lord.

Those five commonly called sacraments—that is to say, confirmation, penance, orders, matrimony, and extreme unction—are not to be counted for sacraments of the gospel, being such as have partly grown out of the corrupt following of the apostles; and partly are states of life allowed in the Scriptures, but yet have not the like nature of baptism and the Lord's Supper, because they have not any visible sign or ceremony ordained of God.

The sacraments were not ordained of Christ to be gazed upon, or to be carried about; but that we should duly use them. And in such only as worthily receive the same they have a wholesome effect or operation; but they that receive them unworthily purchase to themselves condemnation, as St. Paul saith, 1 Cor. xi. 29.

PROOFS.—Christ ordained but two positive sacraments—Baptism and the Lord's Supper. (See Matt. xxviii. 19; Matt. xxvi. 26, 1 Cor. xi. 23.)

NOTE.

The five sacraments of the Catholic Church are confirmation, penance, orders, matrimony, and extreme unction. *Confirmation* in the Roman Church is a service by which those baptized in infancy publicly take upon themselves the obligations of the baptismal covenant, and voluntarily confirm and recognize their Church-membership. The service in itself is proper enough, but not such in solemn dignity as to entitle it to be placed in the same rank with baptism and the Lord's Supper. The same may be said of "orders," or the ordination ceremony of the ministry, and of matrimony. *Roman penance* is a service by which a penitent, having sinned and made auricular confession, the priest grants pardon for sins committed after baptism. This so-called sacrament is founded upon the assumption that the priest has power to forgive sin, which Protestantism regards as blasphemous. *Extreme unction* is a service consisting in anointing with holy oil persons at the point of death, by which sins are forgiven and grace imparted.

XVII. Of Baptism.

Baptism is not only a sign of profession and mark of difference whereby Christians are distinguished from others that are not baptized, but it is also a sign of regeneration, or the new birth. The baptism of young children is to be retained in the Church.

Proofs.—"Arise, and be baptized, and wash away thy sins, calling on the name of the Lord." (Acts xxii. 16.) "Except a man be born of water and of the Spirit, he cannot enter into the kingdom of God." (John iii. 5.) "He that believeth and is baptized shall be saved." (Mark xvi. 16.)

Notes.

A brief argument in favor of infant baptism will be found in another place.

This Article defines baptism to be:

1. *A sign of profession.* It is a profession of faith in Jesus Christ as the Son of God. When a person makes a profession of faith, baptism is a *sign* of that profession and a pledge of loyalty to God and the Church. It is a profession of faith in all the fundamental doctrines of salvation as taught by Christ. " See, here is water; what doth hinder me to be baptized? And Philip said, If thou believest with all thine heart, thou mayest. And he answered and said, I believe that Jesus Christ is the Son of God. and he baptized him." (Acts viii. 36.)

2. *Baptism is "a mark of difference whereby Christians are distinguished from others that are not baptized."* The Jew was distinguished from the Gentile by the significant mark or sign of circumcision. In the Christian Church, baptism in the name of the Trinity takes the place of circumcision. By circumcision the Jew entered into the Jewish Church; by baptism we enter into the Christian Church.

3. *" It is also a sign of regeneration."* The cleansing water is a fit sign of the cleansing power of the Holy Ghost.

XVIII. OF THE LORD'S SUPPER.

The Supper of the Lord is not only a sign of the love that Christians ought to have among themselves one to another, but rather is a sacrament of our redemption by Christ's death; insomuch that, to such as rightly, worthily, and with faith receive the same, the bread which we break is a partaking of the body of Christ; and likewise the cup of blessing is a partaking of the blood of Christ.

Transubstantiation, or the change of the substance

of bread and wine in the Supper of the Lord, cannot be proved by Holy Writ, but is repugnant to the plain words of Scripture, overthroweth the nature of a sacrament, and hath given occasion to many superstitions.

The body of Christ is given, taken, and eaten in the Supper only after a heavenly and spiritual manner. And the means whereby the body of Christ is received and eaten in the Supper is faith.

The sacrament of the Lord's Supper was not by Christ's ordinance reserved, carried about, lifted up, or worshiped.

PROOFS.—"And he took bread, and gave thanks, and brake it, and gave unto them, saying, This is my body which is given for you: this do in remembrance of me. Likewise also the cup after supper, saying, This cup is the new testament in my blood, which is shed for you." (Luke xxii. 19, 20.)

NOTES.

1. *Names.* It is called the "Lord's Supper" because it was first instituted in the evening, and at the close of the passover supper. It is called a "sacrament," which means an oath of renewed allegiance to Christ. It is called the "eucharist," which means the giving of thanks. "He took bread and gave thanks." A "communion" to express Christian fellowship.

2. *The import of the Supper is a commemoration.* "This do in remembrance of me." It took the place of the passover, which commemorated the deliverance of the Israelites from Egyptian bondage. The suffering of Christ delivers the world from Satanic bondage. A father once kept a canceled bond for his family to look upon, and see how he had paid a heavy debt, through much self-sacrifice, to make them happy. So Christ has canceled the claim of justice against us,

"nailing it to his cross." In the Lord's Supper his family look upon this bond.

3. *Transubstantiation is a Romish absurdity.* Being in bodily person in heaven, and at the right-hand of the throne of the Father, Christ cannot at the same time be visibly and bodily in the hands of the priests, nor on hundreds of altars at once. The expression "This is my body" is a Hebraism for "This *represents* my body." It is clearly a figure, as "I am the vine," "I am the door," "I am the way," "The seven good kine are seven years." Besides, if the bread and wine be actually changed into the real flesh and blood of Christ, how could these material things nourish and feed the soul, which is a spiritual substance?" "It is the Spirit that quickeneth, the flesh profiteth nothing" in feeding the soul. While the Lutherans renounce the doctrine of *tran*substantiation, they affirm a *con*substantiation, which is akin to the real presence of the Catholics. But in the light of common sense both the *tran* and the *con* are alike contrary to truth. The true doctrine is, a sacrament is a holy ordinance instituted by Christ, wherein, by sensible signs, Christ and the benefits of the new covenant are *represented, sealed*, and *applied* to believers. The sacrament is to be taken after a heavenly and spiritual manner. Its benefit depends upon the faith of the communicant. The astronomer does not worship the telescope, but looks *through* it out and beyond to the stars in the heavens. So the bread and wine are as a telescope through which the eye of faith looks to Christ dying on the cross for the sins of the world. "*This do in remembrance of me.*"

XIX. Of Both Kinds.

The cup of the Lord is not to be denied to the lay

people, for both the parts of the Lord's Supper, by Christ's ordinance and commandment, ought to be administered to all Christians alike.

PROOFS.—"He took the cup, and gave thanks, and gave it to them (the disciples), saying, *Drink ye all* of it." (Matt. xxvi. 27.) "For as often as ye (believers in common) eat this bread, and *drink this cup*, ye do show the Lord's death till he come. But let a man (the believer) examine himself, and so let him eat of that bread, and *drink* of that cup." (1 Cor. xi. 26, 28.)

NOTE.

Both the bread and the wine were originally administered by our Lord to the apostles, and both elements were ordered to be given to the lay people until the coming of Christ. The command is, *Drink, all* of you. Surely Paul was not addressing the clergy when he wrote his Epistle to the Corinthian Church, in which he said, "Let a man examine himself, and so let him eat of that bread, and *drink of that cup.*"

This Romish error grows out of the greater one of transubstantiation. The papists teach that after the bread and wine are changed into the flesh and blood of Christ, he is whole and entire in either bread or wine, and so, whatever part the communicant may receive, he receives the whole Christ. Therefore that Church has decreed to give "the laity only in one kind." And whoever does not believe with that Church, it says "Let him be *accursed.*"

XX. OF THE ONE OBLATION OF CHRIST FINISHED UPON THE CROSS.

The offering of Christ, once made, is that perfect redemption, propitiation, and satisfaction, for all the sins of the whole world, both original and actual; and there is none other satisfaction for sin but that alone.

Wherefore the sacrifice of masses, in which it is commonly said that the priest doth offer Christ for the quick and the dead, to have remission of pain or guilt, is a blasphemous fable, and dangerous deceit.

PROOFS.—"So Christ was *once* offered to bear the sins of many." (Heb. ix. 28.) "Knowing that Christ being raised from the dead *dieth no more.* For in that he died, he died unto sin *once.*" (Rom. vi. 9, 10.) "Neither is there salvation in any other: for there is *none other name* under heaven given among men, whereby we must be saved." (Acts iv. 12.) "There remaineth *no more sacrifice for sins.* (Heb. x. 26.) "After he had offered *one* sacrifice for sins forever, sat down on the right-hand of God; for by *one offering* he hath perfected forever them that are sanctified." (Heb. x. 12, 14.)

NOTE.

This Article condemns as a blasphemous fable the dogma of the Catholic Church which affirms that Christ is offered afresh for sin every time the mass is celebrated, and teaches the Protestant doctrine that Christ made *but one offering* of himself for sin, and that this offering is perfect, complete in every respect, and forever *final.* Therefore "the Romanist sacrifice of the mass has no sanction, but is utterly condemned in the Epistle to the Hebrews."

XXI. OF THE MARRIAGE OF MINISTERS.

The ministers of Christ are not commanded by God's law either to vow the estate of single life or to abstain from marriage; therefore it is lawful for them, as for all other Christians, to marry at their own discretion, as they shall judge the same to serve best to godliness.

PROOFS.—The Apostle Peter was a married man. "When Jesus was come into Peter's house, he saw his *wife's* mother laid, and sick of a fever." (Matt. viii. 14.) Philip the evangelist "had four daughters, virgins, which did prophesy." (Acts xxi. 9.) Paul says "A bishop then must be blameless, the *husband* of *one wife*." (1 Tim. iii. 2.) "Let the deacons be the *husbands* of *one wife*." (1 Tim. iii. 12.) "Have we not *power* to lead about a *wife*, as well as other apostles?" (1 Cor. ix. 5.)

NOTE.

But the Church of Rome has commanded her ministers not to marry, which command they strictly obey. And forbidding to marry is a sign of an apostate church. (1 Tim. iv. 1–3.) But the Roman Church not only forbids marriage to her clergy, but has exalted the marriage of the laity to the unscriptural dignity of a sacrament. What bold absurdities and gross errors!

XXII. OF THE RITES AND CEREMONIES OF CHURCHES.

It is not necessary that rites and ceremonies should in all places be the same, or exactly alike, for they have been always different, and may be changed according to the diversity of countries, times, and men's manners, so that nothing be ordained against God's word. Whosoever, through his private judgment, willingly and purposely, doth openly break the rites and ceremonies of the Church to which he belongs, which are not repugnant to the word of God, and are ordained and approved by common authority, ought to be rebuked openly, that others may fear to do the like, as one that offendeth against the common order of the Church, and woundeth the consciences of weak brethren.

Every particular Church may ordain, change, or abolish rites and ceremonies, so that all things may be done to edification.

PROOFS.—"As free, and not using your liberty for a cloak of

maliciousness, but as the servants of God." (1 Pet. ii. 16.) "Let every man be fully pursuaded in his own mind." (Rom. xiv. 5.) "Let all things be done unto edification." (1 Cor. xiv. 26.) "The kingdom of God is not meat and drink." (Rom. xiv. 17.)

NOTES.

1. The *doctrines* and *institutions* of the Christian religion are *positive* and *unchangeable*, while her rites and ceremonies are circumstantial. Baptism may be administered by pouring or immersion; the elements of the Lord's Supper may be received sitting or kneeling; prayers may be offered in public kneeling or standing; we may stand or sit in singing, etc.

2. This Article opposes the Catholics, who maintain that the authority of the Church is supreme, and whatever rite she may ordain, though it becomes obsolete and useless, is of supreme and endless obligation. It teaches that whenever a ceremony becomes a hinderance to the real progress of the Church, it is to be laid aside. When new ones are needed they are to be used. The *law of expediency* is to reign as to these matters.

3. This Article also teaches that when rites and ceremonies are "ordained and approved" by the proper authorities of the Church, they are not to be tampered with by private individuals. No person is allowed, "through his private judgment," to set them aside. This secures uniformity of Church ceremonies.

XXIII. OF THE RULERS OF THE UNITED STATES OF AMERICA.

The President, the Congress, the General Assemblies, the Governors, and the Councils of State, *as the delegates of the people*, are the rulers of the United States of America, according to the division of power made to them by the Constitution of the United States, and by the constitution of their respective States. And the said States are a sovereign and independent nation, and ought not to be subject to any foreign jurisdiction.

PROOFS.—"Let every soul be subject unto the higher powers. For there is no power but of God; the powers that be are ordained of God. For rulers are not a terror to good works, but to the evil. For he is the minister of God to thee for good." (Rom. xiii. 1–4.)

NOTES.

"As far as it respects civil affairs, we believe it the duty of Christians, and especially all Christian ministers, to be subject to the supreme authority of the country where they may reside, and to use all laudable means to enjoin obedience to the powers that be; and, therefore, it is expected that all our preachers and people, who may be under any foreign government, will behave themselves as peaceable and orderly subjects."—*Note of the Discipline.*

The above Article was drawn up at the Conference in 1784, when the Church was organized, and incorporated in the body of the Articles in 1786, when the next edition of the Discipline was printed. The explanatory note was appended in 1820.

XXIV OF CHRISTIAN MEN'S GOODS.

The riches and goods of Christians are not common as touching the right, title, and possession of the same, as some do falsely boast. Notwithstanding, every man ought of such things as he possesseth liberally to give alms to the poor, according to his ability.

PROOFS.—"Thou shalt not steal." (Ex. xx. 15.) Stealing implies ownership of property. "Give to him that asketh thee, and from him that would borrow of thee turn not thou away." (Matt. v. 42.) Giving and lending necessarily imply the personal ownership of property. "But whoso *hath* this world's good, and seeth his brother hath need, and shutteth up his bowels of compassion from him, how dwelleth the love of God in him?" (1 John iii. 17.)

NOTES.

1. This Article was drawn up to counteract the teachings of the Anabaptists, who, soon after the Lutheran Reformation, preached "that all things ought to be common among the faithful."

2. The instance of community of goods mentioned in Acts ii. 44 was not such as modern communists advocate. That of the early Christians was *voluntary, local, and temporary*. There was no forcible division of property. Peter said to Ananias, "While it remained, was it not *thine own?* and after it was sold, was it not in thine own power?"—all of which shows that the common fund for benevolent purposes was made up by voluntary contributions. Besides, this instance was not general, but confined to the church at Jerusalem. No mention is made of any similar arrangement in the further history of the Church.

XXV. OF A CHRISTIAN MAN'S OATH.

As we confess that vain and rash swearing is forbidden Christian men by our Lord Jesus Christ and James his apostle, so we judge that the Christian religion doth not prohibit but that a man may swear when the magistrate requireth, in a cause of faith and charity, so it be done according to the prophet's teaching, in justice, judgment, and truth.

PROOFS.—"And thou shalt swear, The Lord liveth, in truth, in judgment, and in righteousness." (Jer. iv. 2.) "Men verily swear by the greater: and an oath for confirmation is to them an end of all strife." (Heb. vi. 16.) "And Jonathan caused David to swear again." (1 Sam. xx. 17.) "I call God for a record upon my soul." (2 Cor. i. 23.)

NOTE.

Judicial oaths are believed to be lawful by all Christians, except the Anabaptists, who flourished about the time this Article was originally drawn up, and the Quakers, and some minor sects. "Though it be said we shall not swear, yet I do not remember it is anywhere read that we should not receive or take an oath from another."—*St. Augustine.*

CHAPTER IV.

THE GENERAL RULES WITH SCRIPTURE QUOTATIONS AND NOTES.

These Rules may be divided into three classes:
1. Those forbidding the doing of evil.
2. Those enjoining the doing of good.
3. Those enforcing the use of the means of grace.

These Rules have become a part of the constitutional law of our Church, and are in perfect harmony with the Scriptures, being mainly apostolic rules of practical Christianity. And being such, no person is to be received into the Church who is unwilling to observe them. It is hardly necessary to state that these Rules contain no doctrinal statements, but only the fundamental principles relating to practical godliness.

These Rules are here arranged, classified, and numbered with the *Bible proofs* on which they are founded. It will be seen that there is not one Rule which is not based on Bible truth.

There is only one condition previously required of

those who desire admission into these societies, a "desire to flee from the wrath to come, and to be saved from their sins." But wherever this is really fixed in the soul, it will be shown by its fruits. It is therefore expected of all who continue therein, that they should continue to evidence their desire of salvation by observing the following Rules:

THE EVILS AND SINS TO BE AVOIDED.

Rule 1. By doing no harm, <u>by</u> avoiding evil of every kind, especially that which is most generally practiced.

BIBLE.—"Abstain from all appearance of evil." (1 Thess. v. 22.) "Be ye therefore wise as serpents, and harmless as doves." (Matt. x. 16.) "Abhor that which is evil; cleave to that which is good." (Rom. xii. 9.)

NOTE.

"Avoiding evil." You must keep at a distance from evil; go wide of it, and thus escape its snaring temptation. "Go not in the way of evil men. Avoid it; pass not by it; turn from it." "Stand in awe, and sin not." "Watch and pray, that ye enter not into temptation." Carry not sparks of fire into a magazine of gunpowder. Sleep not on the giddy height of seductive enticement. Pass not through a field, though it be decked with blooming flowers, where poisonous adders lurk. Let the beauty of harmlessness deck thy whole life as flowers deck the garden.

Rule 2. (Must avoid) The taking of the name of God in vain.

BIBLE.—"Thou shalt not take the name of the Lord thy God in vain; for the Lord will not hold him guiltless that taketh his name in vain." (Ex. xx. 7.)

NOTE.

" Irreverence for sacred things; playing the animal

with sanctities; the degradation of that which is higher than ordinary life, and which should lead men up from the lower depths of experience—that is as accursed as it would be to go through a gallery of art and slime the noblest paintings with mud, and deface or destroy the most magnificent marbles. No man would permit that. The whole world would cry out against the desecration of beauty in art under such circumstances. But men think themselves justified in drawing down the sanctities of heaven—those thoughts and feelings which have in them inspiration and elevation—and defiling them; and yet, here stands this commandment which covers the whole ground of vulgarizing things that are high, and that are necessary to lift men up from low associations. 'Thou shalt not take the name of the Lord thy God in vain' includes the whole latitude and longitude of the realm of thought and feeling in which there is the desecration of whatever is sacred."

Rule 3. (Must avoid) The profaning the day of the Lord, either by doing ordinary work therein, or by buying or selling.

BIBLE.—" Remember the Sabbath-day to keep it holy. Six days shalt thou labor and do all thy work; but the seventh day is the Sabbath of the Lord thy God; in it thou shalt not do any work, thou, nor thy son, nor thy daughter, nor thy man-servant, nor thy maid-servant, nor thy cattle, nor thy stranger that is within thy gates; wherefore, the Lord blessed the Sabbath-day and hallowed it." (Ex. xx. 8–11.)

NOTE.

Keep the Sabbaths holy, and they will be to you as green and refreshing oases blooming in the desert of your earthly pilgrimage. Our Sabbaths should be hills of light and joy in God's presence; and so, as time rolls on, we shall go on from mountain-top to mountain-top, till at last we catch the glory of the shining gate, and enter into the eternal Sabbath of perfect rest and joy. Let the Sabbath be a day of sweet rest and warm devotion; and the sacred influences generated by attendance on public worship will be as a river flowing down through the secular days of the week, spreading freshness and fertility along its course. A world without a Sabbath is a summer without its green lap full of flowers and fruits.

Rule 4. (Must avoid) Drunkenness, or drinking spirituous liquors unless in cases of necessity.

BIBLE.—" Be not among wine-bibbers; for the drunkard and glutton shall come to poverty." (Prov. xxxiii. 20.) "Wine is a mocker, strong drink is raging; whosoever is deceived thereby is not wise. Look not thou upon the wine when it is red at the last it biteth like a serpent and stingeth like an adder." (Prov. xxxiii. 31.) "Woe to him that giveth his neighbor drink, that putteth thy bottle to him, and maketh him drunk." (Hab. ii. 5.)

NOTES.

1. There are two kinds of wine mentioned in the Bible—one, which makes men drunk, is *condemned* everywhere; the other, meaning sweet wine, not *intoxicating*, is spoken of as a blessing. Keeping this fact in view it will not be hard to reconcile the seeming contradiction in the Bible where wine is sometimes condemned, and then again commended.

2. The new rule in the Discipline, enacted 1882, requires our "members to abstain from the manufacture and sale of intoxicating liquors as a beverage." It will be seen that the Methodist Church is squarely opposed to intemperance. It is a total abstinence Church. The making or selling liquor as a beverage

is classed with the sin of drunkenness. There is good reason for it. The making and selling have a close connection with the evils of intemperance. The origin is in making and selling. The still-houses make the poison; the grog-shops distribute it broadly over the land. The first is the deadly fountain, the latter is the channel circulating the liquid poison. The production and circulation of liquor is closely connected. The distillers are busy in loading the Satanic battery; the retail and wholesale dealers are busy in firing it off. The consequence is the battle-field of life runs red with the blood of the slain. Every still and grog-shop is a battery of death. Think of the appalling number of them! There are in the United States eight thousand four hundred and two distilleries and breweries (this is according to official report), and two hundred thousand grog-shops and liquor-saloons! And these batteries, under the generalship of Satan, loaded and fired day and night the year round, pouring bursting bombs, grape-shot, and other missiles of death into the ranks of our people, what wide-spread destruction is wrought!

The Cost of Intemperance.—The Presbyterian *Review* gives the following statistics for the United States: "Paid to all the ministers of the gospel, $12,000,000; support of criminals, $12,000,000; fees of litigation, $35,000,000; importation of liquor, $50,000,000; support of grog-shops, $1,500,000,000. Whole cost of liquor, $12,200,000,000."

Rule 5. (Must avoid) Fighting, quarreling, brawling, brother going to law with brother; returning evil for evil, or railing for railing; the using many words in buying or selling.

BIBLE.—"From whence come wars and fightings among you?

Come they not hence, even of your lusts that war in your members?" (James iv. 1.) "The works of the flesh are manifest, which are these: hatred, variance, emulations, strife, seditions, heresies." (Gal. v. 19.) "Dare any of you, having a matter against another, go to the law before the unjust and not before the saints?" (1 Cor. vi. 1-6.) "Not rendering evil for evil, or railing for railing, but contrariwise blessing." (1 Pet. iii. 9.) "Let your conversation be, without covetousness." (Heb. xiii. 5.) "Let your yea be yea, and your nay, nay, lest ye fall into condemnation." (James v. 12.)

NOTES.

1. "Of all things which are to be met with here on earth there is nothing which can give such continual, such cutting, such useless pain as an undisciplined temper. The touchy and sensitive temper, which takes offense at a word; the irritable temper, which finds offense in every thing, whether intended or not; the violent temper, which breaks through all bounds of reason when once roused; the jealous or sullen temper, which wears a cloud on the face all day, and never utters a word of complaint; the discontented temper, brooding over its own wrongs; the severe temper, which always looks at the worst side of whatever is done; the willful temper, which overrides every scruple to gratify a whim—what an amount of pain have these caused in the hearts of men, if we could but sum up their results! How many a soul have they stirred to evil impulses; how many a prayer have they stifled; how many an emotion of true affection have they turned to bitterness! How hard they make all duties! How they kill the sweetest and warmest of domestic charities! Ill-temper is a sin requiring long and careful discipline."—*Bishop Temple.*

2. A quarrel is stopped by letting the angry person have all the quarrel to himself. A soft answer will

extinguish a quarrel as water fire. Turn away from a querulous man as you would from the path of a roaring lion. When men carry magazines of powder in their temper, better not let the spark of your anger fall upon them. It is too late to avoid disaster when the explosion takes place. Nothing can prevent red ruin then. You must guard *beforehand*, or not at all. Watch and pray.

Rule 6. (Must avoid) The buying or selling goods that have not paid the duty.

BIBLE.—"Provide things honest in the sight of all men." (Rom. xii. 17.) "Render therefore unto Cæsar the things which are Cæsar's." (Matt. xxii. 21.) "Render therefore to all their dues." (Rom. xiii. 7.)

NOTE.

To smuggle goods into a country in violation of the revenue laws of the Government is the sin forbidden by this rule. To buy or sell goods known to be contraband is considered lawless robbery. This Rule condemns also the practice of cheating the Government of its just taxes, or revenues laid on the manufacture of liquors or tobacco, or any other article. Religion requires men to be as just to governments as they are to individuals. As the Government gives us the protection of liberty, life, property, and the pursuit of happiness, every man should obey its laws and cheerfully pay the taxes and revenues demanded.

Rule 7. (Must avoid) The giving or taking things on usury, *i. e.*, unlawful interest.

BIBLE.—"Lord, who shall abide in thy tabernacle? Who shall dwell in thy holy hill? He that putteth not his money to usury, nor taketh reward against the innocent." (Ps. xv. 1-5.) "That no man go beyond and defraud his brother." (1 Thess. iv. 6.)

NOTE.

The Hebrew word for *usury* means exorbitant interest. It means greediness, sharpness, rapacity, which takes advantage of the oppressed. The practice forbidden is receiving more for the loan of money than it is really worth, and more than the law allows.

Rule 8. (Must avoid) Uncharitable or unprofitable conversation, particularly speaking evil of magistrates or of ministers.

BIBLE.—"Let all clamor and evil-speaking be put away from you, with all malice." (Eph. iv. 31.) "Every idle word that men speak, they shall give account thereof in the day of judgment." (Matt. xii. 36.) "Let no corrupt communication proceed out of your mouth." (Eph. iv. 29.) "Put them in mind to be subject to principalities and powers, to obey magistrates to speak evil of no man." (Titus iii. 1, 2.)

NOTES.

Reasons for observing this Rule are:

1. It prevents much evil. "The tongue is a fire, a world of iniquity," when not governed. Like a swollen river whose embankments have given way, it spreads destruction through the country. "It is set on fire of hell," says the apostle. The Indians in the West sometimes set the dry grass afire, and it spreads and roars. The smoke darkens the sun. The running flame, caught up and fanned by the wind, circles far and wide, towering up almost mountain-high. Man and beast have to flee for their lives. It is a world of fire coming from a spark. So unruly tongues set whole neighborhoods to burn and flame with evils.

2. The practice of tale-bearing is *disgraceful*. To be known as a tale-bearer, a tattler, a gossip, a busybody in everybody's business, a backbiter, how mean

and low! A backbiter reminds one of a sneaking dog that makes the attack when your face is turned the other way. Backbiting is a doggish trick. It is said of Domitian that he, though a Roman emperor, "employed his leisure hours in catching and tormenting flies." Such work showed meanness and cruelty combined. And how much better are you employed in catching up and exposing all the little dirty rumors that buzz through your neighborhood?

3. It is a violation of the Golden Rule: "Whatsoever ye would that men should do to you, do ye even so to them." Do you wish men to speak well of you behind your back? Yes, of course you do. Then speak well of your neighbors. Dr. South said that the tale-bearer and listener ought both to be hanged—one by the tongue, the other by the ear.

Rule 9. (Must avoid) Doing to others as we would not they should do unto us.

BIBLE.—"Therefore all things whatsoever ye would that men should do to you, do ye even so to them: for this is the law and the prophets." (Matt. vii. 12.)

NOTE.

Whatsoever is disagreeable to thyself do not to thy neighbor. Treat your neighbor as you would have him treat you. Regard him as your other self. Make his case your own, put yourself into his place; divest yourself of that selfishness which would injure another. Every man desires to be esteemed as his merit deserves—desires his neighbor to be tender with his reputation, not to slander his good name, not to put harsh construction on his conduct, to be kindly disposed toward him, to deal justly, honestly, truthfully candidly with him, to be faithful as a friend and polite and honorable as an acquaintance; and as you desire such treatment from others, be sure to give it to them. "As you would that men should do to you, do ye even so to them." How ennobling and beautiful the observance of this Golden Rule would make the characters of men!

Rule 10. (Must avoid) Doing what we know is not for the glory of God; as the putting on of gold and costly apparel.

BIBLE.—"Whose adorning, let it not be that outward adorning of plaiting the hair, and of wearing of gold or of putting on of apparel." (1 Pet. iii. 3.) "I will that women adorn themselves in modest apparel, not with braided hair, or gold, or pearls, or costly array." (1 Tim. ii. 8, 9.)

NOTE.

This Rule forbids needless *extravagance* in *dress*, and *useless* and *showy ornaments*. The taste for the beautiful must be carefully limited by economical and religious considerations. The text quoted in support of the Rule is a standing rebuke to all ostentation in dress, and reminds every Christian woman that nothing can so adorn a woman as a beautiful character, fruitful of good works. Paul rebuked this extravagance of dress in his day, and it needs to be rebuked in our day, when we read that a certain woman wore a hundred thousand dollars' worth of diamonds on her dress while attending a charity ball. It is sad to see women thinking more of the glittering trinkets than a crown of glory. You may pamper and adorn the body with the flashing blaze of a thousand diamonds, yet remember that this beautiful form, stripped of its glittering jewelry, will be wrapped in a death-shroud, nailed up in a coffin, and become food for worms.

Rule 11. (Must avoid) The taking such diversions as cannot be used in the name of the Lord.

BIBLE.—"Wherefore come out from among them, and be ye separate, saith the Lord, and touch not the unclean thing; and I will receive you, and will be a father unto you, and ye shall be my sons and daughters." (2 Cor. vi. 17, 18.) "Be not conformed to this world." (Rom. xii. 2.) "Know ye not that the friendship of the world is enmity with God." (James iv. 4.)

NOTE.

"Diversions" include those popular amusements, such as dancing, theaters, circuses, etc., which *divert or turn the heart away from God to be fascinated by worldly things.* Our Bishops explain the above Rule as forbidding indulgence in the modern dance, and attending circuses and theaters.

Dancing.—The Church stands squarely and firmly opposed to the modern dance. Even the Roman Catholic Church says: "We consider it to be our duty to warn our people against the fashionable dances, which are revolting to every feeling of delicacy, and fraught with the greatest danger to morals." Bishop Hopkins, of the Episcopal Church, says: "I have shown that dancing is chargeable with waste of time, the interruption of useful study, the indulgence of personal vanity, and the premature incitement of the passions." Dr. Robinson, of the Presbyterian Church says: "It is simply impossible that this question of indulgence in such worldly pleasures as the theater, the masquerade, the card-table, and the dance, can be a doubtful or a debatable question." It is well known that most of the Baptist Churches expel their members for the continued indulgence of dancing. So we see that all these Churches stand side by side with the Methodist Church in opposition to dancing.

Its practice *tends to ruin the virtue of woman*. A New York paper says: "*Three-fourths* of the abandoned girls of this city were ruined by dancing. Young ladies allow gentlemen privileges in dancing which, taken under any other circumstances, would be considered improper. It requires neither brains nor good morals to be a good dancer. As the love of dancing increases the love of religion decreases. Parlor dancing is dangerous. Tippling leads to drunkenness, and parlor dancing leads to ungodly balls. Tippling and parlor dancing sow to winds, and both reap the whirlwind. Put dancing in the crucible, apply the acids, weigh it, and the verdict of reason, morality, and religion is, "Weighed in the balance and found wanting."

Its practice destroys the Christian's influence. "But the wreck of Christian influence will be as complete as that of character. What good can a member of the Church, who is a participator in social dances and a frequenter of balls, do? Is he disposed to exhort, or pray, or sing, who will be disposed to hear him? Can the Spirit of God accompany his message? Will the wicked feel its power? Will not religion seem to them a mockery when presented, if ever such should be the case, by such an advocate? It cannot be otherwise. Says Dr. Wilson, in a sermon to which we have already alluded, and we wish especially to call the attention of Christian young ladies to it: 'I cannot well imagine a more speedy method of teaching a careless young man to despise the Christian name, than for some female acquaintance whom he has seen at the communion-table to become his partner in the dance. Nor is any thing probably more usual in such a case than for those who look on quietly to pass the ungracious whisper, "See that pious dancer! why, she waltzes as if she had been accustomed to it. She seems to love it as much as any of us poor sinners. A pretty Christian, to be sure." This is no fancy sketch; they know little of the world who suppose it to be so; for that which Cicero did not hesitate to call *omnium vitiorum extremum,* "a vice that no one would be guilty of till he had utterly abandoned all virtue," and *umbram luxuriæ,* or that which "follows riot and debauchery as the shade follows the body," I take it is now, in the middle of the nineteenth century, well understood by unconverted men not to consist with what ought reasonably to be looked for in the genuine Christian character.'"—*Bishop Clark.*

Theaters and Circuses. Much of the argument against dancing bears equally strong against theaters and circuses. Plato said, "Public theaters are dangerous to morality;" Aristotle, "They should be entirely forbidden to young people as unsafe;" Ovid, that they were "a grand source of corruption." Archbishop Tillotson found them in England to be "a nursery of vice," and called them "the devil's chapel." To the theater, the ball, the circus, the race-course, the gambling table, go all the idle, the dissipated, the rogues, the licentious, the gluttons, the artful jades, the immodest prudes, the worthless, the refuse, the very atmosphere of whose association is defiling and corrupting. The whole influence of such people is to destroy the good morals of the country. They breed corruption as naturally as putrefying carcasses breed vermin, and fatten on the corruption which they produce. Yet people call these things "innocent amusements;" but hell is populated with their victims. The managers of these amusements are the devil's recruiting officers, whose business is to strew the way to hell with flowers, charm it with music, and deck it with gorgeous pictures.

Rule 12. (Must avoid) The singing those songs or reading those books which do not tend to the knowledge or love of God.

BIBLE.—"Be not deceived: evil communications corrupt good manners." (1 Cor. xv. 33.) "Speaking to yourselves in psalms and hymns and spiritual songs, singing and making melody in your hearts to the Lord." (Eph. v. 19.) "I count all things but loss for the excellency of the knowledge of Christ Jesus my Lord." (Phil. iii. 8.)

NOTE.

The evils of corrupt literature are very great. Dr. Talmage says: "The assassin of Sir William Russell declared that he got the inspiration for his crime by reading what was then a new and popular novel, 'Jack Sheppard.' Homer's Iliad made Alexander the warrior. Alexander said so. The story of Alexander made Julius Cæsar and Charles XII. both men of blood. Have you in your pocket, or in your trunk, or in your desk at business, a bad book, a bad picture, a bad pamphlet? In God's name I warn you to destroy it. Why are fifty per cent. of the criminals in the jails and penitentiaries of the United States today under twenty-one years of age—many of them under seventeen, under sixteen, under fifteen, under fourteen, under thirteen? Walk along the corridors of the Tombs prison in New York and look for yourselves. Bad books, bad newspapers, bewitched them as soon as they got out of the cradle. Beware of all those stories which end wrong. Beware of all those books which make the road that ends in perdition seem to end in paradise. Do not glorify the dirk and the pistol. Do not call the desperado brave, or the libertine gallant. Teach our young people that if they go down into the swamps and marshes to watch their jacks-with-a-lantern dance on decay and rottenness, they will catch malaria and death. 'O,' says some man, 'I am a business man, and I have no time to examine what my children read; I have no time to inspect the books that come into my household.' If your children were threatened with typhoid fever, would you have time to go for the doctor?"

Rule 13. (Must avoid) Softness, or needless self-indulgence.

BIBLE.—"Then said Jesus unto his disciples, If any man would come after me, let him deny himself, and take up his cross, and follow me." (Matt. xvi. 24.)

NOTE.

Self-denial is reasonable. The men of the world practice it when seeking earthly things. Even the brutal prize-fighter will deny himself of all effeminate pleasures when being trained for a pugilistic combat, or a foot-race. Military men submit to all sorts of self-denial to win the fading laurels of earth. "Now they do it to obtain a corruptible crown, but we an incorruptible."

These illustrations are enough, I think, to satisfy you that the principle of self-denial and of self-control not only is not impossible to human nature, but is one of the commonest, one of the most universal principles in exercise, and that when the Christian religion introduces self-denial, symbolizing it by the cross, it does not introduce a new principle, and does not introduce a difficult one. If no man is worthy to be a disciple of Christ unless he take up his cross, and deny himself, and follow the Saviour, he is only saying in regard to himself, and to the world eternal, what this world says in regard to every man that follows it. There is no trade that does not say to every applicant that comes to it, "If you will take up your cross and follow me, you shall have my remuneration." There is no profession that does not say to every applicant, "If you will take up your cross, and follow me, I will reward you." There is no pleasure, there is no ambition, there is no cause that men pursue, from the lowest to the highest in the horizon of secular things, that does not say to every man, "Unless you take up your cross and follow me, you shall have none of me." Now, the Lord Jesus Christ, standing like the angel in the sun, with the eternal world for a background, clothed in garments white as snow, as no fuller on earth could white them, and calling us to honor and glory and immortality, says only in behalf of these higher things what the whole world says of its poor, groveling, and miserable things: "Take up your cross, and follow me."

Rule 14. (Must avoid) Laying up treasure upon earth.

BIBLE.—" Lay not up for yourselves treasures upon earth where moth and rust doth corrupt, and where thieves break through and steal; but lay up for yourselves treasures in heaven, where neither moth nor rust doth corrupt, and where thieves do not break through nor steal; for where your treasure is there will your heart be also." (Matt. vi. 19-21.)

NOTE.

" Hoarding for one's self accompanies poverty toward

God. Not all accumulation is condemnable; Joseph accumulated, but for others, not for himself. Not all desire for wealth is condemnable; but the desire for wealth above my neighbor; the eager, insatiable desire; the selfish, dishonest desire; the desire which puts wealth above honesty, benevolence, piety.

"This is illustrated by the story of King Midas. To him was given the magic power that every thing he touched should turn to gold. It proved a fatal gift. The flowers lost their fragrance and bloom, and became golden; the food turned to metal when it touched his lips, and left him to hunger; finally his daughter turned to a statue of gold when she ran to kiss him, and the poor king cried to be rescued from the horrible gift which he had besought. A glass of water, a crust of bread, a fragrant rose, above all a loving heart, he discovered to be worth more than all golden treasures."

The spirit of the Rule would be met if men bestowed their charities while living.

"Let men be the living executors of their benevolence. Not a few are beginning to do this. Mr. Vassar, of Poughkeepsie, while living, built and saw in operation a very noble monument of his benevolence. He lived to enjoy it. Peter Cooper lived beyond a score of years to have the enjoyment of a wisely disposed charity from out of his large property. Late in life, Mr. Vanderbilt founded and organized the University at Nashville, which is open and in full prosperity. Mr. Durant has built the great college for women at Wellesley, in Massachusetts, and he lives to see to it that his charity is wisely employed. The man who earns money is far more apt to organize it into an institution wisely than any set of trustees into whose hands he can put it. It is a good thing, therefore, for a man who means to give when he dies to consider that he is likely to die to-morrow, and give to-day."

Rule 15. (Must avoid) Borrowing without a probability of paying, or taking up goods without a probability of paying for them.

BIBLE.—" The wicked borroweth and payeth not again." (Ps. xxxvii. 21.) " Render unto all their dues." (Rom. xiii. 7.) "Owe no man any thing. Provide things honest in the sight of all men." (Rom. xii. 17.)

NOTE.

The Rule forbids the incurring of pecuniary obligation when there is no reasonable ground for supposing it can be paid. To do so is to practice a cheat, to be guilty of fraud. Our people are to be taught that to borrow, without a reasonable probability of paying back, or to purchase goods without a probability of paying for them, is to stand before the Church and their own conscience convicted of fraud. We cannot be too careful and conscientious in reference to borrowed property, or buying goods on slender credit. Men should be scrupulous in returning all borrowed property. They should not allow such property to be injured while in their possession, nor return an inferior article for the one borrowed.

GOOD WORKS TO BE DONE.

It is expected of all who continue in these societies that they should continue to evidence their desire of salvation:

Rule 16. By doing good, by being in every kind merciful after their power, as they have opportunity, doing good of every possible sort, and, as far as possible, to all men.

BIBLE.—"Trust in the Lord, and do good." (Ps. xxxvii. 3.) 'To do good and to communicate forget not." (Heb. iii. 16.) "Blessed are the merciful, for they shall obtain mercy." (Matt. v. 7.) "To him that knoweth to do good, and doeth it not, to him it is *sin*." (James iv. 17.) "As we have opportunity, let us do good unto all men." (Gal. vi. 10.)

NOTES.

1. "The opportunities for doing good are continuous and occasional. The continuous are those that belong to the ordinary course and duties of the life of the individual and of society; the occasional are those instances of special emergencies that arise from time to time. And all these may be generalized under the heads of the preventive, the educational, and the reformatory agencies of society. That is, evil is to be prevented, good is to be developed, and the vicious are to be reformed. And in each of these we may class all the good agencies of the world as workers, such as the home, the school, the Church, the press, the State, and all benevolent institutions, with all the common industries of life that go to sustain each of these."

2. *Doing Good is Made a Test Question in the Bible.*— "The rich young ruler is tested by the command, 'Go, sell that thou hast and give to the poor;' the inquiring lawyer by the story of the Good Samaritan, with the added direction, 'Go, and do likewise;' Paul by the command to preach the gospel to the Gentiles. Where is there an instance in the New Testament in which any man is accepted because he accepts a creed, or a ceremony, or a covenant, or is rejected because he does not? To every professing Christian, to every worshiping Church, to every revival with its hosannas, Christ comes seeking if haply he may find fruits. The fruit

of the Spirit is love, joy, peace, long-suffering, gentleness, goodness, faith, meekness, temperance. Does the professing Christian, with his orthodox creed and his water baptism—does the Church, with its sound doctrine and its devout worship; does the revival, with its enthusiastic hosannas—bear this kind of fruit? The tree that bears no fruit dies, for the fruit is the seed-protector; and in the fruit is the promise of reproduction, and so the assurance of immortality. The unfruitful tree lives only long enough to afford a generous opportunity for it to answer the question, 'Wilt thou bring forth fruit?' Leaves cannot save it; for leaves do not reproduce life. The unfruitful professor dies of his own unfruitfulness. Men sometimes ask, almost querulously, 'What have I done that I should be condemned to death?' The New Testament retorts, 'What have you done that you should be preserved unto life eternal?' Who is richer, wiser, better, happier, for your existence? Why should any man live who lives to no useful purpose? Cut him down; why cumbereth he the ground? Give his vacant place to a better man."

Rule 17. (Doing good) To their bodies, of the ability which God giveth, by giving food to the hungry, by clothing the naked, by visiting or helping them that are sick or in prison.

BIBLE.—"Then shall the King say unto them on his right-hand, Come, ye blessed of my Father, inherit the kingdom prepared for you from the foundation of the world; for I was a hungered, and ye gave me meat; I was thirsty, and ye gave me drink; I was a stranger, and ye took me in; naked, and ye clothed me; I was sick, and ye visited me; I was in prison, and ye came unto me. Inasmuch as ye have done it unto one of the least of these my brethren, ye have done it unto me." (Matt. xxv. 34–10.)

NOTE.

Christians are morally obligated to administer to the wants and necessities of the poor, the helpless, the sick, the fatherless, the widow. The beautiful story of the Good Samaritan strikingly illustrates the spirit of Christian philanthropy.

"True Christian philanthropy is a self-denying service. The Good Samaritan put the wounded man on his own beast. He, therefore, had to walk, was delayed in his journey, ran the risk of assault himself. His benevolence cost him something. We are always trying to do good to our fellow-men without bearing any burden ourselves. But Christ bore our burdens and carried our sorrows; he took them on himself. The mother carries in her own person the sins and sorrows of her children. True Christian philanthropy takes up its cross to follow Christ in going about doing good. There is very little charity in giving cold victuals which you cannot eat, cast-off clothing which you cannot wear, old books for which you have no room on your shelves, money which you will not miss from your purse. The benevolence which costs nothing is worth—what it costs. The paring from your apple may be eagerly eaten by the pigs, but there is no charity in giving it to them. No man shows love for his fellow-men except he who puts himself to some inconvenience for their sake.

"To his personal service the Good Samaritan added a money contribution. It was not very great—about equal to two dollars of our day. But the giver added the pledge that whatever was necessary he would pay; at all events, he paid something. To do good with money to the moneyless is of all tasks of benevolence the most difficult. How to give to poverty without increasing pauperism is a perpetual and ever unsolved problem. But he who cannot part with money to do good to others is no follower of Him who, though he was rich, for our sakes became poor. To give service without money, or to give money without service—neither of these givings is true Christian philanthropy. Two pence personally given is worth more than twenty given through paid agents. The love that reaches the pocket is often deeper than that which reaches only the heart.

The Good Samaritan had compassion, went to the sufferer, rendered him personal service, at cost of inconvenience to himself, and accompanied it with gift of money." "Go thou, and do likewise."

Rule 18. (Doing good) To their souls, by instructing, reproving, or exhorting all we have any intercourse with; trampling under foot that enthusiastic doctrine, that "we are not to do good unless *our hearts be free to it.*"

BIBLE.—"Reprove, rebuke, exhort, with all long-suffering and doctrine." (2 Tim. iv. 2.) "Exhort one another daily." (Heb. iii. 13.) "Them that sin rebuke before all, that others also may fear." (1 Tim. v. 20.) "Ye are the salt of the earth and the light of the world." (Matt. v. 13-16.)

NOTES.

1. *As Christians be Instructors.*—Be a teacher of divine truths in the home-circle and at your Sunday-school. Let your light *shine*. The candle can enlighten the room, the lamp the street, the light-house the darkness of the stormy sea, the moon the night, the sun the world. Be ye a luminous light in your sphere of life.

2. *Reprove Sin.*—The reproof of sin is a Christian

duty. When you see your neighbor living in a dangerous sin, have the moral courage to rebuke him. Would it not be cruel to see your neighbor's house on fire, and pass on and give him no warning? Why? Because his life is in danger. But if your neighbor is living in a deadly sin, then his immortal soul is in danger of hell-fire. Timely reproof may save him. Your silence may leave him to perish in his sins. But let your rebuke be bathed in the spirit of Christian love. "Thou shalt rebuke thy neighbor, and not suffer sin upon him."

Rule 19. By doing good, especially to them that are of the household of faith, or groaning so to be; employing them preferably to others, buying one of another, helping each other in business; and so much the more because the world will love its own, and them only.

BIBLE.—"As we have opportunity let us do good unto all men, especially unto them who are of the household of faith." (Gal. vi. 10.) "Be kindly-affectioned one to another with brotherly love; in honor preferring one another; distributing to the necessity of saints; given to hospitality." (Rom. xii. 10, 13.) "If ye were of the world, the world would love his own." (John xv. 19.)

NOTE.

Christian fellowship and mutual helpfulness are two leading duties taught in the gospel.

"What is fellowship? It is more than sympathy, although that is the core of it. It is sympathy expressed or manifested in such a way as to draw others toward you in the bonds of brotherhood. Fellowship is making men feel that they are fellows with you; that they are your brethren; that they are related to you; that they are a part of your person, as it were.

"In the New Testament the Church is considered as a family: 'Of whom the whole family in heaven and earth is named.' In a family, there are two influences that bind persons together. One is the common relation which all the children have to the father and the mother, and that is a very powerful influence. Having the same father and mother, they have the same affection, the same obedience, the same gratitude and love; but then there is also the personal attractiveness of each toward the others—the generosity of the brother, the guilelessness and simplicity of the sister, their mutual helpfulness—various traits in them tend to bring members of the same family together. So the attractiveness of each, in his own disposition and conduct, is one of the elements of fellowship in the family; and the other is a consciousness of a common relation to the father and the mother, whom they love even more than they love each other.

"Now, the same rule of fellowship should exist in the Church, and among all Churches, namely, the consciousness of a common relationship to Christ, and the attractiveness of mutually helpful, loving lives. We are to love one another, in our own Church, and in other Churches, because we feel that all those who are striving to live spiritual lives are recognized by the Lord Jesus Christ, and are dear to him; for whoever is dear to Christ ought to be dear to us, no matter how much they have attained or how little; we are to love all men who, according to the measure of their light and strength, are endeavoring to please Christ.

"If you are going to carry out this doctrine of fellowship you must begin by being yourself lovely, and acting in a lovely manner. Rejoice not in iniquity in other people. Love them. Serve them. Whatever you feel of indignation and vengeance explode on principles; but when you come to persons and Churches, cover them with sympathy. And remember that this doctrine can be practiced singly as well as doubly. You can be in fellowship with men if they are not in fellowship with you. You can rejoice in their wellbeing, and love them with sincerity and truth, though they may not requite it."

Rule 20. (Must so live) By all possible diligence and frugality, that the gospel be not blamed.

BIBLE.—"Not slothful in business, fervent in spirit, serving the Lord." (Rom. xii. 11.) "If a man provide not for his own, and especially for those of his own house, he hath denied the faith, and is worse than an infidel." (1 Tim. v. 8).

NOTES.

1. "In the spirit of this teaching one should measure his social duties. First, it is a part of a Christian man's duty to make provision for his household by a wise prudence. If a man has no means of enlarging his possessions, if he is shut up to the necessity of poverty, that necessity is not a virtue: it is a misfortune; but there may be the virtue of content and patience therein. It is surely a Christian duty in every man who has power over natural law so to organize his affairs as to enlarge and make more and more bountiful the property foundation on which his household stands, for property is the absolute condition of civilization. In the midst of civilization, and in a religious community, a single man may be poor, and yet in every sense manly and useful through life; but, looking at the race, you never can develop men and bring them up from savage or barbarous conditions except by

those energies by which property is developed, and by that leisure which property gives. You sharpen men by industry: you organize the active forces of society by commercial or mechanical law; and you gain freedom from bondage to matter by property, which gives men the opportunity of reflection and of refinement. Property as your master is a tyrant, and mean enough; but as your servant, it is God's noble gift; and men are called, so soon as they assume the family relation, to fulfill certain duties which devolve upon them in the matter of property. These duties are, then, for the most part, no longer optional with them."

2. *Frugality* is economy in small things. "Gather up the fragments that remain, that nothing be lost."

"Looking after little things, that nothing may be lost, is one of the ways in which men learn to be careful. It is one of the ways in which they are taught that kind of sharpness which men's faculties need as much as tools need a sharp and cutting edge. This sharpness comes by the exercise of thoughtfulness at the beginning of life. The wise adaptation of little to little; the making the little more, and the more most; the habit of wise frugality. The knowing how to turn every thing that one touches into some economic use; the being willing to do it; the waiting in the doing of it until by frugality and care you are able to live more largely."

"It is a common saying, in respect to certain people who come among us, that they can live on what we throw away. It is said that a German will support his family on the wastes of our households. It is a complaint which is made in business communities, that profits are small. Men say: 'We cannot do business honestly and thrive; the Jews are taking all our business from us.' Why is this? Are they smarter than you are? Are they more industrious than you are? 'O no; but they are less scrupulous; they have no conscience.' That is not it. It does not take so much to support them as it does to support you. They live on less than you do, and they are willing to live on less. They save what they get. They take care of the fragments, and on the fragments they live; and, so far as that is concerned, they live about as well as you do. The difference is in the amount of care and thought which is put into the living. They give to it more flavor than you do. And, if you demand more than they do, you cannot stand the competition, and they will thrive while you will not. That is according to a law of nature."

Rule 21. (Must live) By running with patience the race which is set before them, denying themselves and taking up their cross daily; submitting to bear the reproach of Christ, to be as the filth and offscouring of the world, and looking that men should say all manner of evil of them falsely for the Lord's sake.

BIBLE.—"Seeing we also are compassed about with so great a cloud of witnesses, let us lay aside every weight, and the sin which doth so easily beset us, and let us run with patience the race that is set before us." (Heb. xii. 1.) "If any man will come after me, let him deny himself and take up his cross and follow me." (Matt. xvi. 24.) "We are made as the filth of the earth, and are offscouring of all things unto this day." (1 Cor. iv. 13.) "Blessed are ye when men shall revile you, and persecute you, and shall say all manner of evil against you falsely, for my sake." (Matt. v. 11.)

NOTES.

1. This Rule requires the culture of patience. Patience is self-control and forbearance under provoca-

tion. It bears the pressure of pain and sorrow bravely. It is willingness to suffer till relief comes; to hold still while under chastisement.

2. "We are to endure hardness as good soldiers. A man may be a good soldier in the armory; he may be a good soldier upon the green; he may be a good soldier at the parade, when he is marching to dainty music, and is gazed upon by flattering eyes; and yet he may not in the field be able to stand the deprivations which belong to campaigning. It is one thing to be a good soldier at home, but it is another thing to be a good soldier in actual service, where hunger, fatigue, all manner of hardships, are to be met cheerfully, and borne with manly resolution. And that which is true of the soldier in the field is also true of the soldier in that spiritual warfare upon which we have all entered. It is not for us to seek religion because we want forever the titillation of joy. Our business in life is to earn manhood and nobility; and for the sake of these not only ought we to have patience, but we ought to be willing to endure sorrow; we ought to be willing to meet opposition; we ought to be willing to be overtaken by poverty; we ought to be willing to suffer reverses of fortune. Whatever may, in the providence of God, be brought upon us, we ought to accept cheerfully for the sake of that glorious victory for which we have become soldiers of the Lord Jesus Christ."

3. "He must take up his cross *daily*. How many there are of us who would like to compromise; who would like to put all our cross-bearing into one great heroic effort; who would like to do it once for all. How many of us there are who would like to bear our

crosses by dreaming of them, reading about them, and listening to exhortations respecting them! How many of us there are who bear our cross on the bed in the morning before we get up, or sitting in our cushioned pew in a well-warmed church, as we listen to exquisite music or to eloquent oratory! This is not the cross-bearing to which Christ invites us. To take up our cross daily is to deny ourselves at breakfast the food which experience has proved disagrees with our digestion, however pleasant it may be to our palate; it is to go to our daily task with a cheerful spirit, though the task be irksome and uncongenial; it is to bear others' burdens, the burdens of their carelessness, their ignorance, their superstition, as Christ bears our burdens, and so fulfill the law of Christ; it is to be wounded for others' transgressions and bruised for others' iniquities, and see others healed with our stripes; it is to do this, not on some great occasion, when all the world is admiring our martyrdom, but day by day, and hour by hour, when no one knows what cross we are bearing except ourselves and our Lord."

It is expected of all who desire to continue in these societies that they should continue to evidence their desire of salvation:

Rule 22. By attending upon all the ordinances of God, such as the public worship of God.

BIBLE.—" One thing have I desired of the Lord, that will I seek after; that I may dwell in the house of the Lord all the days of my life, to behold the beauty of the Lord, and to inquire in his temple." (Ps. xxvii. 4.) "Not forsaking the assembling of ourselves together, as the manner of some is." (Heb. x. 25.)

Rule 23. The ministry of the word, either read or expounded.

Bible.—Christ instituted the ministry, and said: "Go ye therefore, and teach all nations, teaching them to observe all things whatsoever I have commanded you; and lo, I am with you alway, even unto the end of the world." (Matt. xxviii. 19, 20.) "So then faith cometh by *hearing*, and hearing by the word of God." (Rom. x. 17.) "But whoso looketh into the perfect law of liberty, and continueth therein, he being not a forgetful hearer, but a doer of the work, this man shall be blessed in his deed." (James i. 25.)

NOTE.

Every absence from public worship, when it is possible to be there, is a spiritual loss. True, you may not realize a special blessing at every meeting, still some effect, however small, will be felt. Frequent dews, though small and silent, spread beauty and freshness over the garden herbs. And for this reason, perhaps, David said, "I was glad when they said unto me, Let us go into the house of the Lord." Here under the pulpit light is poured upon the ignorant, the thunder of the word awakens the careless sinner, the believer is fed upon the hidden manna of the gospel. "They that wait upon the Lord shall renew their strength." Make it a matter of conscience, then, to attend the public worship of the Church, whether on week-day or Sabbath, whether the meeting be for preaching, or the holy sacrament, or prayer-meeting, or love-feast, or class-meeting, go, and contribute your part to the general interest. Be not one of those who "neglect the assembling of themselves together, as the manner of some is;" who are prevented by a little heat, or cold, or rain, or some other slight, imaginary hinderance.

Rule 24. (Must not neglect) The Supper of the Lord.

Bible.—"And he took bread, and gave thanks, and brake it and gave unto them, saying, This is my body which is given for you:

this do in remembrance of me. Likewise also the cup after supper, saying, This cup is the new testament in my blood, which is shed for you." (Luke xxii. 19, 20.)

Notes.

1. *The duty of members to commune.* It is a divinely ordained as well as an efficient means of grace. In the words "Take, eat, drink ye all of it," we are taught that just as bread and wine—the common food of the people in that day—nourish the living body, supplying the daily waste of that body, and providing material for its growth, so the believing with the heart in Christ crucified will nourish the new man. Our Lord uses the word *believing*, with reference to spiritual life, as the equivalent of eating and drinking, used with reference to the natural life. "I am the bread of life; he that cometh to me shall never hunger, and he that believeth on me shall never thirst." And so the administrator of the Lord's Supper is directed to say to the communicant, "Take and eat this in remembrance that Christ died for thee, and feed on him in thy heart by faith with thanksgiving." When a man approaches the communion-table with a penitent heart, confessing his sins, feeling his dependence on Christ and exercising faith in his atonement, it is reasonable and scriptural to expect that the Holy Spirit will quicken, strengthen, and comfort.

2. *The qualifications of a communicant.* Many persons are kept away from the Lord's Supper by wrong views on the subject. They put the standard of worthiness to commune too high. Who are fit to approach the Lord's table? Dr. Pope, an eminent Methodist minister in England, says: "All who profess faith in Christ's atonement, who desire his salvation, who

are willing to keep his laws, *are invited* to come." Now examine yourself by this rule. Dr. Raymond, another Methodist minister, says: "A credible faith in Christ is the sole condition of membership in the Christian Church, and, being admitted by the rite of baptism, such a person is entitled to the communion." Dr. Armstrong, a talented Presbyterian minister, says: "The conditions prescribed by Christ are two, and only two, viz., (1) membership in the visible Church, and (2) a credible profession of personal faith in him." Our Ritual says: "Ye that do truly and earnestly *repent* of your sins, and are in *love* and *charity* with your neighbors, and intend to lead a *new life*, following the commandments of God, and walking from henceforth in his holy ways, draw near with faith, and take this holy sacrament to your comfort, and make your humble confession to Almighty God, meekly kneeling upon your knees." To be "in love and charity with our neighbors," in the sense of the Ritual, does not require that we should believe that all who appear at the communion-table are good and worthy Christians. The meaning of the invitation is, to be truly sorry for our personal sins, to cultivate good and charitable feelings toward others, and a settled purpose to lead Christian lives.

3. *Open communion.* All the Protestant Churches practice open communion, except the Baptists and Associate Reformed. By open communion is meant a joint participation of the Lord's Supper of all professed believers in Christ. John Bunyan and Robert Hall, of the past, and Charles Spurgeon, of the present generation, all great lights among the English Baptists, repudiate close communion.

Rule 25. (Must not neglect) **Family and private prayer.**

BIBLE.—"As for me and my house, we will serve the Lord." (Josh. xxiv. 15.) "Pour out thy fury upon the heathen that know thee not, and upon the families that call not on thy name." (Jer. x. 25.) "When thou prayest, enter into thy closet, and when thou hast shut the door, pray to thy Father which is in secret; and thy Father which seeth in secret shall reward thee openly." (Matt. vi. 6.)

NOTES.

Prayerless families are like the Egyptian houses on whose door-posts there was no protecting blood of the paschal lamb. They are unsheltered by the shield of prayer, exposed to the destroying angel. *The altar of family prayer should be erected for the benefit of the children.* "It is the molding hand that shapes our souls for time and for eternity. Many a young man has gone down to a premature death simply because in his cradle, in his infancy, he was not prayed for or, what were better still, prayed with. How often it happens that a certain kind of morbid delicacy—so it is called—a certain kind of false sensitiveness exists on the part of the father and mother which prevents their speaking of religious matters to their children! How many mothers are in the habit of gathering their children together to pray with them? How many fathers, on these holy Sabbath days that come one after another throughout the year, take their little ones upon their knees, and talk to them pleasantly and persuasively, and therefore eloquently, about those higher things that are to come when this world shall be burned up as a scroll? Brethren, it seems to me that every child has a claim on his parents in this direction, and a right to look upon their memory with suspicion if they have neglected their duty. These things ought not to be left to the Sunday-school teacher, they ought not to be left to the teachings of the Sabbath-day from the pulpit; they ought to be done in the midst of one's own family. It is not enough to work all the week, that you may leave many thousand dollars to your boys and girls; it is infinitely better for them, and infinitely more satisfactory for you, if you start them on life's journey with that buckler and shield through which the dart of the enemy can never find its way, and against which the steel-point of temptation will be blunted.

"I plead, then, in the first place, with you who have children, to see to it that they are properly prepared to meet the exigences of life as they ought to. I tell you the religion of one's cradle is of infinite importance, and to teach one to pray is better than to give one money, and to teach one to trust in God is far, is infinitely better than to urge the child's ambition toward any earthly goal. It is well enough to see to the intellectual culture of your little ones, but it is of greater importance to them and to you that you give them a sensible religious education."—*Dr. Hepworth.*

The fact has been discovered by actual experiment that two-thirds of the children reared in praying, pious families become members of the Church, while only *one in twelve* becomes religious of those raised in prayerless families. Out of two hundred and seven praying families come sixty ministers of the gospel, and five hundred and thirty-nine professors of religion.

2. *Secret prayer.* Our Saviour prayed much in secret. If he found it necessary, who of his disciples can plead exemption? Secret prayer rightly per-

formed refreshes the soul as the silent dews of the night do the grass; it gets at the hidden sources of life. Behold that beautiful tree, swaying its green branches in the wind, catching the glory of the summer's sun on its foliage, fragrant with bloom and bending with golden fruit! Where is the secret of its abundant life? In the roots, hidden in the ground, but busy all summer pumping up the elements of life. Secret prayer is to the Christian life what the roots are to the tree. "Prayer is the rope up in the belfry; we pull it, and it rings the bell up in heaven." Said Mary, Queen of Scotland, "I fear John Knox's prayers more than an army of ten thousand men." Prayer moves the arm that moves the world.

Rule 26. (Must not neglect) Searching the Scriptures.

BIBLE.—"I will meditate in thy precepts, and have respect unto thy ways. I will delight myself in thy statutes; I will not forget thy word." (Ps. cxix. 15, 16.) "Search the Scriptures; for in them ye think ye have eternal life; and they are they which testify of me." (John v. 39.)

NOTE.

"The Bible is a rock of diamonds, a chain of pearls, the sword of the Spirit; a chart by which the Christian sails to eternity; the map by which he daily walks; the sun-dial by which he sets his life; the balances in which he weighs his action."—*T. Watson.*

To be read daily. The Countess of Suffolk read the Bible over twice annually. Dr. Gouge read fifteen chapters daily. Joshua Barnes read his Bible a hundred and twenty times over. Robert Cotton read the whole Bible through twelve times a year.

How to read it. An old man once said: "Reading the Bible is like eating fish. When I find a difficulty

I lay it aside, and call it a *bone*. Why should I choke over a bone, when there is so much nutritious meat for me?"

Rule 27 (Must not neglect) Fasting, or abstinence.

BIBLE.—"When ye fast, be not, as the hypocrites, of a sad countenance; but thou, when thou fastest, anoint thine head, and wash thy face; that thou appear not unto men to fast, but unto thy Father which is in secret." (Matt. vi. 16–18.)

NOTE.

Observe, Christ did not condemn fasting, but the hypocritical manner of doing it. When you fast—which implies the duty of it—do not appear before men bowed down as a bulrush, with a sad face, but wear a cheerful smile; anoint the head, that thou appear not unto men to fast, but unto thy Father. Let your fasting be internal, not external.

The Church requires its members to fast as a means of grace. Every Friday *immediately preceding* each quarterly-meeting has usually been set apart as fast-day in our Church. A day devoted to fasting and prayer is a preparation for the success of these important meetings. "It is precisely the lack of this preparation and training that we suffer from. When the greatest speed of a horse is to be tested, the trainer does not allow him to run at will over the pasture, nor does he simply put him on a wholesale diet. He almost counts the straws that he gives the horse; he cleans and sifts the oats, and gives him the very best kinds; he measures the horse's exercise; and every part of the horse is under the trainer's watch and care, that he may be in the finest condition when he puts forth his energy in competition. And shall a man do so much for his horse, and nothing for himself? Shall there be no preparation, no discipline, no blanketing, no washing, no care as to diet, no training, nothing but going on through the linked year, Sabbath joined to Sabbath, taking things as they come, allowing themselves to move about as the current sweeps them along? Is that the wisest method of spiritual culture?"

These are the General Rules of our societies; all which we are taught of God to observe, even in his written word, which is the only rule, and the sufficient rule, both of our faith and practice. And all these we know his Spirit writes on truly awakened hearts. If there be any among us who observe them not, who habitually break any of them, let it be known unto them who watch over that soul, as they who must give an account. We will admonish him of the error of his ways: we will bear with him for a season; but if then he repent not, he hath no more place among us: we have delivered our own souls.

CHAPTER V

PROMINENT DOCTRINES OF METHODISM.

I. Universal Redemption.

Methodism teaches that the atonement of Christ is universal in its extent—that it is broad enough to cover all the sins of all the children of Adam from the beginning to the end of time. It teaches that the sacrifice of Christ derived infinite value from the divinity of his person, and is therefore intrinsically sufficient to expiate the sins of the *whole* human race, and was really *so intended*. This is Arminianism.

Calvinism teaches that "Christ died exclusively for the elect, and purchased redemption for them alone, and in no sense did he die for the rest of the race." "That the atonement of Christ is specific and *limited*, that it is neither universal nor indefinite, but *restricted* to the elect alone."

According to Calvinism, the salvation or the non-salvation of each human being depends absolutely and solely on the eternal, irresistible decree of God, made "without *any foresight* of faith or good works in the creature, as conditions or causes moving him thereto." According to this system, God has elected to eternal life a certain, definite, unalterable number, and passed the rest of mankind by unredeemed to perish in their sins. Hence it teaches a partial atonement, irresistible grace, and final perseverance as flowing out from the decrees.

Arminianism teaches that " Christ died for *all* men," for "the whole world," and that the salvation or non-salvation depends not on an arbitrary decree, but upon the *willingness* or *unwillingness* of each man to comply with the gospel conditions of salvation.

1. *That Jesus Christ died for all men is clearly and expressly taught in the following scriptures:*

PROOFS.—"That He, by the grace of God, should taste death for every man." (Heb. ii. 9.) "He is the propitiation for sins; and not for ours only, but also for the sins of the *whole world.*" (2 Cor. v. 15.) "The grace of God that bringeth salvation to *all men* hath appeared." (Titus ii. 11.) "God so loved the world that he gave his only-begotten Son, that whosoever believeth in him should not perish, but have everlasting life." (John iii. 16.) "That was the true Light, which lighteth every man that cometh into the world." (John i. 9.) "God our Saviour. . . will have *all* men to be saved." (1 Tim. ii. 3.) "For the love of Christ constraineth us, because we thus judge, that if one died for all, then were all dead." (2 Cor. v. 14.)

NOTES.

1. If Christ died for all men, then are all placed in

a solvable condition. The sins of every man are atoned for, a pardon for every man is purchased, and every man is welcome to the favor of God and everlasting life. It follows that a decree of reprobation, absolutely predestinating any human being to eternal damnation, is impossible. In harmony with the doctrine that Christ died for all men, the duty to believe in him as a Saviour is enjoined upon all.

Proofs.—"He that believeth shall be saved, but he that believeth not shall be damned." (Mark xvi. 16.) "He that believeth is not condemned, but he that believeth not is condemned already, because he hath not believed in the name of the only-begotten Son of God." (John iii. 8.)

2. In harmony with the scheme of universal redemption, gospel ministers are authorized to preach free salvation to all men.

Proofs.—"Go ye into all the world, and preach the gospel to every creature." (Mark xvi. 15.) "And the Spirit and the Bride say, Come. And let him that heareth say, Come. And let him that is athirst come. And whosoever will, let him take the water of life freely." (Rev. xxii. 17.) "Come unto me all ye that labor and are heavy-laden, and I will give you rest; and him that cometh unto me, I will in no wise cast out." (Matt. xi. 28.)

3. In accord with this doctrine are many precious promises and tender expostulations.

Proof.—"Come now, and let us reason together, saith the Lord; though your sins be as scarlet, they shall be as white as snow; though they be red like crimson, they shall be as wool." (Isa. i. 18.)

4. Then, men are constantly charged with the blame of their own ruin. "For I have no pleasure in the death of him that dieth, saith the Lord God; wherefore turn yourselves, and live ye." (Ezek. xviii. 32.) We might quote every chapter in the prophets to show that the Israelites were blamed as the cause of their own ruin.

But it is needless to enlarge. The whole Bible testifies that men are truly the authors of their own destruction. God often complains that he has striven to save men, but they would not let him. "O Jerusalem, Jerusalem . . how often would I have gathered thy children together, even as a hen gathereth her chickens under her wings, and *ye would not.*" (Matt. xxiii. 37.) He "will have all men to be saved, and to come unto the knowledge of the truth." (1 Tim. i. 4.)

5. Furthermore, the argument from reason is as definite and conclusive. Does not every man's own conscience tell him that he is the author of his own sins, and consequently of the punishment flowing from them? Does not conscience accuse us, holding that we alone are to blame for them? Thus, the testimony of conscience sustains the Arminian doctrine. Yet Calvinism teaches that God, "for the sake of his own glory," created man to be lost—created pain and stamped it with immortality—that "God did create a race, large portions of whom, not being elected, would go on to eternal punishment, suffering forever and ever hopelessly—all "for his own glory." Can there be any *glory* in creating and dooming millions of the human race to perdition just for the sake of seeing them suffer? Is there "glory" in a government over this universe in which there is suffering without any other end than suffering? Can there be any better definition of Satanic malignity given than that it is a voluntary creation of suffering merely for the sake of suffering? Finally, the salvation of every human being is possible, or it is not possible. If it is possible, then the possibility is based on the universality of the atonement, for none can be saved outside of the atone-

ment. If the salvation of every man is not possible, then men are damned for not performing an impossibility, which is too monstrous for any sane man to believe. But, as Methodists, we glory in the full, free, and universal redemption of Christ.

Christ says, *"I am the Light of the world."* The candle is the light of a little room; the lamp is the light of the street; but the sun, standing on the high arch of the heavens says, " I am the light of *the world*." He fills the blue heavens above full of light, and clothes the rolling seas, the earth, its hills, dales, fields, and mountains, with the beautiful robe of radiance. Who owns the sun? Everybody. He is made for the world. The modest spire of grass can look up and say, "Thou art my sun." The spreading oaks, the blooming flowers, the ripening grain in a thousand fields, can look up and say, "Yes, and he is no less our sun." The sun shines not for the few, but for the teeming millions of earth. So Christ is the Light of the world. "He is the Sun of righteousness." The cross is the flaming orb of moral day, spreading impartially glorious light from pole to pole. Its power changes the winter of heathendom into the green and fruitful summer of Christian civilization.

The psalmist says: "As the heaven is high above the earth, so great is his mercy toward them that fear him." The boundless extent of heaven's blue field is an emblem of redeeming grace. The vast circular tent of the broad firmament incloses the whole race of man. None can go beyond and outside of its sapphire walls. Wherever man may stray on the remote frontier and far-off corners of the earth, the deep blue heavens bend over him. So the boundless blue sky of Christ's love bends over the human race, beaming with the stars of promise and hope.

As there is room in the broad ocean for all the ships of the world to float and never crowd each other, so there is ample room in the kingdom of Christ for all men. As all the armies of the world can wash, bathe, and cleanse themselves in the ocean, so in the red sea of Christ's blood the world's vast population may be purified.

"He tasted death for every man." "He gave himself a ransom for all." "He is a propitiation for the sins of the whole world." That all are not saved is no objection. It is suggested by a popular expositor that in material nature much goodness seems wasted. Rain and dew descend upon flinty rocks and sterile sands; floods of genial light come tiding down every morning from the sun on scenes where no human foot has trod; flowers bloom in beauty, and emit their fragrance; trees rise in majesty, and throw away their clustering fruit on spots where as yet there has never been a man; wealth sufficient to enrich whole nations is buried beneath the mountains and the seas, while millions are in want; medicine for half the ills of life is shut up in minerals and plants, while generations die without knowing the remedy which nature has provided. It is no objection, therefore, to the universality of the atonement that all are not benefited by it. Its benefits one day will be universally enjoyed. There are men coming after us who shall live in these solitary wastes, enjoy the beauty and the light which now seems wasted, appropriate the fruits, the wealth, the medicine, which for ages have been of no avail. It will be even so with the death of Christ. There are men coming after us that shall participate in the blessings of that atonement which generations have either ignorantly rejected or wickedly despised.

II. REPENTANCE.

Personal repentance toward God and faith toward our Lord Jesus Christ are always united in the Bible. Repentance implies a certain kind of preëxisting faith, and faith implies a preëxisting repentance. Both are produced by the preliminary grace of the Holy Spirit, but not perfected without the coöperation of man. Repentance is a *means* and faith a *condition* of salvation. The broken and contrite heart, a godly sorrow of soul, a keen sense of sin, prepare the soul to accept Christ as the only Saviour. Such a state of mind leads to a free and candid *confession* of sin; and this leads to reformation. This reformation implies two things, viz., a *turning from sin*, and a *serious effort at obedience*. The Bible commands the penitent, "*Cease to do evil, and learn to do well.*" Repentance is preëminently a *personal* obligation. It is a duty laid upon all men.

PROOFS.—"God now commandeth all men everywhere to repent." (Acts xvii. 30.) "Repent ye, for the kingdom of heaven is at hand." (Matt. iii. 2.) "Repent, and be baptized every one of you in the name of Jesus Christ for the remission of sins, and ye shall receive the gift of the Holy Ghost." (Acts ii. 38.) "Let the wicked forsake his way, and the unrighteous man his thoughts, and let him return unto the Lord, and he will have mercy upon him; and to our God, for he will abundantly pardon." (Isa. lv. 7.) "Repent, and turn yourselves from all your transgressions; so iniquity shall not be your ruin." (Ezek. xviii. 30.) "Except ye repent, ye shall all likewise perish." (Luke xiii. 5.)

NOTES.

1. True repentance must be *thorough*, forsaking all sin. If a ship have three leaks, the stopping of two

of them is not sufficient; the *third* one left unstopped will sink it. *All* must be closed up. Or, if a man have two dangerous wounds, the curing of one is not enough. *Both* must be cured. A tree, fallen upon the bosom of a river, sways up and down on the stream, but does not float off down stream, because it is anchored by a hidden root reaching into the bank. So one secret sin, not given up, will keep the soul from floating on the stream of grace into the kingdom of life.

2. Gospel repentance makes *self-sacrifice*. A certain liquor-seller showed sincere repentance by piling up his liquor-barrels and burning them. Sins dear as right eyes and hands must be given up.

3. True repentance asks pardon, and trusts in Christ alone for salvation.

4. Gospel repentance leads to an open and full confession of sin. "If we *confess* our sins, he is faithful and just to forgive us." The benefit of confession is illustrated in the following story: A German prince visited the Arsenal at London, where the galleys were kept. The commandant, as a compliment to his rank, offered to set at liberty any slave whom he selected. The prince went the round of the prison, and conversed with the prisoners. He inquired into the reason of their confinement, and met only with universal complaints of injustice, oppression, and false accusation. At last he came to one man who *admitted his imprisonment to be just*. "My lord," said he, "I have no reason to complain. I have been a wicked, desperate wretch; I have often deserved to be broken upon the wheel; and it is a mercy that I am here." The prince selected *him*, saying, "This is the man whom I wish released." The application is easy.

III. Justification Through Faith.

"Justification is the divine judicial act which applies to the sinner believing in Christ the benefit of the atonement, delivering him from the condemnation of his sin, introducing him into a state of favor, and treating him as a righteous person." "To be justified is to be pardoned, and received into God's favor; into such a state that, if we continue therein, we shall be finally saved."—*Methodist Minutes.* Justification, pardon, forgiveness of sins, are substantially the same in Methodist theology.

This pardon extends to all sins in the past, little and great. "All manner of sin" is forgiven; so "there is no condemnation to them who are in Christ Jesus."

The *originating cause* is the love of God; the *meritorious* cause is the atonement of Christ; the *instrumental* cause is the personal faith of the believer.

Proofs.—"God so *loved* the world that he gave his only-begotten Son that whosoever *believeth* in him should not perish but have everlasting life." (John iii. 16.) "Christ is the end of the law for righteousness [or justification] to every one that believeth." (Rom. x. 4.) "Being justified by faith, we have peace with God *through our Lord Jesus Christ.*" (Rom. v. 1.) "By him [Christ] all that believe are justified from *all* things, from which they could not be justified by the law of Moses." (Acts xiii. 39.) "To him that worketh not, but believeth on him that justifieth the ungodly, his *faith* is counted for righteousness [or justification]." (Rom. iv. 5.) "Therefore we conclude that a man is justified by faith without the deeds of the law." (Rom. iii. 28.)

We must have that faith that relies on Christ as our *Substitute.* A farmer was seen kneeling at a soldier's grave, near Nashville. Some one said unto him: "Why do you pay so much attention to this grave? Was your son buried here?" "No;" said he. "During the war my family were sick. I knew not how to leave them. I was drafted. One of my neighbors came over and said, 'I will go for you; I have no family.' He went off. He was wounded at Chicamauga. He was carried to the hospital, and died. And, sir, I have come a great many miles, that I might write over his grave these words, '*He died for me.*'" So Christ was our Substitute; *he died for us.* He was wounded for our transgressions.

"When the Son of God was made of a woman, and made under the law, then was heard the most awful voice that ever was heard in the universe yet: 'Awake, O sword! against the man that is my fellow, and smite the shepherd'—smite him! When there was a man in the world that was Jehovah's fellow, then there was one that could magnify the law, in smiting whom justice could obtain its demands. The sword of justice smote him, struck him, cut him. The sword of justice had a commission to smite the Man that was Jehovah's fellow; it smote him in Bethlehem; it smote all along the highway of his life, even to Calvary. On Calvary the stroke of the sword fell heavy; the glances of that sword then darkened the sun; the stroke of the sword shook the earth, shook hell; it kept smiting and smiting the Man that was God's fellow, till at last he cried, 'It is finished!' Then the sword fell down at the foot of the cross, hushed, lulled, pacified; and it lay there till the third hallowed morning, when it was found changed into a scepter of mercy; and that scepter of mercy has been a warning among mankind ever since."

Without Works.—Faith without works renounces every other dependence than the atonement. As an instrument it embraces Christ, rests upon him as a house upon a rock foundation, enters into his righteousness for safety, as Noah entered the ark for protection from the flood. It acknowledges the utter impossibility of being saved by personal obedience to the law. To become righteous in that way is forever out of the question. It confesses past sins, present weakness, and the impossibility of canceling past transgressions by future obedience. Justifying faith is then the trust of the soul in Christ as the only hope of salvation. It is the forsaking of the sinking ship of self-righteousness, and taking refuge in the ark of Christ's atonement. *The genuineness* of this saving faith is proved by evangelical works of righteousness without which the state of justification cannot be retained. The works of faith declare, manifest the life and reality of saving faith. The tree of justifying faith is known by the fruits of good works. The *substance* of faith will project the shadow of good works. Hence there is a justification by faith without the *merit* of works, and a justification by faith *on the evidence of works;* but in both cases justification is based on the grace of the atonement. "As the body without the spirit is dead, so faith without works is dead also."

In conclusion, note the following particulars:

1. "*Importance of Justification.*—Justification is the very king and pillar of Christianity, and an error about justification is dangerous, like a crack in the foundation. Justification by Christ is a spring of the water of life, and to have the poison of corrupt doctrine cast into this spring is damnable."—*T. Watson.*

2. *It is by Faith.*—"Luther sought rest for his troubled breast in self-denial, and retirement as a monk,

but did not find it. In 1510 he started as a delegate for Rome, hoping to find relief from his burden there. As he came in sight of the city, he fell on his knees, exclaiming, 'Holy Rome, I salute thee!' He was shocked at the wickedness which he found there. The people said to him, 'If there is a hell, Rome is built over it.' At last he turned to ascend Pilate's staircase upon his knees. He toiled from step to step, repeating prayers at every one, till a voice of thunder seemed to cry within him, 'The just shall live by faith!' Instantly he rose; saw the folly of his hope of relief through works of merit. New life followed his new light. Seven years after, he nailed his 'theses' to the doors of the Wittenburg church, and inaugurated the Reformation."—*Foster's Cyclopedia.*

3. *Only by the Merit of Christ.*—" Some harbors have bars of sand which lie across the entrance, and prohibit the access of ships at low water. There is a bar, not of sand, but of adamantine rock—the bar of divine justice—which lies between the sinner and heaven. Christ's righteousness is the high water that carries a believing penitent over this bar and transmits him safely to the land of eternal rest."—*Salter.*

4. Justification and regeneration are *coincident* as to time, though distant as to nature. The first is what God does *for* us in heaven—granting pardon for all past sins; the latter is what he does *in us* in regenerating the heart. Like two streams which unite their separate waters to form one river, justification and regeneration are combined in the work of salvation.

IV REGENERATION.

Regeneration is the new birth: that work of the Holy Spirit by which we experience a change of heart.

It is expressed in the Scripture by *being born again;* by being *quickened;* by our partaking of the *divine nature.* The efficient cause of regeneration is the Divine Spirit."—*R. Watson.*

Proofs.—"Except a man be born again he cannot see the kingdom of God." (John iii. 3.) "That ye put on the *new man,* which after God is created in righteousness and true holiness." (Eph. iv. 24.) "If any man be in Christ, he is a new creature." (2 Cor. v. 17.)

Notes.

1. Justification is the removal of *guilt,* while regeneration is the removal of the pollution of sin. Justification is an act taking place in the court of heaven, while regeneration is a work performed by the Holy Spirit *in and upon the soul of the believer.* Justification, therefore, is *objective,* while regeneration is always *subjective.* Regeneration is the birth of a new-born babe. The infant born into the world is the man in miniature. All the parts of the body, and all the faculties of the mind, are there in embryo. So the regenerated person is a saint in embryo. The new principles are there, the new affections are there, the saint is there, but in infancy. The young twig two feet high is an oak, yet there is a vast distance between its diminutive size and the full-grown oak, covering with its wide-spreading branches an acre of ground. "The kingdom of God is like a grain of mustard-seed, which, when it is sown in the earth, is less than all the seeds that be in the earth; but when it is sown, it *groweth up,* and becometh greater than all herbs, and shooteth out great branches."

2. *Regeneration is More than Outward Reformation.*—"Wash me thoroughly from iniquity, and cleanse me from my sin." Mark the thoroughness of this desire.

Not only must sin be blotted out, but the *sinner* himself must be washed and cleansed. There must be not merely a change of state, but a change of *nature*. Not only must the debt be forgiven, but all *disposition* to contract further debt must be eradicated. Outward reformation is cutting the bird's wings, but leaving it with the propensity to fly. It is pulling out the lion's teeth, but not changing the lion's nature. A vicious horse is none the better tempered because the kicking straps prevent his dashing the carriage to pieces. Regenerating grace, like a lump of sugar in a cup of tea, sweetens the heart of man. It makes the tree good to get good fruit. It purifies the fountain of the heart, and then the practical stream of life will be pure.

3. The scriptural images setting forth the nature of the new birth are many. The first is the *new birth*. "So is every one that is *born* of the Spirit." "Christians are born of God; they are the children of God." "That which is born of the flesh is flesh, and that which is born of the Spirit is spirit." Every thing in generation produces its own peculiar kind. This is a universal law. The oak is born out of the acorn; the eagle comes out of the egg of the eagle; serpents beget serpents; corn produces corn; wheat generates wheat; so fallen human beings will generate children of impure fleshly nature. And as the child bears the image of the parent, so those born of God bear the image of God. They have the spirit of Christ. "To as many as received him to them gave he power to become the *sons of God*." Secondly, regeneration is compared to a *new creation*. "If any man be in Christ he is a new creature," or a new creation. *He is created* in Christ Jesus unto good works. This spiritual

creation refers to the creation of the world at the beginning. There were two stages of creation: first the creation of *matter;* then the fashioning the chaotic matter into a beautiful world of order. The latter illustrates spiritual creation. The soul in sin is the chaotic "earth without form and void, and darkness upon the face of it." And as the creative Spirit moved over the huge bulk of matter to bring light out of darkness, beauty out of deformity, life out of death, so must that same efficient and powerful Spirit shed light upon the darkened understanding, fashion the dilapidated soul into the beauty of the divine image, and imbue it with the moving energy of spiritual life. Thirdly, regeneration is likened to a resurrection from a state of death. The regenerated are "those that are alive *from the dead.*" "You hath he quickened who were dead in trespasses and sins." The regenerated man is the same man who was dead in sin. He has the same body, the same intellectual faculties and personal peculiarities. The convert is the same man, but leavened with a new spirit. Christ did not give the blind man *new* eyes, but a new *light* to the old ones. He did not give Lazarus a new body, but imparted life to the old one. The body of Christ was not destroyed, but remained the same body, and was made glorious by the Transfiguration; so the spiritual man is made glorious by grace.

4. *The Evidences of Regeneration.*—Regeneration is never without certain effects which evidence its existence. We have seen that the Bible describes it as "life from the dead," and as "a new creation." All life manifests itself. All nature seems dead in winter. When spring comes, we know it by the signs of vege-

table life. The buds open in new bloom, in new foliage, new verdure, new fruit. The evidence of life is abundant in all departments of nature. So in the work of the Spirit there is new light shining upon the mind. The Sun of righteousness pours its beams upon the darkened soul. There is new love shed abroad in the heart. "We know that we have passed from death unto life, because we love the brethren." Mr. Wesley said, when converted, "*I felt my heart strangely warmed.*" There is a new direction given to the will. The convert will ask, "Lord, what wilt thou have me to do?"

5. *Its Necessity.*—None can go to heaven unless they are made holy. "Except a man be born of water and of the Spirit, he cannot enter into the kingdom of God." *Purity* is a necessary qualification to enjoy heaven. If a sinner were lifted to heaven, he would be blind to its beauties, deaf to its songs, and dead to its joys. While malice remains in the devil's nature, were he admitted into heaven, it would be a place of torment. So a wicked man would meet hell in the midst of heaven, so long as he carries within him sin, for sin kindles the fires of hell in the soul. "The kingdom of God is *righteousness, peace,* and joy in the Holy Ghost."

V Witness of the Spirit.

"By the witness of the Spirit I mean an inward impression on the soul, whereby the Spirit of God immediately and directly witnesses to my spirit that I am a child of God; that Jesus Christ hath loved me and given himself for me; that all my sins are blotted out, and I, even I, am reconciled to God."—*John Wesley.*

PROOFS.—"The Spirit itself beareth witness with our spirit that we are the children of God." (Rom. viii. 16.) "He that believeth on the Son of God hath the witness in himself." (1 John v. 10.) "Because ye are sons, God hath sent the Spirit of his Son into your hearts, crying, Abba, Father." (Gal. iv. 6.) "The love of God is shed abroad in our hearts by the Holy Ghost." (Rom. v. 5.) "The fruit of the Spirit is love, joy, peace, long-suffering, gentleness, goodness, faith, meekness, temperance." (Gal. v. 22, 23.)

NOTE.

Can a Man Know that he is a Christian? Methodistic teaching answers, *Yes.* Mr. Wesley says: "The soul intimately and evidently perceives when it loves, delights, and rejoices in God, as when it loves and delights in any thing. I love and delight in God, therefore I am a child of God." The Bible furnishes certain marks of being a Christian. First, there is the *love* of God "shed abroad in our hearts by the Holy Ghost." The believer *feels, knows, is conscious* that he loves God; "therefore," he says, "I am a child of God." Mr. Wesley says when he was converted he *"felt his heart strangely warmed."* We are just as conscious of the warming influence of love as we are of a fire in a room, or of the genial beams of the sun breaking through the clouds on a cold day, and shining upon us. Love is likened to fire, and fire is something that can be sensibly felt. Secondly, fraternal love is a mark of a Christian. The believer feels that he loves all who love the Lord Jesus Christ in sincerity; therefore he concludes, "I am a child of God." "We *know* that we have passed from death unto life, because we *love the brethren.*" Brotherly love is adduced as a proof of having passed from death to life. Again, "He that loveth his brother *abideth in the light.*"

"Now, there are some things that we know. When

a man is enraged, he knows it; and other people generally know it, too. When a man is full of spirit, he usually knows it. When a man has the inspiration of ambition, and he is a fiery and energetic man, he knows that. A man knows whether he is in distress; he knows whether he is eager; he knows whether he is forceful or mild. A man knows whether it is his pleasure to do good, or whether he does it graciously. These things are within the sphere of positive knowledge. A man knows whether he joys or whether he sorrows. A man knows whether he loves or not; for if he does not know that he loves, he does not love, and he may be sure of it. There are some things that are like fire; and what would you say of one who should put his hand in the fire, and take it out slowly, look at it deliberately, and say, 'On the whole, I think it burns?' Men know what is evil. They know what is good. All the recognized things within the sphere of knowledge they know with positiveness — with all the positiveness that is required; nor does it necessarily infer conceit.

"Take notice, then, in regard to this witness, that light is thrown upon the method of it. We do not have this witness borne in upon us in consequence of any actions of our own, standing upon which we reason to it ourselves. It is not the result of retrospect. It is not from any estimate that we form of our moral worth. The soul's spontaneous affinity for God being disclosed in us becomes itself the evidence. We find ourselves possessed of a certain enthusiasm. We are lifted up, fired with an unusual experience; not a superhuman experience, and yet an experience transcending all ordinary experience; and the nature of it is that of love. It is an experience which, acting in love, draws us by elective affinities to the great Source and fountain of love, as well as of wisdom and power—God; and this condition of the soul which produces filial love is the sign of God's influence upon us. It is the witness of the Spirit."

VI. Holiness, or Sanctification.

"Sanctification is that work of God's grace by which we are renewed after the image of God, set apart for his service, and enabled to die unto sin and live unto righteousness. It comprehends all the graces of knowledge, faith, repentance, love, humility, zeal, and patience, and the exercise of them toward God and man."—*R. Watson.*

PROOFS.—"The very God of peace *sanctify* you wholly; and I pray God your whole spirit and soul and body be preserved blameless." (1 Thess. v. 23.) "This is the will of God, even your *sanctification.*" (1 Thess. iv. 3.) "As he who hath called you is *holy*, so be ye *holy* in all manner of conversation." (1 Pet. i. 15.) "Who gave himself for us, that he might redeem us from *all iniquity, and purify* unto himself a peculiar people, zealous of good works." (Tit. ii. 14.) "We are *sanctified* through the offering of the body of Jesus Christ." (Heb. x. 10.) "Herein is our love made *perfect.*" (1 John iv. 17.)

NOTES.

1. *The Nature of Holiness.*—It is the conformity of the heart and life to the law of God. The casting out of those inbred sins, the purification of the moral nature, and the restoration of the image of God, so that the soul is all glorious within, having the fruit of the Spirit—"love, joy, peace, long-suffering, gentleness, goodness, faith, meekness, temperance." It implies the consecration of the whole body, the whole heart, the whole spirit, the whole mind, property, influence,

family—all to the service of God. Sanctification brings the intellect of the Christian into captivity to Christ, so that he thinks for him; puts the love of God in his heart, so that he is unselfish and beneficent; the life of righteousness into his conscience, so that the law of right is his rule; the life of obedience into his will, so that it is his meat and drink to do the will of the Father.

2. *When is it Attainable?*—It is a work commencing *in* and carried on *after* conversion. It is a *second* blessing, in harmony *with*, yet separate *from*, and subsequent *to*, the work of conversion. There may be *rare* exceptions to this statement. The Catholic Church teaches that sanctification with *some* is attained *after* death through the fires of purgatory. The Calvinists, that it can be attained only in the *article of death*. The Methodists maintain that it may be attained soon after conversion and enjoyed during life. All agree, then, that *holiness*—perfect love, sanctification—is absolutely necessary as a qualification for heaven. The difference is simply in the time of its attainment. The Arminian view is unquestionably correct and scriptural. Our doctrine hereby elevates the plane of Christian experience immeasurably higher than the other view. The Catholic doctrine that men are sanctified in purgatory is simply absurd. To send a soul to hell to purify it, how ridiculous! Why is not the devil purified? He has been in hell long enough to be very pure, if that be the place of purification. The Calvinistic theory has no scriptural foundation. There is no virtue in the mere act of dying to sanctify the soul.

3. That sanctification is attainable during life will be seen: (1) Because *God wills it*. "For this is the

will of God, even your sanctification." God wills our sanctification just as truly and sincerely as he wills the salvation of sinners, or any other desirable thing. There can be no higher law than the will of God. (2) Because God *commands* it. "Be ye therefore perfect, even as your Father who is in heaven is perfect." "Be perfect"—not in knowledge or power as God, but in love and holiness. *Be perfect*—not in degree as God, but in quality, in kind. (3) *Because this great blessing is promised.* "Then will I sprinkle clean water upon you, and ye shall be clean: from all your filthiness, and from all your idols, will I cleanse you." (Ezek. xxxvi. 25.) "If we confess our sins, he is faithful and just to forgive us our sins, and *cleanse us from all unrighteousness.*" (1 John i. 9.) "The very God of peace sanctify you *wholly.*" Does not this passage mean entire sanctification? Do we have to wait till death for this? Then, why does the apostle pray that your "body be preserved blameless?" (4) Because the *possession of holiness is eminently desirable.* Holiness makes us like God. It enables us to enjoy much of heaven while on earth. It makes us more useful. It gives us *meetness* for heaven. The Methodist Church was raised up to spread holiness over the land. For this the precious blood of Christ streamed from the cross. For this the Holy Spirit is sent into the world. For this the lamp of the Bible shines. For this the gospel is preached. For this the world stands, the sun shines, the earth yields her increase, and judgment is delayed. For this God employs the various agencies of the Church. "For he gave some apostles, and some prophets, and some evangelists, and some pastors and teachers, *for the perfecting of the saints.*"

4. *How is this Blessed State to be Attained?*—(1) It is manifest that there must be a deep and abiding conviction of its need. No one will seek it till he feels it to be a duty and a great blessing. Reflect upon the reasonableness and glory of such a state. Can any thing less than the whole heart satisfy God? Supreme love to God is the glory of man. (2) There must be a definite and fixed purpose to seek it perseveringly, and by all possible means. (3) It must be sought by entire consecration of yourself and all you have to God. Consecrating the hands to work for God, the feet to walk in the path of obedience, the tongue to speak truthfully and lovingly, the ears to hear what is good and pure, the eyes to see what is best in men, the heart to be a vessel full of Christian love, the mind to reflect the glory of God as the moon the light of the sun, the property possessed to advance the cause of God. (4) It must be sought in the exercise of implicit faith—faith steadily believing in the ample *ability, willingness,* and *readiness* of God to bestow sanctifying grace. Nothing is hard with the omnipotent God. He that, through the sun, fills the earth with the glory of summer and the wealth of autumn, can fill your heart with the summer of divine grace. The ocean floats magnificent ships as easily as the fisherman's cork; the earth carries massive mountains as easily as mole-hills. It is as easy for God to give sanctifying as justifying grace. Throw yourself into the ocean of divine love, and be filled with all the fullness of God.

VII. THE POSSIBILITY OF FINAL APOSTASY.

The Statement of the Argument.—It is possible for a person who has been truly regenerated to fall away from such a gracious state and be finally lost. This doctrine is clearly taught in the Old Testament Scriptures.

PROOFS.—"But when the righteous turneth away from his righteousness, and committeth iniquity, and doeth according to all the abominations that the wicked man doeth, shall he live? All the righteousness that he hath done shall not be mentioned; in his trespass that he hath trespassed, and in his sin that he hath sinned, in them shall he die. When a righteous man turneth away from his righteousness, and committeth iniquity, and dieth in them; for the iniquity that he hath done, shall he die." (Ezek. xxxiii. 12-20.)

Let the reader observe: 1. The persons referred to in this passage are truly righteous men. Mr. Edwards concedes that a righteous man in Scripture phrase denotes a "godly man." 2. The drift of the whole passage shows that these righteous persons may totally turn away and perish in their sins. 3. Man's life on earth is a period of trial. He has all the endowments necessary to make him a free and responsible agent. In this character there is no time on earth when he is not subject to change of moral character. As a sinner, he may repent, reform, and become a good man all along the path of his probation. There is no point along this probationary road up to the hour of death where he may not repent and believe; or, *being good, may* relapse into sin and perish. If this be not true, then it must follow that man ceases to be a free agent.

SECOND PROPOSITION.—*The possibility of total and final apostasy is expressly declared in the New Testament.*

PROOFS.—"For it is impossible for those who were once enlightened, and have tasted of the heavenly gift, and were made partakers of the Holy Ghost, and have tasted the good word of God, and the powers of the world to come, if they shall fall away, to renew them again unto repentance; seeing they crucify to themselves the Son of God afresh, and put him to an open shame." (Heb. vi. 4–8.)

Let the reader observe, these persons were Christians of deep experience. 1. They were "*enlightened.*" 2. "*Tasted of the heavenly gift.*" This may mean the experience of a gracious pardon. 3. "*Made partakers of the Holy Ghost.*" This includes the work of regeneration, the witness of the Holy Spirit, and his indwelling influence. 4. "*Tasted of the good word of God.*" This means the Christian's relish and comfort in reading the Scriptures. 5. "*Tasted of the powers of the world to come.*" By this we understand the delightful anticipation of heaven. Here are all the marks and fruits of experienced Christians. But these persons may fall away and finally perish. The whole drift of the passage teaches this. The Greek scholars agree that the term "if" is not in the original passage. Mr. Wesley proves that it is not there, and says it should read: "It is impossible to renew again unto repentance those who have been once enlightened and have turned away and renounced the Saviour—the only refuge for sinners." The fall contemplated is total and final. And the possibility of such a fall is borne on the very face of the passage.

The same doctrine is taught by our Saviour.

Proof.—"I am the true vine, and my Father is the husbandman. Every branch in me that beareth not fruit, he taketh it away. I am the vine; ye are the branches. If a man abide not in me, he is cast forth as a branch, and is withered; and men gather them, and cast them into the fire, and they are burned." (John xv. 1–6.)

Observe: 1. The persons here spoken of were branches *in the vine*—that is, in Christ. 2. Some of these branches were *cut off* because they did not *bear fruit.* 3. And being severed from the vine—the only source of life—they hopelessly died, withered, dried up. For further proof-texts, see Luke xi. 12; Heb. x. 26.

THIRD PROPOSITION.—*The possibility of final apostasy appears from the repeated warnings against such danger, and the earnest exhortations to Christian faithfulness.*

PROOFS.—"Because of unbelief they were broken off, and thou standest by faith. Be not high-minded, but fear; for if God spared not the natural branches, take heed, lest he also spare not thee." (Rom. xi. 20, 21.) "Take heed, brethren, lest there be in any of you an evil heart of unbelief in departing from the living God. But exhort one another daily, while it is called to-day; lest any of you be hardened through the deceitfulness of sin. For we are made partakers of Christ if we hold the beginning of our confidence steadfast unto the end." (Heb. iii. 12-14.) "Let us therefore fear, lest, a promise being left us of entering into his rest, any of you should seem to come short of it." (Heb. iv. 1.)

Observe: 1. All these exhortations to *fear*, to be *diligent*, to put forth effort, undoubtedly imply the *possibility of failure*. It is a palpable absurdity to exhort men to hold on to that which it is impossible for them to lose. A Christian can or cannot fall from grace. If he cannot fall, then the exhortation not to fall is absurd and senseless. Suppose a man on some high mountain is chained to a rock with iron fetters that could not be broken; and another should stand off shouting, *"Take heed lest you fall!"* would not the exhortation be ridiculous nonsense? The application is easy.

FOURTH PROPOSITION.—*The possibility of falling from grace is evident from examples contained in the Scriptures.*

PROOF.—"Holding faith, and a good conscience; which some

having put away, concerning faith have made shipwreck; of whom is Hymeneus and Alexander, whom I have delivered unto Satan, that they may learn not to blaspheme." (1 Tim. i. 19, 20.)

Observe: 1. These persons once *had faith* and a good conscience, else they could not have wrecked or cast away what they never had. 2. They made shipwreck of this saving faith. 3. What is shipwrecked is entirely lost. A wrecked vessel is totally ruined. Angels fell from their original state of celestial holiness. Our first parents fell from their original purity. Judas fell from his apostleship by *transgressions*. King Saul was once a good man. "God gave him another heart," but he fatally backslid, and "died for his transgressions which he committed against the Lord." Solomon was clearly, at one time, a saintly man, but he evidently apostatized, and died, said Josephus, "ingloriously."

The dogma, "once in grace, always in grace," is a very fatal error. A man gets a ticket, sits down in the cars, folds his hands, and says to himself: "Well, I bought my ticket, I am *in* the train, and now I will go to sleep. It is the engineer's business to run the train and watch out for danger. It is the business of the conductor to land me safely at my journey's end. I have nothing to do but to sleep." This is about the way men reason who believe in final perseverance. And anyone can see the deadening and sleep-producing influence the doctrine has upon the human heart. But the Bible, instead of encouraging such a state, commands us to *Watch—work out your own salvation—give all diligence* to make your calling and election sure. Hundreds of warnings stand all through the Bible like mountains with a gloomy grandeur—stern, portentous, awful, and sublime, as Mount Sinai when the Lord descended upon it in fire, storm-clouds, and thunders, that shook the hills of the earth, "that the fear of God may be upon us, and that we sin not." They sternly rebuke the folly of supposing that because God has delivered us from our former sins, we need have no anxiety about our final salvation.

CHAPTER VI.

ORDERS IN THE METHODIST MINISTRY.

METHODISM recognizes but two orders in the ministry—*the deacon and presbyter*. It also recognizes a *third office*—that of bishop—which is presbyterial in *order*, but episcopal in office. Methodism occupies medium ground between prelacy on the one hand and parity of the ministry on the other. Roman Catholics and the Episcopalians believe in *three* orders — those of bishop, presbyter, and deacon. Presbyterians, Baptists, and Congregationalists maintain one order only—that of the presbyter. We believe that two orders are recognized in the Bible.

I. DEACONS.

The deaconship is a subordinate grade and order of the ministry. Deacons among Presbyterians and Baptists are simply lay-officers, but among Methodists they are a subordinate order of ministers. Methodism here is on scriptural ground. Stephen was a deacon, one of the first seven. He was a powerful preacher, "being full of the Holy Ghost." When the Jews heard his sermon which is recorded in Acts vii., "they were cut to the heart." He was duly ordained by the apostles. Philip was another deacon, and a preacher.

"Then Philip went down to the city of Samaria and *preached* Christ unto them." (Acts viii. 5.) He had a great revival at that place. "But when they believed Philip, preaching the things concerning the kingdom of God and the name of Jesus Christ, they were baptized, both men and women." "And there was great joy in that city." Philip expounded the Scriptures to the Ethiopian eunuch, and administered to him the rite of baptism. The point we make is that deacons are ministers, which is clearly proved by the above citations of Scripture. A Methodist deacon can perform all the ministerial functions of an elder, except that of consecrating the elements of the Lord's Supper.

II. Elders.

1. *Presbyter*, or *elder*, is a higher order and office of the ministry. It designates an order of men whose duties are to preach, to administer the ordinances, and watch over the Church. "The elders which are among you I exhort, who am also an elder. Feed the flock of God which is among you, taking the oversight thereof." (1 Pet. v. 1, 2.)

2. Elders have authority of governing the Churches. "Let the elders that rule well be counted worthy of double honor." (1 Tim. v. 17.) The people are exhorted to "obey them that have the rule over them, and submit themselves." (Heb. xiii. 17)

3. *Elders have the power of ordination.* Timothy was ordained by "the laying on of the hands of the *presbytery*," or body of elders. (1 Tim. iv. 14.) They were associates of ecclesiastical authority with the apostles. The decrees passed at Jerusalem to regulate the Churches "were ordained of the apostles *and*

elders." (See Acts xv. 2-6, 22, 23; xvi. 4; 1 Tim. v. 17.) As all Churches agree that the eldership is an ecclesiastical order, it is not necessary to dwell longer on this subject.

III. BISHOPS.

"Bishops are not a distinct *order*, but *officers*, elected by the body of elders for general superintendency, and for greater convenience in regard to ordination, and to secure unity and greater efficiency in administration; and this was unquestioned for hundreds of years. Now, Methodism conforms to this primitive arrangement." "Bishops and presbyters, or elders, were originally the same, but as Jerome says, one of the elders was chosen as a president, and called bishop by way of distinction, and some of the functions pertaining to the whole body of the presbyters—as ordination, for example—were committed to him, and, like the name, confined to him. Thus he became *primus inter pares*, first among equals."—*Bishop McTyeire.*

CHAPTER VII.
THE MODE OF BAPTISM.

THE essential elements of baptism are—

1. It must be administered in the name of the Father, and of the Son, and of the Holy Ghost.

2. It must be performed by a gospel minister. No others are commissioned to baptize but ministers of Christ.

3. The element to be used must be water only. This only is mentioned in the Scriptures.

4. The person baptized must be a proper subject.

We conclude, then, that *water applied in the name*

of the Trinity, by a gospel minister to a proper candidate, is Christian baptism. "Go ye therefore, and teach all nations, baptizing them in the name of the Father, and of the Son, and of the Holy Ghost." (Matt. xxviii. 19.)

It will be seen from the above definition that the *mode* of baptism is not one of its essential elements; that all the essentials of baptism will be preserved when administered by the mode of pouring, sprinkling, or immersion. Therefore, the Methodist Church holds that the three modes are equally valid, but that the weight of evidence is in favor of *pouring or sprinkling*. Pouring and sprinkling are really only one mode, they being alike as to mode, the difference being the freer use of water in pouring. The terms are borrowed from the Bible. "*I will pour out my Spirit; and then will I sprinkle clean water upon you.*"

We remarked that the *weight of evidence is in favor of pouring or sprinkling*. Real baptism is the regenerating influence of the Holy Spirit in the heart. Water baptism is the *sign* of this grace in the heart. That mode which is most like the mode of the Spirit's operation is the true one. *How* does the Spirit come upon the soul? Scripture teaches us on this point. "I will *pour* water upon him that is thirsty." (Isa. xliv. 3.) "Then will I *sprinkle* clean water upon you, and ye shall be clean." (Ezek. xxxvi. 25.) Thus, when Peter was addressing the company of Cornelius, "the Holy Ghost *fell* on all them that heard," and "on the Gentiles also was poured out the gift of the Holy Ghost." (Acts x. 44, 47.) Then, Peter baptized those on whom the Holy Spirit was poured out. Now, as the Holy Spirit was *poured* upon the people, it is almost certain that Peter *poured* water upon them as the most fitting mode of baptism. The *sign* as to mode would be like the thing signified, and the thing signified was *poured out*. Again, it is said in reference to Christ's baptism, "The heavens were opened unto him, and he *saw the Spirit of God descending like a dove, and lighting upon him.*" When God shows *how* he baptizes, the element *descends* upon the subject. But immersion requires that the *subject* descend—fall upon—the element. The mode of the Holy Ghost baptism is *pouring*, applying the *Spirit to* the soul; and water baptism, as a sign of this, should be poured, so as to make the *sign* correspond with the thing signified. But there is no resemblance between immersion, applying the candidate to water and covering him up in it, and the pouring out the Spirit *upon the* soul. The Spirit is shed upon us as rain upon the earth.

Dr. Pope, a Wesleyan minister of England, says: "There are many considerations which lead us to regard affusion, or sprinkling, as the ordained form of the rite. The catholic design of the gospel suggests that the simplest and most universally practicable ordinance would be appointed. Again, the most important realities, of which baptism is only the sign, are such as sprinkling, or affusion, indicates. The blood of the atonement was sprinkled on the people and on the mercy-seat; and the gifts of the Holy Ghost are generally illustrated by the *pouring* of water and the anointing."

Richard Watson, in his Institutes, says: "It is satisfactory to discover that all attempts made to impose upon Christians a practice (immersion) repulsive to the feeling, dangerous to the health, and offensive to delicacy, is destitute of all scriptural authority and of really primitive practice." Nevertheless, our Church, believing that the "essence of the rite" consists in applying water to the body in the name of the Trinity, says: "Let every adult person, and the parents of every child to be baptized, have the choice either of immersion, sprinkling, or pouring." Dr. Raymond says: "No Church, as such, except the Baptists, requires any particular form of baptism as a *sine qua non* condition of membership." So it will be seen that Methodists are not alone in allowing the choice of modes.

There is no command to baptize by immersion. The duty of baptizing with water is commanded, but, like the Lord's Supper, the mode of its administration is left undecided by any positive precept. The following Bible examples lead us to believe that the apostles administered it by pouring or sprinkling:

I. BAPTISM OF PAUL.

"And Ananias went his way, and entered into the house; and putting his hands on him said, Brother Saul, the Lord, even Jesus, that appeared unto thee in the way as thou camest, hath sent me, that thou mightest receive thy sight, and be filled with the Holy Ghost. And immediately there fell from his eyes as it had been scales; and he received sight forthwith, and arose, and was baptized." (Acts ix. 17, 18.)

NOTES.

1. Note that the rising up and baptizing are closely connected. Dr. Armstrong says: "In the original the language is much more definite than it appears in the English version." On the expressions "arise and be baptized" (literally, standing up, be baptized) and "he arose and was baptized" (literally, standing up,

ho was baptized), Dr. J. H. Rice remarks correctly: "According to the idiom of the Greek language these two words do not make two different commands, as the English reader would suppose, when he reads (1) '*arise,*' (2) '*be baptized,*' but the participle (*arise,* literally standing) simply modifies the signification of the verb, or rather is used to *complete* the action of the verb; and therefore, instead of warranting the opinion that Paul rose up, went out, and was immersed, it definitely and precisely expresses his posture when he received baptism."

2. "Three days had he been sunk in feebleness and fasting, when he 'arose and was baptized,' and then 'received meat and was strengthened.' Strange that where every movement is detailed with wonderful minuteness, no going forth in his weakness to a river could have been mentioned. The whole air of it is that he just stood up from his prostration in order to be baptized while *upon his feet.*"—*Dr. Whedon.*

II. BAPTISM OF THE JAILER.

"And they spake unto him the word of the Lord, and to all that were in his house. And he took them the same hour of the night, and washed their stripes; and was baptized, he and all his, straightway." (Acts xvi. 32, 33.)

NOTES.

1. Notice a few points in this case. The jailer and his family were baptized at the hour of *midnight* in the prison. "And he took them the same hour of the night, and washed their stripes; *and was baptized, he and his, straightway.*"

2. *The baptism took place in the prison.* We have the authority of the apostles that they did not go out of the prison. Paul refused to leave the prison *privily.*

He demanded that the magistrates themselves should take them out as *publicly* as they had put them in. Now, who can believe that Paul had gone out to some river at midnight—gone privily, secretly—and immersed the parties and then *slipped* back into the prison, and demanded a public and honorable discharge from the prison after he had been already out? Can anyone believe that Paul was capable of such deception as this? The refusal of the apostles to go out privily expressly implied that they had not been out the night before. Their language, if they had already been out, was based on concealment and equivocation. The magistrates might have fairly replied: "With what face can these men pretend that they will not go out without formal and public dismissal, when they have already gone out of their own accord, and are now in prison only by voluntarily imprisoning themselves?" No such hypocrisy can be charged against them; the conclusion is inevitable that they had not been out of prison-bounds.

3. Now, observe another fact: There was no tank or cistern in the prison where immersion could be performed. There is not the slightest ground for the wild supposition that a Roman prison was provided with any thing like a baptistry. The public authority that could thrust the innocent apostles, all bloody with stripes, into the irons of a dark dungeon would not likely provide baths for the comfort of their victims. The Romans were too cruel to mitigate the sufferings of their prisoners. Besides, Philippi was located in the very latitude of "Snowy Thrace," where such things would not be needed. A bath or tank in a Roman prison! As well expect to find a piano in

the wigwam of a flat-headed Indian. There was a baptism in the prison, but most clearly it was not by immersion. To suppose that the jailer took his wife and family out of bed at midnight, and went in search of a river to find some suitable place to have them immersed, is simply absurd. Therefore, the jailer and his family were baptized *in the prison*, and hence by sprinkling or pouring, as immersion would have been impossible under the circumstances.

III. BAPTISM OF CORNELIUS.

"While Peter yet spake these words, the Holy Ghost fell on all them which heard the word. And they of the circumcision which believed were astonished, as many as came with Peter, because that on the Gentiles also was poured out the gift of the Holy Ghost. For they heard them speak with tongues, and magnify God. Then answered Peter, Can any man forbid water, that these should not be baptized, which have received the Holy Ghost as well as we? And he commanded them to be baptized in the name of the Lord. Then prayed they him to tarry certain days." (Acts x. 44-48.)

NOTE.

The clear inference is that Cornelius and his household were baptized by *pouring*. The circumstances prove this. "They went to no river, they are not said to go down to any water, nor are we told that they had a bath adapted for such a purpose in their house. Peter's remark about forbidding water indicates that it was to be brought to him for the purpose of administering this rite. And, above all, it should be noticed that when the apostle saw the Holy Spirit DESCENDING upon them, he was reminded of what Christ had said of John's baptizing with water. (Acts xi. 10.) Whence this instantaneous recollection and association of ideas, but from the fact that the mode of water baptism was in form the same as that of the descent of the Holy Ghost? Had either John or Peter baptized by dipping, the narrative and the allusion would have been grossly inconsistent, and calculated to mislead the most devout and clear-headed student of inspiration."—*Rev. W Thorn.*

IV THE BAPTISM OF THE THREE THOUSAND.

"Then Peter said unto them, Repent, and be baptized every one of you in the name of Jesus Christ for the remission of sins, and ye shall receive the gift of the Holy Ghost." "Then they that gladly received his word were baptized; and the same day there were added unto them about three thousand souls." (Acts ii. 38, 41.)

NOTES.

1. That they were all actually baptized on this day is evident; and it is admitted by our opponents, who assure us that baptism always preceded admission into the visible Church. Now, supposing the twelve apostles to have been engaged in this work, and supposing immersion to have been the mode, it must have been a most laborious, disagreeable, if not an impracticable undertaking to be accomplished in the course of five or six hours. It should be taken into the account, moreover, that at least twenty-four robing-rooms and a dozen dipping-places must have been obtained for the purpose. And if more agents assisted, and lightened the labor of each, a proportionate increase of both kinds of conveniences must have been provided.

2. Now, in Jerusalem itself, there was neither a river nor a fountain of water. Kedron was little better than the common sewer of the city, and was dry except during the early and latter rains. Siloam was only a spring without the walls, not always flow

ing, the contents of which were sometimes sold to the people by measure; and the pools supplied by its puny streams were either used for washing sheep and similar purposes, rendering them unfit for ceremonial lustrations, or they were the property of persons not likely to lend them for washing apostate strangers in. The water used for domestic purposes was obtained from the rains of heaven and preserved in household tanks, and, of course, was guarded with the utmost care, and used with a rigid economy—it raining there at only two seasons of the year. It may be further mentioned that the fountain of Siloam "is the *only* place in the environs of Jerusalem where the traveler can moisten his finger, quench his thirst, and rest his head under the shadow of the cool rock, and on two or three tufts of verdure." (LAMARTINE.) That the case was precisely similar in the time of the apostles may be clearly proved by reference to the writings of Josephus, their countryman and contemporary.

CHAPTER VIII.
OBJECTIONS ANSWERED.

I. BURIED WITH HIM IN BAPTISM.

"Know ye not that so many of us as were *baptized into* Christ were baptized into his death? Therefore, we are buried with him by baptism into death." (Rom. vi. 3, 4; Col. ii. 12.)

OUR Baptist friends falsely assume that the baptism referred to here means ritual or water baptism, whereas it clearly refers to a spiritual baptism.

"Baptized *into* Christ" and "*baptized in the name* of Christ" are two very distinct things. The former means to be in the spirit of Christ, to be like Christ.

to be *in* Christ as the branch is in the vine. As: "For by one Spirit we are all *baptized into* one body;" "For as many of you as have been *baptized into* Christ, have put on Christ." These expressions mean spiritual baptism—and not ritual or water baptism. Wherever *water* baptism is meant the form of expression is, "*In the name* of the Father, and of the Son, and of the Holy Ghost." And so the passage under consideration says, "*Baptized into Christ*," and not in the name of Christ.

The apostle argues that renunciation of sin is death to sin; that as Christ died on the cross, so the old Adam in man is crucified by renouncing sin. As Christ was buried from the scenes of external nature in the rock-tomb, so the Christian, in baptismal dedication, is buried from the world in Christ's body— the Church. As Christ rose into a new life, so the Christian rises into a new life of holiness. No reference whatever to the mode of baptism is found here. It is the *sound* more than the sense that strikes our Baptist brethren.

The Rev. W Thorn says: "Mr. Robinson, the Baptist historian, gives up the passage, justly observing that Paul could not have referred to any thing like an ordinary English interment, as the persons to whom he wrote did not bury their dead, but burned them to ashes. Other leading Baptist writers have admitted that the original idea of burying is not the lowering of a corpse into a grave, but casting earth upon it, and thereby raising a barrow over it. Hence the entire argument founded on these passages in favor of dipping vanishes in a moment."

But supposing the reference had been to the entombing of Christ, the analogy is essentially defective. His precious body was carried into a room hewn out of a rock, and laid upon a side bench; a stone being rolled not upon but against the door, which was low and small. In this process there was not the slightest resemblance to dipping a person under water, no more than when the body of Dorcas was carried up-stairs and laid upon a bed. And he must be sadly at a loss for valid evidence in aid of immersion who seizes on this allusion to uphold his practice.

As a spiritual resurrection, or a rising to newness of life, is avowedly the *result* of this baptism, so, unquestionably, a spiritual interment must be supposed to precede it. In the same connection we are said to be crucified with Christ, and planted together in the likeness of his death. Surely, this can refer only to a spiritual work in the soul, and therefore the burial cannot be consistently regarded as an exception. Mr. Maclean, a leading Baptist, says that in consequence of our covenant union to Christ "we are so comprehended in and counted one with him as to have died in his death, been buried in his burial, and raised again in his resurrection." Here a physical similitude is quite out of the question. Indeed, the passage literally translated conveys not the least idea of such a resemblance: "As many of us as were baptized *unto* Christ Jesus were baptized *unto* his death; therefore, we are buried with him (DIA) *through* baptism unto death." Besides, those who regard this gracious renovation of soul as necessarily taking place at the font, or being the legitimate result of water baptism, and not as effected by the Holy Ghost, independent of that ordinance, will find it difficult to repel the charge of advocating the doctrine of baptismal regeneration."

II. THE BAPTISM OF CHRIST.

"Following Christ into the water," "Going down into the liquid grave," "Being buried with the Saviour beneath Jordan's rolling waves," are clap-trap words of much sound but of little sense. If you follow Christ strictly in baptism, you must wait till you are *thirty years* old, for he was not baptized until he had reached that age. What was the design of Christ's baptism? Christ furnishes the answer: "It becometh us to fulfill all righteousness." To fulfill righteousness is to be obedient to law. This was not the moral law, but the law respecting the high-priesthood. The baptism of Christ was the *public, formal inauguration* and consecration of him to his priestly ministry. He was just entering on the age of thirty—the age at which the Levites began their ministry and the rabbis their course of teaching. The consecration of Aaron to the high-priesthood was by *washing, anointing,* and *consecration*. Observe how this typical law was completely fulfilled by Christ: (1) He was washed by baptism; (2) he was anointed by the Holy Ghost; (3) and then consecrated to the priestly office. Thus we see that Christ was "a High-priest;" that he was "called of God" to this office as was Aaron; that he was ordained and consecrated to the office of "High-priest forevermore, that he might offer both gifts and sacrifice for sins."

III. JOHN BAPTIZING IN JORDAN.

1. It is believed that *immersing* persons in Jordan was altogether impracticable.

The Rev. W Thorn says: "The baptizing spot has been visited and minutely examined by many intelligent and credible travelers, who tell us that here "the river Jordan is of considerable width, the water turbulent, the bottom rocky, the edges of the bank abrupt, and the depth about six or seven feet close to the shore." Volney says, "Its breadth between the two principal lakes, in few places, exceeds sixty or eighty feet, but its *depth is about ten or twelve.*" Monro says, "The river here, at the baptizing spot, forms an angle, etc.; the width of it might be thirty-five yards, and the stream was running with the precipitous fury of a rapid; the bank was steep, shelving off abruptly into deep water." Thompson says, "It is exceeding deep, even at the edge of the inner bank." Dr. Shaw computes it "about thirty yards broad, and *three yards* in depth." Chateaubriand found the Jordan to be "six or seven *feet deep close to the shore.*"

2. Judging, then, from the places chosen, and the fonts constructed for immersion by our opponents, and indeed from the nature of the case (unless men and women in John's time were twice as tall as at the present day!), I contend that dipping persons in the Jordan was altogether impracticable, and unhesitatingly conclude that they were only affused, or sprinkled, with the water of it.

3. That John's baptism was not by immersion is clear from the vast number baptized by him. Dr. Hibbard proves that the population of Palestine at the time of John's ministry could not be less than *six million.* Now, the Bible says: "There went out unto him all the land of Judea, and they of Jerusalem, and all the region round about Jordan, and were

all baptized of him in the river Jordan, confessing their sins." Dr. Hibbard contends that "Jerusalem, all Judea, and the region round about Jordan" must mean the larger part of the population—and puts the number baptized at *three million*—half of the population. John's ministry lasted only about *ten* months. He allows six hours a day and six days in the week for baptizing, and upon this calculation shows that John had to baptize *two thousand and two hundred each hour*. And this calculation shows the utter impossibility of it being done by immersion.

Whatever may have been the mode of John's baptism, one thing is certain—that is, John's baptism was not the Christian baptism.

1. He did not baptize in the name of the Holy Trinity. And this is essential to Christian baptism. "Go ye, therefore, and teach all nations, baptizing them in the *name of the Father, and of the Son, and of the Holy Ghost.*"

2. John's baptism was not *initiatory* into the Church. It did not admit them into the Old Testament Church, since those who received it (being Jews) were *already* members of that Church by circumcision. It did not admit them into the Christian Church, since that Church had not been established. Just before the day of Pentecost the members of the Christian Church numbered only "*about one hundred and twenty.*" Now, of course John had baptized thousands before this, and if his baptism had admitted them into the Christian Church, the count would have been tens of thousands instead of "*one hundred and twenty.*" The fact is, the Christian Church was not instituted till *after* John's death.

3. It is rendered still more evident from the fact that Paul *re-baptized* certain persons at Ephesus, who had received John's baptism. (Acts xix. 5.)

IV BAPTO AND BAPTIDZO.

The argument of the immersionists is: "*My position is that baptidzo always signifies to dip, never expressing any thing but mode.*"—*Dr. Carson.*

The hinge on which the whole argument turns is that the classic meaning of the terms bapto and baptidzo is always but one thing—*to dip, immerse.* Can this be established? No. Let us see. "Dr. Dale (a learned divine of England) renders *bapto* dip fourteen times; dye, fourteen times; imbue seven times; temper, one time; stain, one time; wash, four times; moisten, two times; wet, one time—forty-seven. Of these forty-seven cases, as rendered by him, we have: (1) *thirty-three against* fourteen for dip; (2) in no case was there an immersion, *i. e., sinking.*"—*Dr. Ditzler.*

Dr. Ditzler, in his new work on Baptism, gives the following cases:

1. Of a frog pierced and slain, Homer says: "He fell without even looking upward, and the lake (ebapteto) was tinged with blood." Anybody knows that the lake could not possibly be *immersed* in the blood of a frog, but that the blood of the frog tinged the water with a red color.

2. Hippocrates, a Greek scholar, says of a dyeing substance: "When it drops upon garments they are (baptetai) dyed, or stained." Here we see that immersion is out of the question.

3. Aristophanes, speaking of an old comic writer, says: "Smearing himself (baptomenos) with frog-

colored paint." Here the term cannot mean dip or plunge.

4. Aristotle, speaking of a coloring substance, says: "Being pressed, it moistens (baptei) and dyes the hand." No immersion here.

5. Plutarch says: "Thou mayest be bathed (baptized), but it is not permitted thee to go *under the water*."

6. Clemens Alexandrinus says of a penitent: "He was baptized a second time *with tears*." Could a man be immersed literally in his own tears? An utter impossibility.

We see now, without quoting more instances, that bapto and baptidzo do not always and uniformly mean to dip, plunge, or immerse; and therefore the immersional theory completely breaks down.

Let the reader observe *the distinction between sacred and secular meaning of words*. Words change their meaning in the course of time. In the Greek language the word *presbyter* meant simply "an old man;" in the Bible the same word means a *preacher*, old or young. Timothy, though young in age, was a presbyter in the Church. In the old Greek language a *pastor* meant "a keeper of sheep;" in the Bible it signifies a man in charge of a church. Deipnon in Greek meant a *sumptuous* and royal feast; in the Bible it signifies the Lord's Supper. Ekklesia in Greek meant a political assembly; in the Bible it is translated a church. It follows conclusively that if baptidzo did mean in the Greek classics to dip, or immerse, it proves nothing unless it can be shown that it means the same thing in the New Testament.

The conclusion of the whole matter, to which we come, is:

1. There is nothing in the history of John's baptism, nothing in the practice of the apostles, nothing in the miscellaneous allusions to baptism in the Epistles, nothing in the meaning of the word *baptize*, to authorize the belief that any *particular mode of baptism is essential to the validity* of this rite.

2. While it cannot be determined with absolute certainty whether sprinkling, pouring, or immersion was the mode of baptism practiced by the apostles, *immersion is the least probable of the three, most inconvenient, and the least expressive of Holy Ghost baptism.*

3. To require immersion in order to admission into the Church is contrary to the teaching of the Bible, and to "teach for doctrine the commandments of men." And to exclude pious Christians from the Lord's table because they have not been immersed is narrow-hearted bigotry.

4. Baptism is enjoined upon all nations, and pouring is adapted to all climates, but immersion is not. How could immersion be performed in those countries where, for six months in the year, every pond, river, and ocean is converted into solid ice?

5. Baptism by sprinkling can be performed on persons who profess religion on a dying-bed, but immersion cannot.

6. Baptism by pouring comports with decency and propriety, but does immersion?

CHAPTER IX.

INFANT BAPTISM.

I. INFANT BAPTISM AS TAUGHT IN THE OLD TESTAMENT.

In tracing back the history of the Jewish Church, we find that infants were members of that Church.

1. This right of infant membership was established when that Church was organized. "Every man-child among you shall be circumcised." "He that is eight days old shall be circumcised." "The uncircumcised shall be cut off from his people."

2. The door through which children entered into the Old Testament Church was circumcision.

3. The visible Church of God has always been the same. The Christian Church to-day is the Old Testament Church purged from the apostate Jews. And around this purged Old Testament Church, as a nucleus, the New Testament Church was formed. John the Baptist said of Christ: "Whose fan is in his hand, and he will thoroughly purge his floor [the old Church], and gather his wheat [those remaining true] into the garner."

The good olive-tree representing the Church of the Jews was not plucked up and a new one planted in its place.

PROOF.—"Boast not against the branches. But if thou boast, thou bearest not the root, but the root thee. Thou wilt say then, The branches were broken off, that I might be grafted in. Well; because of unbelief they were broken off, and thou standest by faith. Be not high-minded, but fear; for if God spared not the natural branches, take heed lest he also spare not thee. For if thou wert cut out of the olive-tree which is wild by nature, and wert grafted contrary to nature into a good olive-tree; how much more shall these, which be the natural branches, be grafted into their own olive-tree?" (Rom. xi. 18–21, 24.)

REMARKS.—By the "good olive-tree" Paul can mean nothing but the Jewish Church. And what does he say about it? Was this good olive-tree plucked up by the roots? No. He asserts the *continuance* of the good olive-tree in life and vigor. The unbelieving Jews as worthless branches were cut off, while the believing Gentiles are being grafted into the fatness of the tree. But mark that the *trunk* of the good old olive-tree remains the same. The ingrafted Gentile partakes of the *root* and *fatness* of the olive-tree. It certainly was not cut down, nor rooted up, but is still flourishing in great beauty and fruitfulness. But furthermore the apostle, in the light of prophecy, foresees the restoration of the Jews. "These," says he, "the natural branches, shall be grafted in *again*—shall be grafted into *their own* olive-tree." When the Jews come into the Christian Church now existing, they will come into their own Church. But how could this be unless the Church be essentially the same under the old and new dispensations?

4. The right of infant membership existing in the Church *has never been repealed*. It stands intact to-day. No change has occurred. No proclamation has been made repealing the law of infant membership. And it is a well-known fact that a law once passed remains in force until formally repealed.

Now, as infants were members of the Jewish Church, and as the gospel Church is but a *continuance* of the Jewish, and no repeal of this law of infant membership having taken place, the conclusion is inevitable that the right of infant membership remains intact.

5. Circumcision, with other forms of the Jewish Church, gave way to baptism in the Christian Church. Baptism, like circumcision, is an initiatory rite of admission into the visible Church. As circumcision was the gate for the Jew and the Gentile proselyte into the Jewish Church, so baptism is the door into the Christian Church. Again, baptism, like circumcision, is a solemn dedication to God's service. Once more, baptism, like circumcision, is a sign and seal of God's covenant. The children of believers hold a similar relation to the Christian Church, as the Jewish children did to the Jewish Church; the former entering the Church by baptism, the latter by circumcision.

II. Christ's Recognition of Infant Membership.

Proofs.—"Then were there brought unto him little children, that he should put his hands on them, and pray; and the disciples rebuked them. But Jesus said, Suffer little children, and forbid them not, to come unto me; for of such is the kingdom of heaven. And he laid his hands on them and departed thence." (Matt. xix. 13-15.) "And they brought unto him also infants, that he would touch them; but when his disciples saw it, they rebuked them. But Jesus called them unto him, and said, Suffer little children to come unto me, and forbid them not; for of such is the kingdom of God. Verily, I say unto you, Whosoever shall not receive the kingdom of God as a little child, shall in no wise enter therein." (Luke xviii. 15-17.)

"Suffer little children to come unto me, *for of such is the kingdom of God.*" What is the meaning of *kingdom* of God? The kingdom is sometimes used to signify the visible Church on earth. "The kingdom of heaven is like unto a net that was cast into the sea, and gathered of every kind." (Matt. xiii. 47.) Then again, it is used to mean the Church of God in a state of glory. "Now this I say, brethren, that flesh and blood cannot inherit the kingdom of God." If we take the first meaning, then the passage would read: For of such is the visible Church, or, Such belong to the Church on earth. The Church was then the Old Testament Church. The day of Pentecost had not come when the Christian Church came of the old into the new. These children being the children of Jewish parents had been introduced into that Church by circumcision. They were then members of that Jewish Church. Hence he says *such are members* of the Church—of the kingdom of God. Or, let us take the other meaning—that the kingdom of God means the heavenly state. Then, it teaches that all children are born into a salvable state. The atonement of Christ puts them in a state of salvation. All believe that children dying in infancy are saved. They are then in a salvable state. If they have then the moral state of salvation, we think it is right to give them the sign of that state. Baptism is an outward *sign* of an inner grace. You say when a man is born of the Spirit he is in a state of salvation, and is a fit subject for baptism. Having saving grace, the thing signified, you give him the sign of it. That is your reason for baptizing adults. For the same reason we baptize children. The Bible authorizes us to baptize all persons who are *fit subjects*, be they infants or adults. The moral state decides the question of baptism, and not ages or classes of persons. If a grown person be a fit subject, or if a child be a fit subject, baptize him. And for this reason it is not necessary to have an express command to baptize infants. There is no command to baptize persons ten, twenty, fifty, or one year old. The authority is to baptize *all who are fit subjects* of the kingdom, young or old.

We are shut up to one of two conclusions—either infants are not fit to go to heaven, or admit their fitness for baptism. For if you admit their fitness for heaven, that implies that they have saving grace, and saving grace is universally conceded to be the ground of baptism. We must believe then either the horrid doctrine of infant damnation or the doctrine of infant baptism.

III. THE APOSTLES PREACHED THE DOCTRINE OF INFANT CHURCH-MEMBERSHIP.

Peter in his Pentecostal sermon expressly declared, "The promise is unto you and *your children*." The promise referred to is that which is contained in the Abrahamic covenant. Never was there a better time for Peter to declare the repeal of the law requiring the children to be brought into the Church than this. If that law had been repealed, now that they were passing out of the old into the new Church, Peter, it seems to me, would have said: "Repent and be baptized, for the promise is unto you, but *your children* are excluded under the new dispensation." But he said, "The promise is unto you *and your children*." Christ had commanded him before, "Feed my lambs," and he knew what he was talking about.

IV. FAMILY BAPTISMS.

PROOFS.—"And a certain woman named Lydia, a seller of purple, of the city of Thyatira, which worshiped God, heard us; whose heart the Lord opened, that she attended unto the things which were spoken of Paul. And when she was baptized, and her household, she besought us, saying, If ye have judged me to be faithful to the Lord, come into my house, and abide there. And she constrained us." (Acts xvi. 14, 15.)

Notice, nothing is said about her family exercising any religious duty, but it is said of her, "The Lord opened *her* heart, and *she* attended to the things spoken by Paul." As an adult person, she repented and believed. And as nothing is said about her family repenting and believing, but that they were baptized, the inference is that her family consisted of children too young to believe, and that they were baptized on the faith of the mother.

THE JAILER'S FAMILY.

"And they said, Believe on the Lord Jesus Christ, and thou shalt be saved, and thy house. And they spake unto him the word of the Lord, and to all that were in his house. And he took them the same hour of the night, and washed their stripes; and was baptized, he and all his, straightway." (Acts xvi. 31–33.)

The term "household," in the ordinary sense, includes all the children in a family. When it is said, "Joseph nourished his father and his brethren, and all his father's household, with bread, according to *their families*," little children are included. When the industrious mother is described as "looking well to the ways of her household," the term includes her children; for it is said, "Her children rise up and call her blessed."

Many attempts have been made to prove that there were no children in these families, but all such attempts are vain. The probabilities are against all such reasoning. Besides these families, Paul baptized "the household" of Stephanas. As households or families generally include children, we have no right to exclude them from these mentioned in the Bible. "Who can believe that not one infant was found in all these families, and that Jews accustomed to the circumcisions, and Gentiles accustomed to the lustration of infants, should not have also brought them to baptism?"—*Bengel.* "The practice of infant baptism does not rest on *inference*, but on the continuity and identity of the covenant of grace to Jew and Gentile, the *sign* only of admission being altered."—*Alford.*

The apostolic practice was that of baptizing entire families. That is certain. Now, if modern preachers follow them, they will baptize entire families; and if they go on in doing so, it is certain that they will baptize infants, for the continued practice of baptizing entire families will necessarily result in the baptism of infants. To follow apostolic example is to baptize entire families, and the continued practice of baptizing entire families is to baptize infants.

Historical Statement.

"From the year 400 A.D. to 1150, no society of men in all the period of seven hundred and fifty years ever pretended to say that it was unlawful to baptize infants. Irenæus, who lived in the second century, declares expressly that the Church learned from the apostles to baptize children."—*Watson.* So far as history affords any light, the baptism of children was practiced down to the eleventh century. About 1130, a body of Christians called Waldenses entertained the idea that infants were incapable of salvation, and therefore rejected infant baptism. About 1520, the Anabaptists renewed this objection, which the Baptists took up and stoutly maintain.

Since the Reformation of Luther, by far the greater portion of Christians have believed and practiced the baptism of infants. The number of Christians in the whole world is put down by Prof. Schem at four hundred and eighteen million; all of these—except about four million belonging mainly to the Baptist Church—believe in and practice infant baptism.

OBJECTIONS.

It is asked, "What is the benefit of baptism to children?" "What does the child know about it?" But don't you see that these objections bear just as hard against circumcision instituted by God as against infant baptism? What was the benefit of circumcision to children only eight days old? What did these infants know about it? We answer, God saw benefit in it, else he would not have commanded it.

Again, the stale and standing objection is, "There is no express command for infant baptism." But there is a command for circumcision in the Old Testament, and baptism takes the place of circumcision. But waiving this point, will you show an express command for *admitting women* to the communion-table? There is none. There is no command requiring baptism as a *prerequisite* to the communion, yet a certain Church acts as though there was. There is not a remote hint—much less a command—in the Bible authorizing the practice of *close communion*, yet the very Church that objects to infant baptism because there is no express "Thus saith the Lord," rigidly enforces the law of close communion without a single hint of Bible authority for so doing.

CHAPTER X.
GOVERNMENT OF THE CHURCH.

I. THE GENERAL CONFERENCE.

THE supreme government of the Church is vested in the General Conference. It is a law-making body. It is composed of the Bishops of the whole Church, and of ministerial and lay delegates who are elected by the several Annual Conferences. The clerical members of each Annual Conference elect one representative of their number for every twenty-eight of the whole body. An equal number of lay delegates is then elected by the lay members.

THE BUSINESS OF THE GENERAL CONFERENCE.

1. The election of Bishops when deemed necessary.
2. To create and readjust the boundaries of the Annual Conferences.
3. To revise the laws and rules of the Discipline.
4. To superintend the interest of Foreign Missions.
5. To elect officers to conduct the business of the general Publishing House.

These items embrace the leading matters of the General Conference work. That body, however, has full powers to make rules and regulations for the Church, under the following restrictions: (1) They cannot change the Articles of Religion, or the standards of doctrine; (2) cannot change certain ratio of Annual Conference representation; (3) cannot destroy the episcopacy; (4) cannot change the General Rules of the United Societies; (5) cannot destroy the privileges of trial as prescribed in Discipline; (6) cannot appropriate the produce of the Publishing House otherwise than specified in Discipline. No change can be made in reference to the subjects protected by the Restrictive Rules except by a majority of *two-thirds* of the General Conference, and the concurrence of *three-fourths* of the members of the several Annual Conferences. Our Articles of Religion and doctrinal standards cannot be revoked or altered even by such a large vote as the above. The General Conference meets once in four years, its sessions lasting about four weeks, and is presided over by the Bishops, each one presiding in turn, a day at a time.

The lay delegates appeared for the first time in the General Conference in 1870, the General Conference of 1866 having recommended it, and the Annual Conferences having concurred, it became a law and took effect in 1870. The introduction of the lay element into the General Conference puts the actual government of the Church equally into the hands of the laymen and the ministry. It is the *only law-making* power in the Church, the Annual Conferences being only administrative and judicial. "The General Conference carries out its laws through an executive arrangement consisting of the Bishops and presiding elders. By their agency, it exercises a general superintendence over the Church."

II. ANNUAL CONFERENCES.

1. The ministers within certain boundaries assemble each year, and this meeting is called an Annual Conference. It is composed of all the itinerant ministers in full connection, and of four lay delegates (one of whom may be a local preacher) from each

presiding elder's district. The lay members have equal rights with the ministerial, "to participate in all the business of the Conference, except such as involves ministerial character." The Bishops, by virtue of their office, are presidents of the Annual Conferences. In the absence of a Bishop, a president is elected by the Conference. The Bishop presiding, after careful consultation with the presiding elders, appoints annually each minister to his field of labor.

2. *The Business of the Conference.*—The principal items of business are the following: (1) To receive from each pastor a report of his year's work; (2) to admit candidates for pastoral work on trial, or into full connection; (3) to inquire into the life and administration of each pastor; (4) to try any who may be accused of immorality or heterodoxy; (5) to examine into the qualifications of candidates for deacon's and elder's orders, and elect the same to such orders; (6) to inaugurate measures to promote the work of missions, Sunday-schools, and education, within the boundaries of the Conference; (7) to distribute the collected funds for the relief of the worn-out ministers, and the widows or orphans of the deceased ministers who died members of the Conference; (8) the appointment of the preachers. Whatever may be the size and number of the Conferences, they are all organized on the same plan and governed by the same laws. There are thirty-eight Conferences in the M. E. Church, South.

III. DISTRICT CONFERENCES.

1. A District Conference is held annually in each presiding elder's district. It is composed of all the

traveling and local preachers within the bounds of the district, and a certain number of laymen from each pastoral charge, which number is fixed by each Annual Conference. The presiding elder is the president unless a Bishop be present.

2. *The Business of this Conference.*—(1) It is the duty of this Conference to inquire respecting the spiritual condition of each pastoral charge, and as to the attendance of the people upon the ordinances and social meetings of the Church; (2) to inquire respecting new fields for establishing missions, and what existing missions ought to be raised to circuits; (3) to inquire if the collections for Church purposes are properly attended to, and as to the comfortableness of churches and parsonages; (4) to inquire into the condition of Sunday-schools, manner of conducting them, and adopt suitable measures for insuring success, and also as to the educational enterprises of the district, and take a general oversight of all the temporal and spiritual affairs of the district, subject to the provisions of the Discipline; (5) to elect four lay delegates—one of whom may be a local preacher—to the ensuing Annual Conference; (6) these Conferences give prominence to preaching, prayer-meetings, love-feasts, and revival exercises.

IV THE QUARTERLY CONFERENCE.

The Quarterly Conference is an official meeting held four times a year, for the purpose of transacting the business of each one of the pastoral charges. It is composed of the pastor in charge, the local preachers, exhorters, stewards, trustees, class-leaders, superintendents of Sunday-schools, and secretaries of the Church Conferences. The presiding elder—in his absence the preacher in charge—is president of the meeting. He also appoints the times of holding the meetings, signs the records, and decides all questions of law.

Its business. (1) It takes account of the temporal and spiritual welfare of the church; (2) elects trustees, stewards, superintendents of Sunday-schools; (3) licenses persons to preach or exhort; (4) tries local preachers when accused, and is a court of appeal to laymen tried in the church; (5) recommends suitable persons to join the Annual Conference, and such local preachers as desire deacon's or elder's orders.

The minutes of this Conference must be regularly recorded, signed, and preserved. All ministers of every office and grade must first be licensed by a Quarterly Conference. None can get into the Annual Conference, except they be recommended by it. The functions of this body are organic; its work is executive and judicial, and is closely related to the order and prosperity of the Church. It is the great wheel moving the business machinery of each circuit, station, and mission, and is indispensable to our system.

V The Church Conference.

This is a meeting of *each* society in a pastoral charge. The pastor is president; a secretary is elected to note the proceedings; the roll of members is called. All the members of the society have a right to participate in the meeting. It is a kind of mass-meeting of that particular church.

The object of the meeting is to lay before all the members reports, (1) of the pastor as to the state of his work; (2) of the class-leader; (3) of the superintendent of the Sunday-school; (4) of the stewards.

The meeting further inquires into what is being done for the *relief* of the poor, for the cause of missions, for the circulation of our religious literature, and any other matter that may advance the good of the church. The meeting "may strike off the names of any who, on account of removal or other cause, have been lost sight of twelve months: provided, however, that if such member appears and claims membership, he may be restored by a vote of the meeting."

The information given by the above reports is designed to enlist the energies of the whole church in its local work of benevolence and spiritual enterprise. The main end of the Church Conference is to put every member to work for the cause of Christ.

CHAPTER XI.
CHURCH OFFICERS.

In the Ministry: Bishops, Presiding Elders, Pastors, Local Preachers.

I. BISHOPS.

BISHOPS are constituted by the election of the General Conference and the laying on of the hands of three Bishops. Their duties are: (1) To preside in the General and Annual Conferences; (2) to make the appointments of the preachers; (3) to form the districts, circuits, and stations; (4) to ordain Bishops, elders, and deacons; (5) to decide questions of law; (6) to prescribe a course of study for young ministers; (7) to change preachers in the interval of Conferences whenever necessary; (8) to travel through the Connection at large and oversee the temporal and spiritual welfare of the whole Church. The episcopacy of

Methodism is not diocesan, like that of the Protestant Episcopal Church, but is *coëxtensive* with the territory of the Church at large. It differs from the Episcopal Church, mainly, in not claiming apostolic succession. Methodist Bishops have neither legislative nor voting power in the Conferences. They, according to our theory, are elders as to ministerial *order*, and episcopal as to the high office of general superintendency. Our moderate episcopacy does not claim any *divine right* for its existence, but affirms that no specific form of Church polity is prescribed in the New Testament, and therefore the Church is free to adopt such a form as in its judgment will best promote the cause of Christ. We claim that our episcopacy preserves the *unity* of the Church, is itself a connectional bond, and serves to strengthen and maintain all other bonds by which the several churches are united in one great connectional Communion. It is the most efficient agency in distributing ministerial talents over the world. So far as human wisdom is competent to judge, it is the most effective form of Church government known among men.

The distinction between the non-Episcopal branches of Methodism and the Episcopal is clearly marked. Wherever Methodism has abandoned the episcopacy and the presiding eldership, the connectional bonds have been loosened, difficulties have arisen, and serious losses have been sustained. "English Methodists have failed to hold their affiliated Conference, and one after another seeks distinct government." The non-Episcopal Methodist Churches, both of America and England, have not prospered so abundantly as the Episcopal Methodist Churches in the two countries named. The vast superiority in numbers of American Methodism over that in England is attributable mainly to our episcopal form of government. Dr. Dixon, one of the leading Wesleyan ministers, said, "We must look to American Methodism to find the model Church of Mr. Wesley."

II. PRESIDING ELDERS.

The presiding elder is appointed by the Bishop, and is put in charge of a district having from twelve to twenty pastoral charges in it.

No class of ministers in the Methodist economy fill a more important position than the presiding elders. This will appear when we consider:

First. Their broad field of ministerial usefulness. They preach over the widest scope of territory, to the largest congregations of appreciative hearers, and under the most inspiring circumstances. Quarterly-meeting occasions have always been, among Methodists at least, the most attractive and fruitful of good results. There is usually the fullest attendance of the members of the particular church where these meetings are held, and also official brethren of other churches. And furthermore, it is the privilege of the presiding elders to preach to such congregations almost every Sunday in the year. And on such occasions they preach their select, most powerful and impressive sermons. The field of ministerial usefulness, then, opened to the presiding elders is vastly superior to that of other preachers. In the light of these facts, it seems strange to hear the question asked—as it is sometimes—"What is the use of presiding elders?" If, as it is conceded cheerfully, the pastors of stations and circuits deserve to be well paid, highly esteemed, and dearly loved because of their ministerial usefulness, then the presiding elders have a higher claim for the same benedictions of the people.

Secondly. The official duties of the presiding elder are many and weighty, and for the information of the people it may be well for us to specify. The duties of the presiding elder are: (1) To travel through his district in order to preach and oversee the spiritual and temporal affairs of the Church; (2) to take charge of all the preachers in his district in the absence of the Bishop; (3) to change, receive, and suspend preachers in his district during the intervals of the Conferences; (4) to hold four Quarterly Conferences in each pastoral charge during the year; (5) to decide all questions of law which may come up in the regular business of the Quarterly Conference; (6) to see that every part of the Discipline is enforced in his district, etc.; (7) if any preacher dies, or leaves his work, the presiding elder, as far as possible, fills his place with another; (8) he is *ex officio* president of the District Conference in the absence of the Bishop. There are some other minor duties not mentioned, but we have specified enough to show the importance of this office.

Thirdly. One of the most important functions of the presiding eldership is the relation it holds to the Bishop in making the appointments of the preachers. Every appointment must be made with a thorough knowledge of the qualifications of the preacher appointed and the demands of the work to which he is appointed; and the Bishop can get such knowledge only through the presiding elders. The presiding elders, then, must *see* and *hear* for the Bishop, and *speak* for the people and the preachers, in the matter of appointments. As they have traveled through all the field, and watched carefully the work of each pastor and wants of each charge, they are admirably well prepared to represent the wants of the people and the claims and adaptation of the preachers; so their advice becomes *essential* to the Bishop in order that his appointments may be judiciously made. They are *middle-men*, and, like all men occupying such a position, they are likely to be blamed, though they may have done their best both for the people and the preachers. There is no work so carefully and prayerfully done as making the appointments of the preachers.

III. PASTORS.

The preacher in charge of work is one who has the pastoral care of a station, circuit, or mission, by the appointment of the regularly constituted authority of the Church. He may be an elder, deacon, or an unordained preacher on trial, or a local preacher employed by the presiding elder. His duties are: (1) To preach; (2) to receive, try, and expel members convicted of immorality; (3) to appoint class-leaders; (4) to see that the sacraments are duly observed; (5) to hold quarterly-meetings in the absence of the presiding elder; (6) to report to the Quarterly Conference the general condition of his work; (7) to promote all benevolent collections of the Church; (8) to report the number and state of the Sunday-schools.

Pastors are represented in the Bible as having "authority" and "rule" over the churches. "Obey them that have the rule over you." They are to "preach the word," to "teach, baptize, to feed the flock." They are sometimes called "elders," because of their oversight; called "pastors," because of their watch-care; "ministers," because of the services rendered; "watchmen," because of their wide-awake vigilance; "embassadors," because of their authority to effect peace between God and man. The three functions of *preaching* the word, *watching* over the congregation, and *ruling* in the congregation by the exercising of discipline, are clearly laid down in the New Testament. The responsibility of all these rests upon the pastor.

IV LOCAL PREACHERS.

Local preachers are constituted by the authority of the Quarterly Conference, and are amenable to that body. They must come before that body properly recommended by the individual church of which they are members. Such applicants are licensed to preach when, on examination, the Conference is satisfied that they have *gifts*, *graces*, and *usefulness*. Local or lay preachers began with the early years of Methodism. They have always been a powerful arm in the Methodist work. They support themselves by secular labor, and preach in their neighborhood on Sundays, and render a very valuable service to the Church. Philip Embury, Captain Webb, and Robert Strawbridge, three local preachers, founded Methodism in America, and their successors have planted it in the new States of the West. Throughout the entire range of the Methodist Connection the local preachers are still an effective and faithful body of ministerial laborers. From their ranks comes the great army of the itinerants. They usually begin as exhorters, graduate to the local ministry, and thence into the itinerancy.

No feature of Methodism shows more practical wisdom than this threefold arrangement and graduation of her ministry. The exhorter must show improvement before he can become a local preacher, and the local preacher must show capacity before he can reach the itinerant ranks.

LAY OFFICERS OF THE CHURCH.

Exhorters, Class-leaders, Stewards, Trustees, Superintendents of Sunday-schools.

I. EXHORTERS.

An exhorter is one licensed by the Quarterly Conference to read scriptural lessons and make a practical application of their truths to the public congregation. They are not expected to select a text and preach a regular sermon. Their service is confined to singing, prayer, and public exhortation. They are useful laborers in our Church. Mr. Wesley permitted none of his members to exercise even the function of an exhorter without license, and so it is ingrafted in our economy that *license* to exhort must be given and annually renewed by the Quarterly Conference, to which body the exhorters are responsible for their official conduct.

II. CLASS-LEADERS

are appointed by the preacher in charge. In 1771 Mr Wesley said: "That it may be more easily discerned whether the members of our societies are working out their salvation, they are divided into little companies called classes. A leader is appointed whose duty it is (1) to see each person in his class once a week, to inquire how their souls are prospering, to advise, reprove, comfort, or exhort them; (2) to report to the pastor any that are sick or walking disorderly."

III. Stewards.

Stewards are elected by the Quarterly Conference. Their business is (1) to attend to the financial interest of the charge; (2) to advise and confer with the pastor as to the general management of the work. Their duties are many and weighty. First, the question of a liberal and generous salary for the pastor *depends* upon them. Second, whether the salary allowed shall be paid *depends* almost exclusively on their efforts in collecting the money. *No other persons are* authorized to collect the estimated amount. If they fail, the failure is remediless. *Faithfulness* in this office is of the highest importance to the welfare of the ministry and the prosperity of the Church.

IV. Trustees.

All Church property—such as meeting-houses, parsonages, cemeteries—held according to the Discipline, is vested in a board of trustees, who hold it in trust for the use of the members of the Methodist Episcopal Church, South. The ministers have never claimed, nor do they hold in law, any title to such property. Churches thus held are obliged to be opened to ministers duly sent by Conference. These churches are held for the sacred purpose of divine worship, and are to be closed against all political or secular meetings. The trustees are elected by the Quarterly Conferences, and are responsible to the same.

V Superintendents of Sunday-schools.

The Quarterly Conference elects superintendents of Sunday-schools on the nomination of the preacher in charge. The office of the superintendent is one of vast importance to the future prosperity of the Church, and therefore great care should be taken to put in men of the greatest efficiency.

CHAPTER XII.
PECULIAR USAGES OF METHODISM.
I. CLASS-MEETINGS.

IN order to raise money to pay a Church debt, Mr. Wesley divided his people into classes of twelve, requiring "every member to give a penny a week." These classes, meeting weekly to contribute their pennies, became also meetings of religious experience. Thus what were at first business-meetings finally developed into class-meetings, which have become one of the peculiar institutions of Methodism. These meetings have been of vast benefit in building up the spiritual manhood of Methodism. But for many years they have been in a state of deep declension. The signs of restoration are beginning to appear in various parts of our Zion. It will be a happy day for Methodism when they are restored to their primitive prevalence and vigor. There are sundry passages in the Bible on which the institution of the class-meeting may rest as a scriptural basis.

While we do not find class-meetings in the Bible in the same form that Methodists hold them, still they are substantially recognized in the word of inspiration. David (in Ps. lxvi. 16) says: "Come and hear, all ye that fear God, and I will declare what he hath done for my soul."

1. Here we see that the godly man is anxious to *impart* to others his experience. "Come and hear." This experience is related to congenial hearers. "All

ye that fear the Lord." These were the spiritual brethren of the psalmist. Spiritual men only comprehend the experience of a godly man, and are therefore greatly benefited by it. They are confirmed and refreshed in their own experience. No man ever related a good experience that did not benefit others. It falls as dew upon the grass. It often disperses the clouds of doubts as the sun clears the skies of clouds. Paul often told the experience of his conversion to the edification of thousands. Wesley's experience, where he states, "*I felt my heart strangely warmed,*" has been a lamp to the feet of thousands. The experience then of godly men is one of the most powerful elements in Christianity. Now, class-meetings afford a constant opportunity for the wielding of this power.

2. Again: The man who relates his experience is perhaps more benefited than the hearers. It makes religion intensely a *personal* matter. "Come, hear what he hath done for *my soul.*" In this matter we talk about ourselves without egotism. It puts a man to thinking about the dealings of God with his soul. It leads a man to obey the apostolic injunction, "Examine yourselves whether ye be in the faith." Self-examination is very important. The lack of it swamped the foolish builder spoken of in the sermon of Christ. It shut the door against the foolish virgins. These meetings are then especially valuable in leading persons to frequent personal examinations.

3. The class-meeting promotes the spirit of fraternal sympathy—the communion of saints. "I believe in the communion of saints." It is a spiritual feast. It is a foretaste of heaven. The fragrance of the blooming garden is not so sweet and refreshing.

It is more genial than the beaming of a warm sun after a season of cold, cloudy weather. "Behold, how pleasant it is for brethren to dwell together in unity."

4. Class-meetings accomplish great good in leading men to a *confession* of their faults. There is nothing here like the Romish confessional. The confession is *voluntary*, not enforced. Voluntary confession is good for the health of the soul. So James thought, "*Confess your faults one to another*, and pray one for another, that ye may be healed." It leads a man to abandon his faults, it enlists the prayers of his brethren, and thus has *healing* and curing effects. When the prodigal son confessed—"I have sinned"—he arose and came to his father.

5. Class-meetings are eminently pleasing to God. "Then they that feared the Lord spake often one to another; and the Lord hearkened and heard it; and a book of remembrance was written before him for them that feared the Lord, and thought upon his name. And they shall be mine, saith the Lord of hosts, in that day when I make up my jewels." The eloquent speeches of legislative halls and kingly parliaments may be written down by ten thousand editors of political journals, but they are not written in the book of God; but the class-meeting talks of God's people are. God thinks so much of these meetings as to have angel reporters there to take down every word, and have it put in the celestial journals.

7. These meetings serve to kindle religious feelings. In such a meeting the heart is drawn out in sympathy, prayer, and desire, and thus a warmer, purer flame is kindled; a fresher love toward God and man is aroused.

When Christ held a kind of class-meeting with his disciples on their way to Emmaus, they said one to another, "Did not our hearts burn within us while he *talked* with us by the way?" These disciples were in the gloom of spiritual winter, but their feelings soon began to kindle, burn, and flame as Christ talked with them. Their clouds were gone, the winter was over, the life of spring began to bud and blossom—balmy air, clear skies, and the warm Sun of righteousness were now pouring a tide of gladness into their souls. How many have gone to these meetings with the darkness of spiritual winter upon them, and have come out with the brightness and beauty of spring all around them!

II. THE ITINERANCY.

A marked peculiarity of Methodism is the itinerancy of her ministry. It is a simple and easy plan of shifting the ministers from one field of labor to another. It requires *three things:*

1. That the congregations give up their right to choose their pastors.

2. That the ministers surrender their right to select their own field of labor.

3. That the appointment be referred to a competent, impartial, untrammeled, but responsible authority arranged by the law of the Church.

Both the people and ministers, however, are at liberty to make known their peculiar condition, wishes, and circumstances to the appointing power. And thus, under this elastic system, all parties have their own choice, when it is clear that the good of the work will be served. While the Bishops have the sole authority of making the appointments, yet they always do so under the advice of the presiding elders. They are *eyes* and *ears* for the Bishop and *mouth* for the people and the preachers. Having traveled through all the work, and being intimately acquainted with the wants of the people and the peculiar qualifications of the preachers, they rarely fail in so advising the appointing power as to secure the best disposition to be made of the ministers. Under this system a minister is liable to be moved after one year's service, yet he may remain *four* years, if all the parties concerned think it best; but beyond this term he cannot go.

The theory of the Methodist itinerancy is based upon the fact that "the world is the parish" of Methodism —that all men everywhere must be called to repentance. It is based upon the great commission, "Go ye into all the world, and preach the gospel to every creature." "Go ye," not wait until the people come to you. In the *settled ministry*, the people call the preacher; in the itinerant system, the minister seeks the lost sheep. Jesus Christ himself was an itinerating preacher. His *circuit* embraced Judea, Samaria, and Galilee. The apostles were commanded "*to go to* the lost sheep of the house of Israel;" the Seventy were *sent forth*, two and two, "into every city and place." "Paul said to Barnabas, Let us go *again*, and visit our brethren in *every city* where we have preached the word of the Lord." Philip traveled the new circuit of Samaria, which embraced Cesarea, Gaza, Azotus, and all the cities on toward Cesarea; and on the first round he had a great revival at Samaria, and was instrumental in the conversion of the Ethiopian eunuch in the south part of his circuit.

Peculiar Advantages of the System.—1. It keeps all

the churches constantly supplied with pastors. The weak and poor churches are as regularly supplied as rich ones. Though such churches be out of the way, and able to pay but little, yet they always have a pastor. Consequently we never have what is so frequently found in other denominations, viz., *vacant churches*.

2. No effective preacher in this system is ever found without a pastoral charge. We have no unemployed ministers waiting, year after year, for some congregation to call them. The ministerial waste of time in other denominations in this respect is enormous. We noticed in a paper not long since that some eight hundred ministers of the Presbyterian Church in the United States were without any regular pastorates.

3. It furnishes our people with a great *variety* of ministerial talent. One year they have a logician to defend the doctrines of the Church, next they have a son of thunder to awaken and arouse the sleepers; this year a revivalist to get the people converted, the next an experienced disciplinarian to train them.

4. It readjusts annually the whole machinery of pastoral relations, so as to secure the greatest efficiency possible.

5. It takes out of and puts into pastoral charge ministers without that violence and strife which attend the dissolution of pastoral relations in the other denominations.

6. Finally, it is well known that the changes in the settled ministry, on an average, are quite as frequent as among the Methodists, but without the harmony and efficiency of the itinerant system. We believe the plan to be providential; it has worked wonders, and we expect to adhere to it till the trump of judgment sounds

III. LOVE-FEAST.

The design of the love-feast is to cultivate and exercise fraternal love and good-fellowship. It is done by eating and drinking the simple elements of bread and water as a beautiful evidence of the same, and to speak together of religious experience for the purpose of strengthening each other's faith and magnifying the goodness of the Lord. The feasts of charity were held by the primitive Church very much as Moravians and Methodists now hold them. Dr. Neander, in his Life of Christ, says, "At the *agapæ*, or love-feasts, all distinctions of earthly condition and rank were to disappear in Christ." Tertullian says, "Our supper shows its character by its name; it bears the Greek name of love." The following scriptures allude to it: "And they continued steadfastly in *breaking* of bread, and in prayers." (Acts ii. 42.) "Upon the first day of the week, when the disciples came together to break bread," etc. (Acts xx. 7) "These are spots in your feasts of charity, when they feast with you." (Jude 12.) The love-feast in the Apostolic Church preceded immediately the communion of the Lord's Supper. The Discipline says, "Love-feasts shall be held quarterly, or at such other times as the preacher may consider expedient." They are to be held by partaking of "a little bread and water *in token of brotherly love.*"

CHAPTER XIII
MINISTERIAL SUPPORT
THE GROUNDS OF MINISTERIAL SUPPORT.

It is certain that God would not, and most assuredly

did not, establish his Church on earth without making ample provisions for its support and perpetuation. In the beginning God instituted a system of tithes for the express purpose of maintaining divine worship. The gold and silver of earth were stored away to do this. "The earth is the Lord's, and the fullness thereof." Churches cannot be built without money. Missionary operations cannot be carried on without money. The question of the world's conversion is largely one of money. The efficiency of the ministry is largely dependent upon a competent support.

I. THE DIVINE LAW ON THE SUPPORT OF THE MINISTRY.

If we turn to this law as recorded by Moses, we shall find it to be specific, definite, and divinely authoritative. Here it is: "And all the tithe of the land, whether of the seed of the land, or of the fruit of the tree, is the Lord's; it is holy unto the Lord. . And concerning the tithe of the herd, or of the flock, the tenth shall be holy unto the Lord." (Lev. xxvii. 30–32.)

This *one-tenth of the annual increase is that which was required from the beginning as the least that would meet the requirements of God's law.* This was emphatically *the Lord's tenth*, and by him was wholly applied to the support of his ministering servants in the temple. To withhold this was to steal God's property. "Will a man rob God? Yet ye have robbed me. But ye say, Wherein have we robbed thee? *In tithes and offerings.*" What follows? "Ye are cursed with a curse; for ye have robbed me, even this whole nation."

This law was not repealed by the gospel dispensation, but fully indorsed by New Testament writers. Paul says: "Do ye not know that they which minister about holy things live of the things of the temple? and they which wait at the altar are partakers with the altar? *Even so hath the Lord ordained that they which preach the gospel should live of the gospel.*" (1 Cor. ix. 13, 14.) Thus we see that the law of the tithe is fully indorsed by the apostle. Jesus sanctioned the great liberality of Zaccheus when he gave "half his goods," commended the example of the poor widow who gave "all her living," and said concerning the law that he "came not to destroy, but to fulfill." The Church is the same through all ages, and the law to support her ministers must be the same.

"The earth is the Lord's and the fullness thereof; the world and they that dwell therein." The earth is God's great plantation, and man is his tenant, and nothing can be more reasonable than that he should require *a tenth* to support his ministers—this is his rental money. "Now this truth is a simple and even a self-evident one: God has made me, and I and all my powers belong to the Maker. He has made the earth, and stored it with all its wealth; he has created the natural forces and laws which are used in the creation of wealth, and he has put all these at my service. My labor is his, because I am his handiwork; because I am dependent upon him for my existence; because, therefore, my supreme allegiance is due to him; and all that by means of my labor I get out of the earth is his, because I am merely taking from the treasure-house that which he previously put there. All the wealth which is dug out of the earth in coal, and silver, and gold, or which is gathered from its surface in wheat and corn, and various cereals and fruits, or which is indirectly produced by changes of form, structure, and location, by the power of steam, or by water-power, or by the wafting winds of commerce, is gathered from stores which he has accumulated and made valuable by means of powers with which he has endowed us. To take these stores and employ these powers for our own uses and purposes is just as truly an act of dishonest defalcation as for the clerk to take money from his employer's till for his own pocket."

II. The Immense Benefits Arising from the Diffusion of the Gospel.

The gospel is worth immensely more in its temporal benefits than the money paid in building churches and supporting ministers. Let us look at this point.

1. *The Gospel Indirectly Increases Property.*—It inspires industry, sharpens the intellect, forbids prodigality, all of which tend to the accumulation of property. Educated mind *finds* the hidden gold, silver, coal, oil, and utilizes the resources of nature, which lie neglected by a savage people. On this continent, where Indians lived for ages in a state of abject poverty, Christian people have made princely fortunes. The richest nations on earth are Christian nations. Wherever a Christian church is built, it adds value to the property surrounding it.

2. *The Gospel Gives Security to Life, Property, and Liberty.*—The sense of sacred regard for the rights of others has been developed by the preaching of the gospel and organized into laws of protection. The blood of the Cross has made man and his rights sacred. In ancient Rome human life was trampled upon as dust. "Prisoners taken in battle were bought

up by traders, who followed the victorious army, and sold as cattle. These prisoners were often highly educated men—Greeks, Gauls, Thracians, Spaniards. The Roman emperors sported with human life. Crassus crucified *ten thousand* prisoners at one time. Trajan made *ten thousand* fight in the amphitheater for the amusement of the people, and prolonged the bloody feast for four months."

3. *The Intellectual Benefits of the Gospel.*—The common schools for the education of the masses were unknown till the introduction of the gospel. "The earliest endeavors to educate all the people originated in the Christian Church." (Johnson's Cyc.) In Greece and Rome, education was confined to the few sons of the noble and the rich. In the wake of the gospel, schools for the education of the common people have sprung up. Another fact is equally clear, namely, the ministers of the gospel have been the leaders in founding educational institutions. They first established them in Europe. The oldest college in America—Harvard—was founded by John Harvard, a minister. He gave $3,500 to start it. Yale College was founded by eleven ministers. And it is well known that the colleges in North Carolina owe their existence and prosperity to ministers. Of the three hundred colleges in the United States, two hundred and seventy were founded by the Christian Churches, only thirty by State authority.

The healthiest and most luminous literature of the world is the fruit of the gospel. It is a noted fact that Columbus who discovered America, Galileo who discovered the satellites of Jupiter, Newton who discovered the law of gravitation, and other famous discoverers and inventors, were all born and educated in countries enlightened by the gospel. The pulpit itself is a great *popular educator*. It presents the grandest and most stirring truths to arouse the popular mind to a sense of right and truth. Christ said to his apostles, "Ye are the light of the world." Through the press, Sunday-schools, books, and the pulpit, the ministers of the gospel are as so many moons catching the light from "the Sun of righteousness" and reflecting it upon the people.

4. *The Benefits of Christian Civilization.*—Look at the worth of the gospel in building up the comforts and conveniences of Christian civilization. Pagan governments were made for the benefit of the rulers, while the governed millions lay under the iron heel of despots. The king was the god, while the people were sheep fleeced by him—a cluster of grapes crushed to fill his cup of royal gratification. Think of Nebuchadnezzar casting the Hebrew children into a fiery furnace because they would not obey his whim to worship a golden image; of Herod slaughtering "all the children that were in Bethlehem;" of a petty prince slaying a man to warm his feet in his blood! What a change has come over the world! The government now is from the people and for the benefit of the people.

Before the gospel came, children were supposed to have no rights. The polished Greeks *murdered* deformed infants; the Carthagenians sacrificed theirs to Moloch; Spartan laws *compelled* parents to cast their sickly children away into deep pits; Roman law allowed parents to murder their children with impunity; China for ages has legalized the assassination of one-third of her infant population; in East India, mothers cast their infants into the river Ganges to feed the crocodiles; but Christ says, "Suffer the little children to come unto me, and forbid them not, for of such is the kingdom of God." Behold the Sunday-schools organized for their instruction; see how parents work for them. What tenderness is exercised toward those that are deformed, sickly, blind, or otherwise unfortunate! What a change the gospel has wrought!

In heathen lands, when parents grow old, blind, and helpless, their children carry them away into the woods and kill them. Behold how differently the old, the blind, the poor, the insane, are treated in Christian countries. We build costly asylums for their comfort. Look at your comforts in this Christian land as compared with ancient times.

"When Christ came, there was not a palace in Palestine that possessed the comforts which have become necessaries in Christendom to-day. There was not probably a glass window, certainly not a chimney; books, none; lights to read them by at night, none. There were few roads, almost no carriages, no banks, no postal conveniences. There was not honesty enough in the world to make either banking or post-offices possible. If Cicero wished to send a letter from Rome to Athens, he must find a friend or hire a special messenger. Even so late as the present century the Shah of Persia endeavored in vain to establish a postal system in his empire, and could not for want of integrity in his people. To-day there are neither banks, railroads, telegraphs, nor post-offices except in Christendom, or where Christians have carried them. Taxation robbed the industrious of all their earnings, leaving them not always enough even to live upon. Famines were common. Money was hid in the ground or concentrated in garments, jewelry, and precious stones; no other investments were possible. Poverty in Rome was so wide-spread that the people were saved from starvation only by the building of great granaries by the government and the distribution of corn at a merely nominal price. The pagan religion did so little for the common people that in Rome they were excluded from public worship and denied the use of the omens. Herds of beggars, armies of tramps, mobs that finally made wreck of Rome herself, were everywhere. And wealth and culture had no pity, only contempt, for them. "Repel a poor man with scorn," "Fling your alms to a beggar, but avoid all contact with him," were Roman maxims to be found in such authors as Quintilian and Seneca. To such a world the proclamation "One is your Father in heaven, and all ye are brethren," was indeed glad tidings to the poor. The post-office, the bank, the home, are all Christian institutions. They are Christ's gifts to man.

5. *Spiritual Benefits of the Ministry.* — In whatever country Christianity has been established, it has been done through the labors and sufferings of the preachers. At first the disciples of Christ numbered but twelve; then a hundred and twenty; then three thousand were added. Thus we see that Christianity was once but a mustard-seed. But it has grown to be a great tree, overshadowing much of the world. Under the healing influence of this tree of life, now whole nations repose in peace. Planted in our country, its

fruitful boughs extend from the Atlantic to the Pacific Ocean, from the frozen regions of the North to the ever-blooming flowers of the South. But let us remember that it was planted by the hands of the preachers—it was watered by their tears and fertilized by their blood. That great army of Christians, numbering its hundreds of millions, that are the salt of the earth and light of the world, marching on their way to heaven to-day, were converted by the instrumentality of the ministers.

III. The Cheapness of Preaching.

Sometimes the people complain that the preachers require *too much* money. Now, we assert that there is no class of men of the same ability and culture who work so cheaply as preachers.

1. We think the ministers are equal in ability and mental culture to any other class of men; yet, while lawyers, doctors, and good business men average about two thousand dollars a year, the salary of preachers will not average more than five hundred dollars a year. The amount paid to the lawyers of this country is put down at thirty-five million, that paid to the ministers at seven million—a difference of twenty-eight million.

2. Then compare the expenses of the ministry with the injurious luxuries of the people, and what a difference! Thousands are paid for liquor, useless jewelry, and gaudy raiment. For every dollar this nation spends for the ministry, it spends seventy-six dollars for intoxicating liquors. North Carolina spends twelve dollars for liquor where one is given for the gospel.

3. It is a sad fact that heathen spend more in keep-

ing up their forms of idolatry than Christians do in supporting their preachers. The annual cost of a heathen temple in India is set down at four hundred and fifty thousand dollars—a little more, perhaps, than is paid to all the ministers in North Carolina. The annual expenses of keeping one idol in Khundoba is put down at thirty thousand dollars. Dr. Duff says that one pagan festival cost two million dollars.

4. It is stated on good authority that the *dogs* cost this nation more than the preachers. It is estimated that the dogs cost the country sixteen million dollars, while preachers cost only seven million dollars. Let us hear no more nonsense about the high cost of preaching, since it is demonstrated that there is nothing in all this land so cheap as the ministry when we consider their talents and the benefits of their preaching.

IV THE ABILITY OF THE PEOPLE TO PAY.

That the professed followers of Christ in our day and country possess a large share of this world's riches is plain to the most casual observer. They own broad acres of fertile land on which the great staples of cotton, corn, wheat, tobacco, and fruits are grown under the warmth of God's sun and the showers of his rain. Others are engaged in the profitable business of merchandising, mining, manufacturing, banking, and other spheres of trade. There are engineers, architects, lawyers, physicians, authors, editors, school-teachers, belonging to the Church of Christ. Most of the immense wealth of this country is in the hands of professed Christians. The wealth of this country is not held by infidels. Why, then, does the cause of the Lord languish for the want of money? *Why, then, do Church interests languish for the want of money?* We call attention to the following reasons:

1. It cannot be denied that the love of money is too prevalent among the professors of religion. There is a grasping spirit that will not let money go to pay the expenses of the gospel. Covetousness is the *plague-spot* of the Church. It is a consuming cancer, eating up the spirit of liberality—a fatal upas-tree, blighting all that is green around it. It is the opium that makes the Church sleep and snore over the plain duty of giving liberally to the cause of the Lord. And this covetousness, this inordinate love of money, the apostle boldly defines to be *idolatry*. This golden calf, worshiped in so many families, keeps the car of the gospel from rolling around the earth to spread the gladness of salvation to earth's remotest bounds. O that this money-loving spirit was rooted out of the Church!

2. Another reason why so many Churches fail to get the amount needed is due to the fact that they do not *reach the masses*. Drops, though small in themselves, when combined make the mighty rivers and flowing oceans, and oceans water the world. When even pennies are collected from the million, they constitute vast sums of money. Governments have millions of dollars in their treasuries, because they so levy taxes and revenues as to reach *all classes*. The great secret of the Roman Catholic Church having such vast pecuniary resources lies in the fact of collecting pennies from the million masses. The pecuniary resources of English Methodism are far in

advance of American Methodism, because their system reaches all the poor classes.

3. Another cause of failure is found in the use of bad plans. The worst of all plans is:

(1) *The Annual Payment Plan.*—While this plan is the worst, it is the most prevalent in our Church. It has many bad features about it—such as forcing the preacher to contract large debts to procure the necessaries of life. It seems much heavier to the members to pay twenty dollars at the close of the year than to have paid in four or twelve installments. The preacher loses a great deal by the collection being put off until the last of the year. Many who could and would have paid, if applied to in the early part of the year, have moved away, died, become unable, or cannot be seen when the preacher is leaving.

This plan is a failure as seen in the amount it secures. It allows a present and pressing duty to be put off to the remote future. It gives time and space to the growth of selfishness and covetousness. Constant giving tends to abate the force of avarice, but these annual payments nourish the besetting sin of covetousness, which is idolatry.

(2) *The Quarterly Payment Plan.*—The quarterly payment plan is a great improvement on the annual. Assess every member of your church something and be sure to collect one-fourth of it quarterly, and it will revolutionize our Church finances. We have remarked before that one of the most potent causes of failure lies in the fact that our system does not reach the entire membership—it leaves out a large number, who therefore contribute nothing.

To illustrate: South Fork Circuit has six hundred and thirty-two members, and paid last year to the pastor and presiding elder, $509. Let us suppose that three hundred of these members should agree to pay quarterly each 25 cents—that would make for the year $300; two hundred to pay quarterly each 30 cents, $240; one hundred to pay quarterly each 50 cents, $200; twenty to pay quarterly each $1, $80; twelve to pay quarterly each $2, $96; which would make a total of $916, and a difference of $407 more than was paid by the same people worked under the old plan of annual payments.

Now, observe that in the calculation it is the many small sums which swell the amount. Second, that it is perfectly easy for nine-tenths of the poorest classes to raise and pay in twenty-five cents during the space of three months—which would be but two cents a week.

(3) *The Monthly Payment Plan.*—The working of this plan is simple and successful. To illustrate: We will take Double Shoals Circuit. It has 700 members. It paid to the pastor and presiding elder less than $500 last year. Let us try it on another plan:

```
   5 persons give each $2.00 monthly,    $120
  10       "         "   1.00    "        120
  20       "         "    50     "        120
  50       "         "    25     "        150
 100       "         "    10     "        120
 515       "         "     5     "        309
 ----                                    ----
 700 members.                            $939
```

This amount is nearly double what that circuit is in the habit of giving, and no doubt it will startle the members when they read it; and yet by assessing all the members according to this plan, and collecting monthly, it would certainly be realized.

(4) *The Weekly Payment Plan.*—The plan of paying weekly has many excellent features. This plan has been crowned with more signal success than any other. It secures the largest amount of money, and is less burdensome upon individuals. This system secures the small gifts of the congregation and swells them into one large volume. It is much easier to pay twenty-five cents a week than thirteen dollars once a year. It is easier to pay a dollar every week than fifty at one time. It is simply astonishing to observe how fast little sums paid weekly amount to great ones. A certain pastor says: "How much do you think the contributions of five cents a week amounted to in my church last year? Fifty-eight persons gave five cents a week, and the sum total was $153.70. Fifty persons gave ten cents each every week, and the sum total of their offerings was $265—two hundred and sixty-five dollars in ten-cent pieces. Thirty-three persons gave twenty-five cents each week, and it amounted to $437.25, and the entire amount given in sums ranging from one cent to twenty-five cents was $1,119.84. Thirty-two persons gave fifty cents each week, and their total was $848. Fourteen persons gave one dollar each week, and together contributed $742; while the whole amount in sums of from one cent to one dollar a week was $3,094.14, and was given by two hundred and sixty-two members."

Here is the weighty argument in favor of constant and frequent paying. The serious blunder in the old method is that the few give and not the many

The second great blunder is the wide-stretching space between the times of giving. The two points in the pecuniary reformation are very plain—frequency as to time, and universality as to the payers. Let everybody pay, and pay quarterly, monthly, or weekly. All at it and always at it will generate pecuniary steam enough to shoot the gospel-car around the world in a few years. "The successful plan, then, is the one that secures the small gifts from many givers, at regular and frequent intervals."

V THE AMOUNT TO BE GIVEN.

The grand cause of failure is that *payers pay too little*. It is a sad fact that men do not give *enough* who are in the habit of giving. Hardly one man in a hundred does his *whole* duty as to the *amount* he ought to give.

1. How much should a Christian give?

Ans. One-tenth of his income.

2. Does the Bible require the payment of one-tenth to the Lord?

Ans. Yes. Abraham paid tithes. (Gen. xiv. 20.) Jacob promised one-tenth of his income, and kept his promise. (Gen. xxviii. 22.) The language of the fourth commandment, "The seventh day is the Sabbath of the Lord thy God," is no more emphatic than the law of the tithes. "All the tithe of the land, whether of the seed of the land, or of the fruit of the tree, *is the Lord's:* it is holy unto the Lord." (Lev. xxvii. 27.) *Holy* means devoted or consecrated to the Lord. In Num. xviii. 21, he says: "I have given the children of Levi [the priests] all the tenth in Israel for an inheritance." This one-tenth of the increase is that which was required from the beginning as the *least* that would meet the requirement of God's law. This is still emphatically the Lord's tenth, and by him it was wholly assigned to the support of his servants.

3. Was not a portion of the Jewish tithes applied as taxes to the support of the state as well as the support of the priests?

Ans. No. God appropriated the tithes to the support of the Levites—the priests. The government was supported by presents, by the products of the royal flock, by vineyards, by the spoils of conquered nations and of merchants passing through the country, by taxes and tolls. The treasuries of the Lord's house and the king's were distinct.

4. Was the law of tithes perpetual in Hebrew history? Was it always binding?

Ans. Abraham paid tithes, so did Jacob; so it is fair to presume did all the patriarchs. More than a thousand years after the death of Moses, God, through Malachi, denounced the Jews for not paying their tithes. They were uniformly prosperous when they paid them, and adversity was certain when they did not.

5. Were not the blessings promised for payment of tithes spiritual rather than temporal?

Ans. Both temporal and spiritual. God united them, why should we separate them? Read the third chapter of Malachi, perhaps the strongest in the Bible on that subject. The promises there have almost sole reference to temporal blessings.

6. Did our Saviour sanction the payment of tithes?

Ans. Yes. Read Matt. xxiii. 23 and Luke xi. 42.

7. But did he *command* that tithes be paid?

Ans. Not directly, that we know of; but he recognized the law, commended it, and did not abrogate it. He did not *command* the keeping of the Sabbath, but neither did he abrogate the law, and we all regard it as binding. There was no need to command the Jews either to keep the Sabbath or to observe the law of tithes. They did both so scrupulously, and in such detail, that, while our Saviour commended the observance of both laws, he reproved them for sacrificing the spirit for the form.

8. I cannot *afford* to give one-tenth of my income.

Ans. How do you know? Did you ever try it? ever know anyone who had practiced it that was not thereby prospered, no matter how rich, no matter how poor, no matter how small the income, no matter how large the family? Do you think your Heavenly Father will make an exception in your case and not keep his promise with you? Can you afford *not* to do it? To which of two men would you rather lend money without security, one who observed this rule, or one who did not, both being equally honest, equally worthy, and possessed of equal advantages and abilities?

9. Why not practice the New Testament rule— "Give as God has prospered you?"

Ans. Certainly. That is an Old Testament rule also. But how much? what proportion—one-twentieth, one-fifth, one-tenth, or just as you happen to feel at the time? One-tenth of the prosperity was God's rule then; when was it changed, and what is the New Testament proportion?

10. Suppose I should resolve to be, and should be, liberal in my gifts, may I not count upon equal temporal and spiritual blessings as if I gave proportionately?

Ans. No. God's estimate of liberality may differ

from yours. To which of two men would you rent land or lend money, one promising, "I will be as liberal as I can afford in the matter of payment of rent or interest, I will from time to time pay what I think is right, but *I intend to be liberal;*" the other, "I will do the best I can with what you intrust to my care, and I will pay you a definite proportion of the income?" Which would you honor most? Which would most honor you? Which would serve you and your interests best? To your possible objection that there is too much of a business air about this illustration, the reply is that there is a wonderful amount of business in God's dealings with us. The Bible contains very many of the truest business maxims ever written, and God's promises apply both to our temporal and spiritual interests.

11. Should a young man just commencing to make his own living, or a poor man with a family to support, set apart one-tenth of the income?

Ans. Yes; and because the remaining nine-tenths will have God's promised richer blessing, and go further. Suppose you were asked a parallel question, "Do you think a poor man can afford to spend every seventh day resting, doing nothing, wasting it so far as income is concerned?" Your answer would be—and you would be right—that no matter what his circumstances he would be poorer, in dollars and cents, if he worked than if he rested on the Sabbath. Remember we are dealing in *facts*, not theories, and the facts are all on one side, both as regards the spending for our own use seventh of time and tenth of income.

12. A farmer asks, "How shall I arrive at one-tenth of my income?"

Ans. The common way with most persons is to set

apart, harvest, market, and keep separate the proceeds of every tenth acre or part of an acre. This is the "one-tenth fund" from which you will draw and pay out as you deem best. Another and, to many, an easier way is to put into this fund one-tenth of the proceeds of every article sold from the farm. When this plan is adopted, a yearly estimate should be made of the value of the products of the farm consumed by the family, and this also should be tithed.

13. A minister asks, "Shall I tithe my income?"

Ans. Yes; upon precisely the same principle that others do.

14. "Suppose my people do not pay me what they agree?"

Ans. Tithe what you receive.

15. A physician asks, "Shall I deduct from the tenth the value of services I gratuitously render to the poor?"

Ans. No. It is in the line of your profession, a part of your business losses or business expenses, and probably pays you better than any form of advertising known to business men.

16. When should I commence?

Ans. Now. Or, if you desire, you can make an estimate of your income back to any given time, and also what you have given for the same time. Keep a correct account to the end of the year, then close the account, and carry forward any balance.

17. Suppose I am in *debt*, should my debts be paid first?

Ans. No. Your debt to God is paramount. It is one-tenth of your weekly, monthly, or yearly income. Pay that as it accrues, and his *promised* blessing will enable you the more easily and rapidly to pay what you owe to others.

18. Should I tithe my capital?

Ans. No. Your capital, whether brains, or hands, or money, or property in any form, is that out of which you make your income. Pay the tenth of your income, or, as the Bible has it, of the "increase."

19. How shall I keep the account?

Ans. Use a memorandum-book, or a page of any blank-book, putting down every item you give. Add up and look over the account frequently, in order to keep the matter well in mind. Another and often a better way is to have a "one-tenth box," and be scrupulously exact in putting into it one-tenth of the income when it is received. This will be the Lord's treasury from which you will draw to give to worthy objects, as your judgment may dictate.

THE PROSPERITY OF LIBERAL PAYERS.

What evidence is there outside of the Bible that all who observe this law will be prospered in temporal interests to a greater degree than if they did not?

Ans. The accumulated testimony through all ages of those who have tried it is that it is true.

Within the last four years a circular has been sent to more than fifteen thousand evangelical ministers in the United States, in which occurs the following statement and question:

"My belief is that God blesses in temporal as well as in spiritual things the man who honors him by setting apart a stated part of his income to his service. I have never known an exception. Have you?"

A little pamphlet containing the same question has

been carefully distributed among more than five hundred thousand laymen, asking if they knew of any exceptions to the rule. Hundreds, probably thousands, of facts and experiences have been collected. A few are inserted. So far as is known, there are no real exceptions. Do *you* know of any? If so, will you tell your pastor, and ask him to give the circumstances?

A large portion of the following testimonials were published first in 1879, and were selected within a short time largely from replies to the circular which was then being sent to Methodist ministers. Probably a greater proportion of similar replies were received from Presbyterian, Congregational, and **Episcopal** ministers, and a slightly less proportion from Baptist. Similar testimonials have been received almost every day for years. These are published only to emphasize and add stronger proof if possible to the advantages of paying back to God one-tenth of our income.

From a pastor in New Jersey: "I commenced the practice when in a condition of deep financial embarrassment, and the way brightens in that direction each step I take."

From a pastor in Michigan: "My father lived that rule and prospered. I have for eight years since leaving the seminary, and have prospered. The wealthiest man in my church and community has lived by it."

From a pastor in Indiana: "One brother in my charge made a written contract that he would give to the Lord one-tenth of his annual income. He was poor then; he now gives hundreds of dollars annually."

From a pastor in West Virginia: "During a recent

pastorate in Baltimore city, I was struck with the fact that the only business man in my church not seriously affected by the hard times was the solitary individual who gave proportionately."

From a pastor in Maine: "I have known some ministers who have done this for many years. Such have invariably had prosperity. The Bible doctrine and practice are safe and true."

From a pastor in Pennsylvania: "Mr. —— told me that from the day of his conversion he commenced giving one-tenth to the cause of God, and during the following eleven years he gave more than he was worth when converted, and that God prospered him so that he was worth after the eleven years of giving ten times more than before."

From a pastor in Ohio: "One man in my congregation has practiced this course. He was at one time very prosperous, then he almost failed in business; yet one-tenth of his gross income always found its way into benevolent enterprises. People were astonished at his tenacity, and now he is better off than ever. His offerings are increasing from year to year."

From a pastor in Ohio: "I have an uncle, who, until he decided to give systematically one-tenth of his income, was in straitened circumstances. For several years of late, giving as above, he has been greatly prospered spiritually, and especially financially. He is now quite independent."

From a pastor in Georgia: "An intelligent lady of my church, on the death of her husband, adopted the rule, and not only has she been blessed personally, but her four daughters, and indeed all of her seven children, seem to be the objects of Divine favor. All are prospering temporally, and all save the little boy are consistent Christians."

From a pastor in Pennsylvania: "I was in doubt for a long time that I ought to give largely to benevolence while I was in debt. I began to doubt, however, after a hard and unsuccessful struggle to get out of debt, that I should ever succeed. At length I was persuaded that I was 'robbing God' to pay my creditors. My wife and I consulted over the matter, and decided to give a tenth, which we have done, and God is prospering us beyond any previous experience."

From a pastor in Northern New York: "In a former charge I had one member who gave a tenth of all to the Lord, and to-day he is worth forty thousand dollars. When I first became acquainted with him, twenty years ago, he was worth perhaps two thousand dollars. He is a farmer."

From a pastor in Northern New York: "A wholesale merchant of my acquaintance came to this country from England when a young man, and on arriving had some three hundred dollars, which he loaned, and worked as a journeyman tailor. He opened an account at that time, giving one-tenth of his income to benevolence, and has conscientiously continued until this time, giving in the aggregate many thousands of dollars. He is now distributing thousands annually."

From a pastor in Iowa: "One of the richest and most influential men of this State is a layman in the M. E. Church in ——. He has religiously adhered to the one-tenth plan, and great prosperity and honor have been his. Numerous such instances have come to me in my ministry."

From a pastor in New Jersey: "For many years I have adopted the plan of giving one-tenth, never going below it, and in all these years have steadily prospered in worldly things. When my giving was irregular, small, and spasmodic, my temporal affairs followed in the same line."

From a pastor in Ohio: "A gentleman of my acquaintance formerly had a little wagon-shop. It was with great difficulty that he made a living for his family. He was called poor, and also had the reputation of being close. One Sabbath, at our missionary anniversary, he surprised us by giving a liberal contribution. The wonder was, What made him do it? It soon became known that he had resolved to give one-tenth to the Lord. It seems from that time he began to prosper. Business increased, opportunities opened before him. To-day he lives in one of the finest houses in the city, is one of the wealthiest men in the —— Church in C——, and is a whole-souled, generous Christian."

From a pastor in New York: "I have been in the active work of a pastor thirty-seven years, and have been an observer of the results of Christian giving, and I have never known one case where a Christian faithfully and uniformly gave conscientiously and proportionately who was not highly prospered in his temporal affairs. These are the very men God can trust with earthly goods."

From a pastor in Missouri: "I have been personally acquainted with but two men who have made it a rule to give unto the Lord the tenth of their increase, and they were prospered exceedingly."

From a pastor in Kentucky: " Proportionate giv

ing, as it has passed under my observation, has been in every instance attended with prosperity; I may say with double prosperity. The givers have prospered in worldly good, and also in spiritual life."

From a pastor in Pennsylvania: "Some time ago I was receiving from a Christian gentleman in Philadelphia certain things needed in my church. He told me to make my own selection from the Lord's portion; and remarked that for thirty years he had been giving the tenth of his increase to the Lord. He commenced business on this principle; and during all that time he has been enabled to pay one hundred cents on the dollar, and every year has had more and more to give back to Him from whom he received every good and perfect gift."

From a pastor in Maryland: "I have had a great deal to do with the finances of the Church for years, and believe the systematic plan is the best. I know a brother in the Church who commenced on a small business capital, and covenanted with God (wrote his pledge in a book) if he would prosper him he would give one-tenth till he was worth ten thousand dollars, and then would give one-fourth until worth twenty-five thousand dollars, and after that give his whole income. In 1858 and 1859 I was his pastor, and he was then giving one-fourth. Since that time he has become worth twenty-five thousand dollars, and now gives all his income."

From a pastor in Philadelphia: "Twenty-five years ago, when I had nothing but my salary of one hundred dollars a year, as a junior traveling minister of the Philadelphia Conference, I adopted the plan of devoting regularly one-tenth of my income to charitable and religious objects. I have adhered to the plan. God has graciously favored me in my ministry and blessed me in temporal things. I have been enabled to give away thousands, and have thousands left."

From a pastor in New York: "I commenced giving a tenth years ago, when I found that I was spending all my salary and it was hard to give any thing. I have found it a great comfort and pleasure to me ever since. One of my younger elders commenced the practice some years since, and no one among us has been so prospered in business as he, or gives so much. I know a wealthy banker, a Presbyterian elder, who commenced to do the same when a young man, with little means, and now his gifts are large."

From a pastor in Iowa: "I knew a merchant who gave ten per cent. of his income. His business prospered, and better still, he grew as a Christian, and was one of the most devout, humble, and spiritually-minded Christians I ever knew. If he was thanked for a gift to some good object, his reply was, 'You don't need to thank me, it is the Lord's money;' referring to his custom of laying aside a certain portion of his profits for the Lord's work."

From a pastor in Ohio: "I have practiced giving the tenth of my income to the Lord for years, and find that I give more money and give it more cheerfully, and I think more intelligently, than before. I have known several who adopted this rule, and in every case it worked well. One man who gave a tenth, and was greatly prospered (giving one year, to my knowledge, eighteen hundred dollars), was broken up in business by a company with which he was connected; but I saw him in his adversity, and he was the same happy Christian man as formerly. He labored to glorify God with his wealth when he had it, and when it took wings and flew away he did not mourn over it. The last I heard the Lord was blessing him again in temporal matters."

From a pastor in Indiana: "It is my judgment that there is nothing that will so foster exact and honest business habits in all other things as systematic paying to the Lord what we owe him. This, of itself, will make for any of us many more dollars than it costs us in tithes and offerings. Really, to be honest with God is one of the most selfish things I know of, for it comes back a hundred-fold or more every time. I have a friend (one of the most prominent physicians here) who pursues this plan. It is a pleasure to see and hear him when I present any case to him: if it commends itself, he gives freely, and with the greatest manifest pleasure. He says, 'It is not giving, only directing the gift.' He has been greatly prospered in every respect."

From a pastor in Iowa: "Some years ago I was in business and in debt, and, after making a covenant with the Lord (I had not learned that God had already made a covenant with me if I would come to it) to give him one-tenth of all my increase, I gave all my affairs into his hands, asking him to just give or withhold as would be most for his glory. From that time my business increased; I had all I could attend to, and all seemed to turn to money. In a short time (about two years) I was out of debt. I have kept on giving one-tenth of all I received, and have never lacked means. I have known others who have done this, and all have been prospered. It is not so much the money we get, but *O the joy of giving!* There is no work in the vineyard of the Lord that gives more pleasure than doing duty in this way."

From a business man in Chicago: "My grandfather followed the plan you suggest, and his sons after him; coming in the third generation, I follow in their teachings. I began about eighteen years ago, and while I have been steadily prosperous, I have never seen the year when there was not apparently some strong reason why I should not pay the tenth that year. The habit or plan has been the influence that carried me through. I know one Christian man who was the soul of generosity, until one year he overgave largely, and then balanced by undergiving for two or three years; the result, his gifts for ten years or longer have dwindled to a mere nothing. In this, as in other matters, the good Lord knows what we need to make character that will, in the long run and on the broad scale, be most of a success in satisfaction to its possessor and usefulness to the world."

From a pastor in Central New York: "I have men in my church who have acted upon this principle for years. They are the largest givers, but not the richest men. One of them said to me the other day that he was always surprised to find how much he had to give, and giving was a great pleasure. He is among the prosperous men of my church, and no blight of any kind has ever rested on his family. His children are prosperous and happy. All are grown up, doing for themselves, and are an honor to their names.

Many men in my church are what the world calls rich. I run my mind over all the most prominent of them, but who are small givers, and I find that there is not one of them who has not a skeleton in his closet. I have never known a man who gave the one-tenth, or who gave proportionately, who was not blessed with a competency, if not great prosperity. I take time to write you this because I feel if such facts as the above can be collected and given to the Church, they must produce a profound impression."

NOTE.—Many of the questions and answers, and the testimonials in the above, were taken from a pamphlet published by a Methodist layman in Chicago.

APPLICATION OF THE PLANS.

No plan, however good, can work itself. But any one of the plans mentioned can be easily worked.

To illustrate: Let the stewards take the church-register, call every name, and assess every one, on the quarterly, monthly, or weekly payment plan—whichever one they may choose to work under—then at a Church Conference read out these assessments, and get each member's consent to the amount.

The next thing to be done is to apply the means of collection. There are two ways of doing this. The first is the envelope plan. In 1873 the envelope system of weekly contributions was introduced in the Churches of New England, and it secured the most satisfactory results. This system is working remarkably well in many Churches in the South now. It is very simple. Suppose a man agrees to pay thirteen dollars a year to be given weekly. Then every

Sabbath he would inclose twenty-five cents in an envelope, and write on the back:

> For Pastor—25 cents.
> Date......................
> Name..................

and drop it into the collection-basket, and the treasurer finding the envelope would give the contributor credit on the general subscription-book; and receiving credit for all thus given every Sabbath, the whole amount could be easily summed up at the close of the year.

This envelope system can be just as easily applied to the quarterly and monthly payment plan. A man proposes, or is assessed, to pay eight dollars a year. Then, at each quarterly-meeting, he would inclose two dollars in an envelope and send it to the steward, with name, amount, and date written on the back. The advantages of this system are many.

1. It develops the habit of giving unto the Lord into a steady, self-acting principle. It makes giving a spontaneous, thoughtful, cheerful duty. And "the Lord loveth a cheerful giver," and so do men.

3. It pays the preacher his money as it becomes due, and enables him to meet his current expenses without being embarrassed with debts.

3. It relieves the stewards of a vast deal of unpleasant work.

4. It introduces the apostolic principle of foresight in giving. "Let every one of you lay by him in store as God hath prospered him." Look ahead, and get ready to pay your Church dues, is what he means. Get up the amount, and lay it by in store against the time it will be called for. Be thoughtful about this

matter. Things done without premeditation are generally badly done. Have it all arranged and ready beforehand, then you have nothing to do but to go to what is laid up for the Lord and pay it. A certain man was always ready to pay. Being asked how it was that he was always so prompt, he replied: "Do you see that safe? In that safe is a secret drawer. The drawer is marked 'The Lord's Drawer.' Into that drawer, at the end of each week, I put one-tenth of all that I have made during the week, and when called upon to pay to the cause of the Lord, I go to that drawer and get it."

THE WORK OF THE STEWARDS.

The duties of the stewards are numerous and responsible. They estimate the amount to be raised; and their estimates should always be liberal and generous. Stewards are examples to the people as to the spirit of liberality. Their closeness is apt to spread the same spirit among the people. The actual amount paid to the pastor depends almost exclusively upon the energetic and effective efforts of the stewards. Those who rely on spasmodic efforts fail. Those who are patient, skillful, and persevering are the ones that succeed. The steward should remember if he fails to discharge his duties the cause of God will inevitably suffer. No other member of the Church feels at liberty to act in his place, and he therefore should do his work well or resign promptly. He should do his work heroically, yet prudently. Let there be no shrinking back from duty; no cowardly apologies; no cold indifference. Giving is a means of grace to givers. No one, therefore, can be excused. It is more blessed to give than to receive. Giving builds up the spiritual manhood of the giver as well as pays the preacher. Non-giving churches perish out. It is stated that fifty years ago thirty Baptist churches in the State of Maryland declared themselves opposed to giving, while two alone stood in favor of it. The two churches that cultivated the spirit of giving grew to thousands, while the others dwindled away to only eight persons. "He which soweth sparingly shall reap also sparingly; and he which soweth bountifully shall reap also bountifully."

The steward will meet with many cold repulses while collecting. The excuses must be met. A common one is, "I do n't like the preacher." Such persons should be reminded that the giving is to be unto the Lord, not to men. The blessedness of giving is lost when the popularity of the preacher is made the ground of giving, instead of the goodness of the Lord. If you withhold money due the Lord, he says, "Ye have robbed me." Another will say, "When will this everlasting begging for money cease? I am sick and worn out with it." The answer will be easy. It will never cease. It is God's law. While there remains the necessity for preaching—while there remains an unsaved soul on earth till the light of the gospel shall have gilded the hills and valleys of the entire globe and wrapped the blue seas into eternal calm—there will be a necessity for preaching, and so a necessity for paying for it. Others will say, "I am so poor, can give so little, that it is no use for me to pay any thing." The answer here is easy also. The obligation to give a penny, when one has it, rests upon the same ground as that of giving a thousand dollars. The ground of obligation is the same. What does the parable of the talents teach? It teaches that the man of one talent was held just as rigidly responsible as the man of ten. "It is so little," said he, "that I won't try to improve it." But his lord cast him into outer darkness for the failure. Remember how the Saviour commended the two mites of the poor widow. It is the rills uniting that make the Nile-like river of beneficence. "Hard times" will be offered as an excuse for not contributing. But the undismayed steward can reply: "Don't begin with the Church to cut down your expenses. Better spend less money for jewelry and finery, foolish and sinful fashions, and pay the Lord's demand in full. It is not very consistent for a Christian to stop giving to the Church, and then keep up all other outlays to the old standard."

Let the steward remember the responsibility of his position, and devote his energies to his work. Paul says, "Moreover, it is required in stewards that a man be found faithful." Be faithful to the duties of your office. Remember how much depends on your activity and skill. By all means let the stewards raise the preacher's claims by quarterly installments. Be sure to square the account at every quarterly-meeting.

REWARDS OF GIVING.

"Blessed is he that considereth the poor: the Lord will deliver him in time of trouble. The Lord will preserve him, and keep him alive; and he shall be blessed upon the earth: and thou wilt not deliver him unto the will of his enemies. The Lord will strengthen him upon the bed of languishing: thou wilt make all his bed in his sickness." (Ps. xli. 1–3.)

"Trust in the Lord, and do good; so shalt thou dwell in the land, and verily shalt thou be fed. (Ps. xxxvii. 3.)

"Honor the Lord with thy substance, and with the first-fruits of all thine increase: so shall thy barns be filled with plenty, and thy presses shall burst out with new wine." (Prov. iii. 9, 10.)

"There is that scattereth, and yet increaseth; and there is that withholdeth more than is meet, but it tendeth to poverty. The liberal soul shall be made fat; and he that watereth shall be watered also himself." (Prov. xi. 24, 25.)

"And if thou draw out thy soul to the hungry, and satisfy the afflicted soul; then shall thy light rise in obscurity, and thy darkness be as the noonday; and the Lord shall guide thee continually, and satisfy thy soul in drought, and make fat thy bones; and thou shalt be like a watered garden, and like a spring of water, whose waters fail not." (Isa. lviii. 10, 11.)

"Bring ye all the tithes into the store-house, that there may be meat in mine house, and prove me now herewith, saith the Lord of hosts, if I will not open you the windows of heaven, and pour you out a blessing, that there shall not be room enough to receive it. And I will rebuke the devourer for your sakes, and he shall not destroy the fruits of your ground; neither shall your vine cast her fruit before the time in the field, saith the Lord of hosts." (Mal. iii. 10, 11.)

"Give, and it shall be given unto you; good measure, pressed down, and shaken together, and running over, shall men give into your bosom. For with the same measure that ye mete withal it shall be measured to you again." (Luke vi. 38.)

"I have showed you all things, how that so laboring ye ought to support the weak, and to remember the words of the Lord Jesus, how he said, It is more blessed to give than to receive." (Acts xx. 35.)

"Every man according as he purposeth in his heart, so let him give; not grudgingly, or of necessity: for God loveth a cheerful giver. And God is able to make all grace [the word "grace" here refers to temporal blessings] abound toward you; that ye, always having all sufficiency in all things, may abound to every good work." (2 Cor. ix. 7, 8.)

These promises are *conditional*. We have no right to claim them except we *comply with the conditions*. If we meet them, we *shall realize true prosperity* both in spiritual and temporal interests. The conditions and promises go together.

If you decide to adopt Christian paying as the rule of your life, the "pledges" sent herewith may be found useful. "*Prove* the Lord now herewith."

SUGGESTIONS.

Giving, or *paying*—for that is the better word—should not be spasmodic or impulsive; it should be from *principle*. We should know how much we receive and how much we give, and our gifts or payments should always have a certain definite proportion to our income.

While we may speak of *giving*, the thought in the heart should be that of *payment*. Giving, properly speaking, commences when the tenth has been *paid*.

Proportionate giving makes our Heavenly Father a partner in all our business tranactions, and he will most surely bless a business or occupation in which he is recognized as a partner. By paying the one-tenth we become partners in his work, and transmute some portion of our little treasure into an imperishable possession, and we shall find it again—treasure laid up in heaven. There may be instances in which men, with mistaken motives, may give too much for their temporal prosperity, but such men are never *proportionate* givers.

Under the impulse of excited feeling men sometimes give too much to one object, and the effect is to render them unable or unwilling to consider objects equally worthy. Such giving is *not* liberal; it is in fact illiberal, just as a man would be illiberal who should will all his property to one child, cutting off brothers and sisters equally worthy.

God loves and will bless a *cheerful giver*—one who sets apart a proportion of his income as a debt to be paid back to the great Giver, and who is watchful to bestow it where it will do the greatest good. If some one should intrust a sum of money to you, to be bestowed as you thought best, leaving the choice of objects to you, you would of course give the matter thought, and use your best judgment in the selection. So it should be in all our gifts, for while they may be *gifts* to those who receive them, they are *payments* to God; and his blessing follows the cheerful giving of what is due to him to the most worthy objects, not forgetting that even in our giving we may be selfish, and remembering that to be liberal we must not confine our gifts to our own church or neighborhood.

Proportionate giving unites religion and business. Those who adopt it as a rule of life struggle to make more money that they may have a larger percentage of income for the Master's cause. They are also saved that absorbing spirit of worldliness that makes shipwreck of many a promising Christian manhood.

We want to give while we *live*, with warm hands from loving hearts. There is no pleasure in giving with a dead man's hand; and the miser who on his death-bed gives largely to benevolence goes still a miser into the presence of his Judge. We want to dispense our charities from day to day, in small sums if need be, not waiting for large ones, and making our lives, like that of our Saviour, a constant benediction.

God's plan is that of constant but limited supply, and the great need of the Church and the world is that Christians should give constantly, regularly, and proportionately as God prospers them. Let us give as an act of worship, as a blessed privilege; give not to receive the approbation of man, but the reward God gives; give increasingly as God prospers with increasing wealth, with thanks to our Heavenly Father that he enables us to give, and for the happiness we thereby receive as well as that we confer on others.

There is no argument for the genuineness of Christianity that men so universally respect as a Christian giving. They care little for large or impulsive giving, as they know that enthusiasm or over-persuasion may have had the controlling influence, but they cannot withstand the argument of a charity which is ceaseless in its flow, and is constantly on the watch for right objects for its bestowal.

The all-important thought on this subject is that of *proportionate giving, or paying*. Paul says to the Corinthians: "Upon the first day of the week let every one of you lay by him in store as God hath prospered him." The plain inferences are, first, regularity—"on the first day of the week;" and, secondly, a certain proportionate, definite share—"as God hath prospered him." Notice, first, that this is not an exhortation, but a *command*, or *order*. He does not say, "Get ready, and when I come I will preach you a sermon on charity, and while under the influence of the preaching, and while your hearts are warm with love and sympathy for the poor brethren at Jerusalem, we will take up a large collection;" but he says, "Have every thing in readiness, that there be no gathering when I come." Also notice that this order is not addressed to a few, or to the rich, but to "every one of you;" and again, that the Epistle is directed not to the Christians at Corinth alone, but also to "all in every place that call upon the name of Jesus Christ our Lord."

CHAPTER XIV
CHURCH MEMBERSHIP

I. WHO ARE ADMITTED INTO THE METHODIST CHURCH?

ADULTS *who have been converted.* Such persons of course who have realized a change of heart, who have felt that their sins have been pardoned, their hearts regenerated, and experienced the fact that "the love of God has been shed abroad in their hearts by the Holy Ghost given unto them," are admitted into our Church. It has ever been characteristic of Methodism to insist on experimental religion. The early Methodists preached experience, told their own experience; and this living experience constitutes the very *salt* of Methodism, and keeps it from taint and mold. This experience gives it a *vital spirit.* "Life and power" is a familiar note among our people.

Methodism is a free spirit. "Liberty" is its watchword—liberty from sin, from bondage, body and soul; liberty to pray loud or low, to speak, to use all the gifts bestowed, whether one talent or ten, whether among men or women; liberty for all, learned or unlearned, rich or poor, young converts or old ones; liberty to sing, whether by note or by rote, with the spirit and with the understanding, to sing in the choir or in the congregation—liberty for all to sing, not one in ten only.

It is a simple spirit. Simplicity is characteristic of it:

no affectation, no pompous, mechanical, and strained dignity.

It is an earnest spirit. Dr. Chalmers said, "Methodism is Christianity in earnest."

It is a liberal spirit. Universal redemption for its theme, "the world for its parish," "perfect love" to God and man its *animus*, it cannot be otherwise than liberal and catholic. It has often been repelled, but it repels none who "truly and earnestly repent." It receives as candidates even those who evince "a desire to flee from the wrath to come, and to be saved from their sins." It welcomes to communion all the members of Christ's body.

It is a fraternal spirit. Both the life and forms of Methodism lead directly to strong fraternization. Love is its life, and the mutual freedom and equality in Jesus Christ which characterize all its social meetings and religious forms tend to centralize the sympathy and feelings of the whole community. And it is from this, in part, that the power of Methodism as a system arises. Unity is power; life is power. They sing truly,

> Our fears, our hopes, our aims are one,
> Our comforts and our cares.
>
> We share our mutual woes,
> Our mutual burdens bear;
> And often for each other flows
> The sympathizing tear.

The class-meeting and the love-feast contribute much to foster this fraternal spirit. "The rich and the poor meet together; the Lord is the maker of them all." Hence the cordial greeting, the familiar "brother" and "sister"—"all one in Christ Jesus," not however, to the exclusion of "other sheep which are not of this fold." Free communion with all the body of Christ is the token of its catholicity.

It is a happy spirit. Methodists believe in getting happy in religion. "Rejoice evermore, pray without ceasing, in every thing give thanks," is one of its favorite proof-texts. Here is one of its notes of triumph:

>How happy is the pilgrim's lot!
>How free from every anxious thought,
>From worldly hope and fear!

>This happiness in part is mine,
>Already saved from low design,
>From every creature love!

Take another excellent specimen strain:

>While the angel choirs are crying,
>Glory to the great I AM!
>I with them will still be vying,
>*Glory! glory to the Lamb!*
>O how precious
>Is the sound of Jesus' name!

Hence "shouting" is but the legitimate expression of the happiness within; at least it is a legitimate offspring. It is not to be manufactured, and under some circumstances should not be suppressed if the soul would enjoy its freedom.

Now, who that has seen Methodism on its own feet, and in its own native attire, and "dwelling under its own vine and fig-tree," does not know that these are characteristics of its spirit, its genius? How strange, then, that Methodists themselves should ever be ashamed of their characteristics! How strange that they should seek to accommodate it to the fastidiousness of other denominations, or to the proud conceits of the world! They may do it, but it will be at the expense of its power and true glory. One fact is remarkable and significant. Generally when any special revival interest appears among other denominations they are found to have adopted more or less of our peculiarities—our hymns and tunes, our free-salvation preaching, our altar labor to a considerable extent, and our free social exercises; so much so that the remark is common even among the world and others, "Why, they preach and pray, etc., just like the Methodists." Amen! let them do so. But, then, mark two or three things: 1. This remark recognizes Methodism as the standard in these things, and that is no small compliment. 2. It shows that other denominations recognize these peculiarities as the secret of success, so far as means are concerned. 3. It rebukes the folly of Methodists in ignoring, or discountenancing, or neglecting these characteristics.

This spirit of Methodism appeals strongly to the moral sensibilities of mankind, to their felt necessities, and even to the spiritual among other denominations. In trying to improve Methodism, let us not lose sight of its genius, its spirit, remembering that the Church is to be "a habitation of God through the Spirit," and is to be conformed in its spirit and worship to the "pattern seen in the mount."

II. PENITENT SEEKERS.

The Methodist Church, besides opening her doors to adult converts, takes in also penitent seekers. The condition for the admission of such persons is this: "*There is only one condition previously required of those who desire admission into these societies, a 'desire to flee from the wrath to come, and to be saved from their sins.'*"

This condition implies a *willingness* to be saved. This willingness to be saved implies also a readiness to *be all* and to *do all* that the gospel requires of those who become partakers of salvation—a willingness to accept of salvation "from sin." To be willing to accept of salvation, therefore, implies a desire to be delivered from the dominion of sin. It implies such *repentance* as hates sin and desires purity of heart, and a *fixedness* of purpose to use the means of grace prescribed by the Church in order to attain actual salvation. Hence, such persons coming into our Church pledge themselves (1) *to abstain from all evil;* (2) *to do good of every kind;* (3) *to attend upon all the ordinances of God.* This "desire to flee from the wrath to come, and to be saved from their sins," is a deep, moving, stirring desire "fixed in the soul." It is not a feeble, transient desire, but such a desire as brings forth fruit meet for repentance — a desire ripening into repentance toward God and faith in Jesus Christ. Repentance implies preëxisting faith, and faith implies preëxisting repentance. Both are produced by the preliminary grace of the Holy Spirit, to be perfected by the willingness of man using the means of salvation. Now, when such persons come to us desiring to be saved, we admit them into the Church, where complete salvation may be attained. Much has been said by way of objection to the Methodist Church for admitting such penitent seekers of religion; but we think our practice is in harmony with scriptural teaching. We think it may be laid down as a safe rule *that the man who is authorized to claim the gracious promises of God is a fit person to join the Church.* To the sincere penitent, desirous "to flee from the wrath to come, and to be saved from sin," the promises of saving grace are offered.

Proofs.—"The Lord is nigh unto them that are of a broken heart, and saveth such as be of a contrite spirit." (Ps. xxxiv. 18.) "The sacrifices of God are a broken spirit: a broken and a contrite heart, O God, thou wilt not despise." (Ps. li. 17.) "Thus saith the high and lofty One that inhabiteth eternity, whose name is Holy: I dwell in the high and holy place, with him also that is of a contrite and humble spirit, to revive the spirit of the humble, and to revive the heart of the contrite ones." (Isa. lvii. 15.) "I will turn their mourning into joy; I will comfort them, and make them rejoice from their sorrow." (Jer. xxxi. 13.) "Jesus began to preach, and to say, Repent, for the kingdom of heaven is at hand." (Matt. iv. 17.) "Repent, and be baptized every one of you in the name of Jesus Christ for the remission of sins." (Acts ii. 38.) The men of Nineveh were saved, "because they repented at the preaching of Jonah."

Notes.

1. A purpose to be a Christian, a state of penitence, a desire to be delivered from sin, were clearly the terms of admission to the Christian Church, at the very commencement of it. This will appear from the following:

"From that time Jesus began to preach, and to say, Repent; for the kingdom of heaven is at hand. And Jesus, walking by the sea of Galilee, saw two brethren, Simon called Peter, and Andrew his brother, casting a net into the sea; for they were fishers. And he saith unto them, Follow me, and I will make you fishers of men. And they straightway left their nets, and followed him. And going on from thence, he saw other two brethren, James the son of Zebedee, and John his brother, in a ship with Zebedee their father, mending their nets; and he called them. And they immediately left the ship, and their father, and followed him." (Matt. iv. 17-22.)

Notice.—Peter, Andrew, James, and John were engaged, when Christ found them, in their daily toil. Christ commanded them to follow him. The command was very simple. The thing to be done was not mysterious, and there was no difficulty in obeying it. The thing was practicable. It lay in the scope of their ability to forsake their calling and follow him. Christ is the Head of the Church, and they united themselves to him. There is no profession of regeneration preceding their joining themselves to Christ. There is no relating of their experience. There is no demand made by Christ requiring them to be converted before they become his disciples. So far as we can see, there was only a desire to be saved, and "they immediately left the ship, and their father, and followed him," in order to be saved.

Again, Christ, in his Sermon on the Mount, says, "Blessed are the poor in spirit, for theirs is the kingdom of God." To feel poor in spirit is to feel humble, penitent, empty of all good. Just such persons as our General Rule describes. Such persons are blessed because "theirs is the kingdom of God." "The kingdom of God" here means either the Church on earth, or the Church triumphant in heaven, or the kingdom of grace in the soul. But if the penitent has the kingdom of grace in his soul, then he is a fit and suitable person to become a member of the visible Church. Such persons were admitted into the primitive Church. Justin Martyr says of such that "when they had given good proofs of their *resolutions* to lead a pious, religious life, and had protested their assent and consent to all the Christian verities, they were baptized," and of course admitted into the Church.

That true penitents may be baptized and admitted

into the Church is scriptural is clear from the following: "Then Peter said unto them, Repent, and be baptized every one of you in the name of Jesus Christ for [unto] the remission of sins, and ye shall receive the gift of the Holy Ghost." (Acts ii. 38.) Here we see that repentance and baptism plainly preceded the gift of the Holy Ghost, that regenerates the soul. These penitents were baptized and added to the company of Christians. It must be clear to all impartial minds that the Methodist practice of receiving penitent seekers into the bosom of the Church, rests upon broad scriptural grounds.

When Christ called men to be his disciples, he did not seek perfect men. He says, "Come and join my school; be my scholar." The Church is a spiritual school. But is a man to be kept out of school because he is ignorant? Schools are opened for illiterate people, not for ripe scholars. If a man desires to be a soldier, he joins the army; and as soon as he joins the army he is a soldier, though he is far from being a trained veteran. He is a soldier just as really when his name goes down on the roll, and he goes out with awkwardness to be drilled, as after he has been in the army ten years. Therefore, when we find men having a spark of grace in their souls, we encourage them to join the Church, where the spark can be kindled to such a flame of love as illumines and warms the whole man. They have germs which, being planted in the garden of the Lord, may become fruitful trees.

Bishop Marvin says: "God has ordained in the Church many efficient aids, and many means of grace, through which the earnest penitent and more advanced believer are alike strengthened and helped forward in the Christian race. The fellowship of saints and the ordinances of religion quicken the spiritual perception and sensibility, and encourage and strengthen faith. The mere fact of membership in the Church exerts a most wholesome effect on the mind and heart." In one sense the Church is a spiritual hospital, where sick and wounded penitents may be carried for the purpose of having nursing and healing influences administered to them by the members of the Church. Who does not see that it is infinitely easier to work out the salvation of the soul in the Church than out of it.

Let it be understood once for all that we do not open our Church to sinners, to impenitent men, nor merely to well-wishers to religion, nor to men who are moralists, but to penitent seekers of religion.

We ask them to come in, no matter how infirm they may be, and no matter how small their religious experience may have been. Babes in Christ, they need nourishing; and here is the motherhood into which they may come. I have seen a great many persons come in with flash and flame who went out ashes; and I have seen a great many persons come in like the little germ of a plant that just breaks the ground, without leaf or apparent power to live, and they have grown until the birds of the air lodged in their branches. We do not ask persons to come in with grandeur of attainments, but if there are any babes, according to the understanding of Christ, who said, "Except ye become as little children, ye shall not enter into the kingdom of heaven," we ask them to come in. If there are any who long to be better, who are determined by the help of God to transform their lives, and who are willing to be helped, to be loved, to be borne with, to be instructed, and to be put forward in the Christian life, it is our office to take them in. We are nurses of just such children. We are school-masters of just such scholars. They, by and by, will be able to render unto others that very service which they have had bestowed upon them; and so the work will go on. We do not ask them to come in because they have got through a supernatural experience, however high or low. We want them provided the work of grace is begun in them. We ask them to come in on the same ground that we ask tender plants to step in under glass in March when frost is in the air. They cannot afford to stay out, they are so tender and so poor.

2. *Growth in Grace.*—While the Church admits penitent seekers, she at the same time urges them never to stop seeking until they feel their sins pardoned and the love of God shed abroad in their heart. Then she sets a very high standard of Christian character before them, to be attained by growth in grace. To begin well is only a starting-point to go on to perfection. To join the Church is only a stepping-stone to reach the full assurance of salvation. We are exhorted to go on to a state of entire sanctification. As the sun, emerging from the horizon of the east, rises upward to his noontide splendor, so the path of the just is to shine more and more unto the perfect day. As the river flows on and on to the expanse of the great ocean, so the stream of repentance flows on and on until it swells out into the full river of sanctification. That mustard-seed of spirit-

ual life is to grow up into a lofty tree, among whose branches the birds of joy are to sing. That spiritual babe must grow up into a full stature of Christian manhood.

3. *The Means of Grace.*—Remember that there are means instituted by God which we are to observe that we may grow in grace. So far as we know, God always works through instruments in producing results. This is the case in nature. The beautiful heavens and the fruitful earth are made, but they are made by the word of his power. God enlightens and warms the world, but it is through the instrumentality of the sun, moon, and stars. He imbues the soil with the productive principle—sends clouds to pour down rain, provides the seeds, light, and heat; but there God leaves the matter. Man can plow the fields, and accordingly God leaves him to do so, or he will have no food to sustain him. Man can sow and cultivate, and God leaves him to do so; otherwise he will reap no golden harvests to fill his barns. It is the same in grace. God has established a system of saving grace for the benefit of man. The Bible, the Sabbath, prayer, the preaching of the everlasting gospel, songs, faith, the communion of the saints—through these he conveys saving grace, as he does light and heat through the sun, and rain through the clouds. But upon whom? Not upon the careless and the disobedient, but upon those who regularly and prayerfully wait upon him in the faithful use of these means. " Work out your own salvation," is the great command.

It is well to begin a religious life, but something more than beginning is necessary to secure salvation.

After a man has laid a good foundation, he must go on to rear up and finish the superstructure of his house. After a man has planted his crop, he must go on to cultivate in order to insure a matured crop. Ripeness of piety comes slowly as sweetness is wrought into the green fruit. It does not blossom suddenly into life. It is not a garment woven in heaven and dropped upon the shoulders of a believer. God clothes us with his own righteousness as he clothes trees with verdure, by a process of growth from within. It begins within and works out into the beauty of holiness. The desire begins within and goes out into holy living. "Blessed are they which do hunger and thirst after righteousness, for they shall be filled."

The figure of "hunger and thirst after righteousness" indicates an indescribable longing for it—one that cannot be denied. You shall have this righteousness, says the Scripture, when you search for it as for hid treasure. The silver is dug out of the hills by pick and gunpowder. It is put under the hammer and beaten into fine dust; it is put into one furnace and melted; into a second furnace and melted again; into a third furnace and melted again; and so through five or six refinings, before it is ready for the mint or jeweler. Dreaming of godliness will no more give you godliness than dreaming of knowledge will give you knowledge. It is given only to him who says: "I will work for it with a pick, and if I cannot get it with a pick, I will use gunpowder; and when it is once got in the crude state, I will not be content with that. If God puts me in the furnace once, twice, thrice, I will rejoice. I will not be content until he has burned me, and burned me until the dross is all consumed, so that I may be ready to be his coin on earth and his crown in heaven." Did Abraham find the road to godliness an easy one, when he turned his back upon home, and friends, and country, and worship, and went out to be the first emigrant to a strange land—not to seek more wages or better earthly conditions, but that he might find liberty to serve God according to his own conscience? Did Moses find it easy, driven into the wilderness, and repressing the powers that seemed to be calling him to greater work, to be forty years a herdsman of cattle, and for forty years a herdsman of imbruted slaves? Did David find it easy, fleeing from cave to cave before the huntsmen of Saul? Did Paul find it easy, thrice beaten with rods, five times receiving forty stripes save one, shipwrecked, stoned, in perils oft on sea and land? Read the autobiographical reminiscences of Paul in Corinthians; see how he was put under the hammer and beaten out, and then cast into the furnace again and again, that so he might receive God's answer to his perpetual prayer: "Nearer, my God, to thee; nearer to thee!"

III. THE INTRODUCTION OF BAPTIZED CHILDREN INTO THE CHURCH.

The Discipline says: 1. "Let the minister diligently instruct and exhort all parents to dedicate their children to the Lord in baptism as early as convenient. 2. Let him pay special attention to the children, speak to them personally and kindly on experimental and practical godliness. 3. As soon as they comprehend the responsibilities involved in a public profession of faith in Christ, and give evidence of a sincere and earnest determination to discharge the same, *see that they be duly recognized as members of the Church agreeably to the provisions of the Discipline.*"

Here we see that baptized children, coming to the years of accountability and giving "evidence of a sincere and earnest determination" to live as Christians, should be taken into the Church. To admit them into the Church is a disciplinary duty laid upon every Methodist pastor—a duty as clearly defined as that of taking in believing adults. And yet how generally this duty is neglected! How few are in the Church! Thousands of Methodist children duly baptized are left to grow up in ignorance and wander off into forbidden paths. They are as fully out of the Church as those unbaptized. They grow up in open *non-membership*, and are regarded as outside sinners. Who are to blame for this? Generally, parents and pastors. Is not something wrong among us as to this matter?

"Churches, parents, and teachers are to bring up the children under their care in the nurture and admonition of the Lord;" but to a very large extent Christians have brought up their children in the hope that when they shall have arrived at years of discretion (which are usually supposed to be somewhere from fifteen to twenty-one years of age) they will then themselves become Christians. I hold that it is possible so to rear our children that they shall be converted from the cradle, and grow up in the nurture and admonition of the Lord—some without a break, and some subject to these normal disturbances which come from physical causes in the readjustment of the system at its maturity. If Christian parents and

Christian teachers were consistent, and were in the true faith of Christ Jesus, I believe that generations of children might be brought up who never would know the point at which the transition was made. They would be taught to love Christ, and to adopt the great Christian element of character—love—and, by it, to cast out evil, to build, and to acquire habits and experiences, so that when they came to man's estate it would not be through all the tanglements, besetments, and soilings of an ordinary earthly experience. They would come honorable, truthful, loving, full of faith, full of hope, full of purity, from the cradle to the Church. And I do not simply believe this to be possible in rare cases. I do not believe there will ever be a day of millennium till it is done. I do not believe there will ever be a prevalence of Christianity, until, instead of trying to fish for the few adults that can be brought from evil into good, we learn to take life at its beginning, and to train generations from the first to true manhood, passing through infancy and youth into the full development of Christian life.

Persons, we all know, are more susceptible at the early age than at any other. Children are not superior to men in knowledge, nor in strength, nor in discrimination. There are a thousand of the acquirements by which a man battles with the world that they are not superior in. But there is one all-important principle which belongs to childhood, and not to any other time, viz., that peculiar development of the soul by which it knows how to take hold of another, and to borrow its light from that other.

To borrow an orchard illustration, there is but one period of the year in which you can graft well. It may be possible to graft successfully at other times, but there is one period when you must make the transfer if you would take a bud from one tree and graft it into another and have it produce its kind and do the best that it is capable of doing. There is but just one season when the bark lifts easily, and the staff is in the right condition.

There is a time, also, when the little natures bud easily and graft easily. It is possible to graft them at other times by extra elaboration, but more than half of the grafts will blow out, as the saying is. There is a period, however, in which ninety-nine out of a hundred will stick and grow; for all the adaptations of the child at that time are such as to incline it to borrow its life from another. It feeds upon another instinctively. It is a little parasite. It is but the transfer of that which is its need and instinct to the blessed Saviour. And then it becomes a Christian child. And so, adhering to Christ by love and by trust, and drawing its little life from Christ, it begins the Christian career. And they would go on and grow in thousands and thousands of instances, if it were not that parents have an absurd notion that when Christ is born into persons he is a self-registering and self-taking-care-of Christ, so that they say, "If my child is born of God, God will take care of his own work." As if a pomologist should come in and say, "I have put a graft into that tree, **and if nature is true to herself she will take care of that graft.**" Nobody says so about trees. The man binds up the graft so that it shall be held in its place, so that the water shall not get in, and so that it shall not be blown out until it gains strength sufficient to take care of itself, and then he leaves it to the force of nature.

But many people, in bringing up their children in the nurture and admonition of the Lord, look with great suspicion on early Christian experiences. They are afraid of abnormal growths; they are afraid of such material as Sunday-school libraries and biographies are made up of; they regard early conversions as indicating disease at the root or in the body of the tree; they do not believe in children being really Christians because they do not see in the child that which they would look for in a ripe Christian. But if they would look for a babe Jesus in a little babe, they would find that there; and if they would treat the babe Christ as they would the babe boy or the babe girl, and nourish it and carry it in their arms, and rear it step by step; if they would treat it as a little child embosomed and arm-encircled; if they would shield it as it goes through all temptation and all trial, they would make straighter Christians, better branched Christians, more fruitful Christians, than those that are made at last out of old and bad growths by lopping away the pernicious boughs. There never will be the ripest and most symmetrical characters in the Church of Christ till we learn how to bring them up from the seed in the spirit of the blessed Master.

There are many persons whose children give every evidence of being truly Christian, but whose parents shrink from bringing them into the fold. "Ah!" say they, "what if they should fall away?" The shepherd's boy comes in and says, "The ewe has dropped a lamb far out in the pasture, shall I bring it up to the barn and put it inside of the yard?" "No," says the shepherd; "let it stay out to-night, and if the wolf does not get it, and the cold chill does not kill it, and it lives till to-morrow and the next day, it will be worth keeping, and you can bring it in." But if the lamb can live in spite of the cold and wind, and without the care of the shepherd, he does not need to bring it in then.

There are many persons who say of the young: "Shall they be gathered into the Church? shall we run the risk of their bringing disgrace upon the Church by their fall?" Which is the most important, in the name of God, the Church or the souls of men for which Christ died? The Church, looked at as the servant of God's dear people, rises before my thought most beautiful; but if the Church dare to take the place of a soul of a man and make itself more precious and nobler than the soul, the poorest and lowest and least, I will regret it. The servant has usurped the place of the master under such circumstances; for the Church is God's slave, sent to take care of God's children, and if the Church is good for any thing it is good to take in little children and shelter them; to take in the wayfarer and to shelter him; to take in the spiritually poor and to shelter them.

Suppose that they do break down and do not get on well in the Church. Is a hospital brought into disgrace because patients die there whom the doctors have tried to cure? Is a school brought into disgrace because some dullards go in fools and come out idiots? And shall a Church be always trying to take care of itself instead of taking care of that which God loves better than any thing else—the souls of his dear children? Bring your little children into the Church; let Christ be born in them the hope of glory; let there be a babe Christ in their little experiences; let them be formed into classes. Do not leave them out with the wolf; do not leave them until they are strong enough to go along without a Church and then bring them in. See that they are taken care of and nourished.

Those who have been brought into the Church young within the circuit of my own experience have, on the whole, with single exceptions of miscarriage here and there, endured and come out into a true Christian life, with far better prospects and more symmetrical dispositions than those who have been brought in late in life.

One may be a Christian who is yet very far from the beauty and symmetry and manhood of piety. We are not to suppose that they only are Christians who are beautiful Christians, or who are embellished with all Christian graces. A man may be a Christian and his Christ may be a babe; a man may be a Christian and the Christian nature in him may yet be, as it were, in its boyhood.

There are but two kingdoms, one of truth and goodness and light, the other of falsehood and selfishness and darkness. The little children do not belong to the kingdom of the devil till some one has rescued them in Christ's name; they belong to Christ unless the devil carries them off and makes them captives to sin and death, from which they may still be rescued by Christian chivalry. The little children are not to wait till they become as men before they can enter into Christ's kingdom; the grown men are to be converted and become as little children before they can enter it. All children are Christ's; it is the duty and the privilege of parents not to wait with anxiety till they grow to years of discretion and then hope to convert them from evil to him; it is their privilege to train them for him from the cradle, to so train them that they shall always go steadily forward, growing in grace and in the knowledge of God, going on from victory to victory. In their earliest and feeblest struggles they have Christ's sympathy and help; in their earliest life, before the first shoots have begun to appear above the ground, they are his. The Sun of righteousness does not confine his shining to the great trees; it shines on the hidden seed and makes trees of them.

We have a right to hope, to pray, to expect for our children that, like John the Baptist, they will be filled from their mother's womb with the Holy Spirit. It is a most dangerous error to suppose that they cannot have the divine help and inspiration till they have come to be old enough to comprehend its desirability and to ask for it. It is a most dangerous error to suppose that our children must live in the wilderness till they are old enough to seek the promised land of their own accord. Not till the Church learns to train its own children, not only for Christ but *in* Christ, from the cradle, so that they shall always be Christ's, will it begin to really vanquish the world. Till then it can hope for nothing more than to make reprisals.

I believe that those of us who really believe this should carry out our belief consistently; that we should regard our children as members of the Church as truly as they are citizens of the commonwealth; that we should repudiate in stronger terms than we are wont to do the notion that they cannot be members of the outward community of saints till they have reached years of discretion; that we should accustom ourselves to regard them as members with us of the household of faith, and should accustom them to so regard themselves; and that we may well use the rite of baptism as a sign of this faith that brings our children into Christ's household with ourselves.

Baptized children, then, ought to be enrolled by name in the register of each Church, as composing a distinct class of *candidate members*, and thus be held in expectancy till the time when they are to be examined, and those that are found to meet the prescribed conditions of the Discipline should be admitted into the full membership of the Church.

IV THE DUTY OF JOINING THE CHURCH.

1. Every one desiring to save his soul should seek a spiritual home in some branch of the Church of God. That this is a duty is seen from the teaching and practice of the early disciples. The converts on the day of Pentecost immediately joined the band of disciples. "And the same day there were added unto them about three thousand souls." (Acts ii. 4.) Also the converts in Lystra, Iconium, and Antioch were organized into churches. Hence, it is said of the apostles: "They returned again to Lystra, and to Iconium, and to Antioch, confirming the souls of the disciples, and exhorting them to continue in the faith." (Acts xiv. 22.) Within the Church thus organized are the ordinances of the gospel, which are means appointed by God to help us work out our salvation—such as spiritual discipline, the communion, and the pastoral watch-care.

2. Consider, too, the benefit of pulpit instruction. How much light and warmth it sheds upon the world

in this way! Think of seventy thousand ministers in the United States, men of culture and well skilled in preaching, pouring every Sabbath streams of moral light and truth upon the people! What a vast amount of good is done! What a great help it is to sit under the enlightening and stirring ministrations of the pulpit! It has pleased God to save men by preaching.

3. Then, again, in the Church is the stirring influence of sacred song. The hymn-book is a power in the land. There can never be such a bond of union as sweet and animating song. How often on the wings of song our dull souls begin to take fire and rise heavenward! How often it comes as a refreshing rain on parched fields!

4. Furthermore, the Church generates spiritual warmth. "It is difficult for single individuals, unless they be very highly endowed, to create in themselves fervor when alone. Now and then there is a nature that can generate its own fire; but ordinarily you must put stick upon stick, and spark to spark, and flame to flame, in order to make fervor; and it is the association of feeling, it is feeling in the multitude, whose thought kindles in each individual the highest forms of emotion. There are very few who have the power of solitary zeal; and there are very few who have not the power of associated zeal. The Christian religion depended at the first, and has ever since depended, and will to the end depend very largely, on Church conditions; for a religion whose element is love and not awe, a religion whose very life is sweet and pure emotion, must thrive by the social principle. It was never meant that Christians should be solitary; it was never meant that they should feed themselves.

It was meant that they should thrive in their combined and associated capacities."

5. "In Church association also the feeble and ignorant get from the gifts of all an education which is not possible in any other way. A Church that has a real Christian life in it is one of the best schools to which men can go. If, when the disciples had professed the name of Christ, each one had made his own house the center, and his own relatives exclusive companions, there would have been hundreds and thousands in the course of time who would have been almost without instruction. But by the gathering together of the humble and lowly with those of culture and refinement in intimate association, the under classes gained and the upper classes lost nothing."

6. Church-membership cultivates brotherly love and mutual assistance. "As soon as the idea of brotherhood was once introduced, as soon as men felt that God was their Father and that Jesus Christ was their elder brother, and that they were all brethren, and they began to come together with that feeling, instantly there took place a process of evolution and of education which never can be measured, and which can scarcely be overestimated. There is an education of the books, and there is an education in the higher forms in schools; but the general education which the community receive depends largely upon the association of men with men. It is the unconscious and general action of the higher natures upon the intermediate or lower that is perpetually working in society. Therefore a Church that gathers together its members, if there be a sweet and blessed affection flowing through the Church, then the best lives in the Church become

instructors, and all the poorest lives, the lives of the whole spiritual household, are pervaded by a common religious sentiment; the gifts of all belong to each, and the gifts of each belong to all. For general instruction, then, and for the development of emotive life, it is wise for those who love the Lord Jesus Christ to gather themselves together."

These are some of the reasons for joining the Church that existed in the past, and will still exist to the end of time. We invite men into Church-fellowship because it is a duty; it is a happier life and a more useful one.

OBJECTIONS MET.—"Well, but," says one, "I do not feel that I am worthy to join the Church." If you mean by this that your unworthiness arises from living in the commission of some sin—secret or known—and you do not mean to abandon sin, then you are not fit. There can be no advance made in securing salvation, either in or out of the Church, till a man makes up his mind to forsake evil and learn to do well. But if you mean, as is most generally the case, that you are not worthy because you have not reached the *standard of spiritual excellence*, then our reply is that you are like a sick man who does not feel worthy to be cured, or a boy hanging around a school-house, saying, "I am too ignorant to go in and become a scholar." What is a hospital for but to cure sick men, or school-houses for but to educate illiterate persons? The Church is a curative institution; it is an educating institution; it is a household where spiritual babes are to be fed and raised.

"O well," some say, "we do n't like to take upon ourselves the duties and obligations of Church-membership." There is not a duty resting on a member of the Church that does not rest on men outside of the Church. Moral obligations rest upon men whether they be in or out of the Church. There is not a single duty that will be incumbent upon you when you go into the Church that is not incumbent upon you now. Is there any obligation greater than this: *"Thou shalt love the Lord thy God with all thy heart and mind and soul and strength, and thy neighbor as thyself."* And does this royal law not become binding till a man joins the Church? Why, its obligations fell on you the very hour you crossed the line of accountability. It rests upon you in or out of the Church. The Church does not create moral obligation; it only helps us to perform the duties that *God* has laid upon us.

CHAPTER XV

METHODISM AND SUNDAY-SCHOOLS.

I. ORIGIN.

WHILE Mr. Wesley was a missionary in Georgia, "he established a school of forty children, which he placed under the care of Mr. Delamotte, a man of good education, who endeavored to blend religious instruction with secular learning; and on Sunday afternoon Wesley met them in the church before evening service, heard the children recite their catechism, questioned them as to what they had heard from the pulpit, endeavoring to fix the truth in their understanding as well as in their memories. This was a regular part of his Sunday duties, and *it shows that John Wesley, in the parish of Savannah, had established a Sunday-*

school fifty years before Robert Raikes originated his noble scheme in Gloucester, and eighty years before the first school in America on Mr. Raikes's plan was established in the city of New York. Mrs. Susannah Wesley, mother of John Wesley, had a Sunday-school in England in 1764, seventeen years before Mr. Raikes organized his school in 1781. In 1783, Bishop Asbury organized a Sunday-school in Virginia.

II. Eminent Usefulness of These Schools.

1. Think of the hundreds of thousands of children who have been led to Christ through these schools! General statistics show that during the past eighteen years 285,730 converted souls have passed from the Sunday-schools into the bosom of the M. E. Church, North. And what is true of this Church is no doubt true of others. Truly these schools are the nurseries of the Church.

"Some years since a noted horticulturist took me to see his orchard of young peach-trees. It was a splendid sight—thousands of trees standing in long rows and comprising all the rich varieties of that delicious fruit! I said to him, 'I presume you are very careful in the selection of your peach-kernels in order to get the rarest quality of fruit?' 'No,' he replied, we plant whatever comes to hand, and then we bud them. Every one of these trees was budded.' This brought to light a curious fact in horticulture. Does the gardener wish to raise a rare and splendid fruit, he takes a bud or sprout from a bearing tree and grafts it. No matter how poor a variety the stock may be upon which he grafts it, the bud will preserve its own identity; it will grow up and bear its own fruit. Thus the tree will be made to bear fruit entirely different from, and infinitely superior to, that which its own nature would have produced. Our Sunday-school system is a system of spiritual horticulture; it is designed to ingraft into the young heart the 'incorruptible seed' of the word of God. No matter how unpromising the variety or individual, it will take root, it will grow up, preserve its own identity, blossom in unfading beauty, send forth heavenly odors, and ripen into immortal fruit. My brethren, let us learn a lesson from the horticulturist. Let us have more faith in the vitalizing and regenerating power of that 'incorruptible seed' which it is our business to ingraft into the mind and heart of the child."—*Bishop Clark.*

2. Think, again, of the distinguished statesmen, lawyers, physicians, merchants, mechanics, ministers, and missionaries, who owe their eminence and usefulness to Sabbath-school instruction. We need to trace the influence of these schools in quickening the whole Church, and in opening wide and promising fields for all Christian workers. We talk of reflex influences. Was there ever a more striking example of it than we have here? Christians meet to teach children; their services are gratuitous, and they look perhaps for a reward in heaven, but God so orders events that they themselves are taught. Agencies and influences surround them and press them in vast numbers to the word of God, where their intellects are filled with divine truths, where they drink of the river of the water of life and are refreshed, where they receive *stimulus* and strength to work for the Master. Since the introduction of the International Lessons, the

Sunday-school has become the greatest theological seminary in Christendom.

3. Think of the hundreds of thousands of well-educated and pious men and women who are engaged every week in the careful study of God's holy word, with the varied and abundant helps furnished by commentaries, and the expositions and illustrations given in religious periodicals and newspapers! Consider how their own minds are profited and enriched by these studies, and their hearts warmed by the simultaneous contemplation of the precious doctrines and glorious hopes that shine from the sacred page! Before this great theological institution — every day becoming greater — in which God himself is the Teacher, and over which the Holy Spirit hovers to answer the prayer from any lips, "Open thou mine eyes, that I may behold wondrous things out of thy law;" before this institution, with its vast array of students hungering and thirsting after knowledge and righteousness, I stand filled with admiration, and with gratitude to God. I see here a theological institute, capable of indefinite enlargement, with its doors open to all who will come in and sit at the feet of Jesus and learn of him.

4. As a missionary organization the Sunday-school has done a great work in establishing and sustaining schools in destitute localities and in remote regions, where it has kindled the first gospel light, and furnished the means for the instruction of the ignorant and neglected classes. Its influence has been sensibly and extensively felt in foreign fields through its contributions, its missionary bands recently so largely increased, and especially in the numerous and able

missionaries whom it has raised up and sent forth to preach the gospel.

III. Sunday-school Statistics.

Methodist Episcopal Church, South: Schools organized, 7,226; officers and teachers, 57,867; scholars, 391,693; total, 449,560.

Methodist Episcopal Church, North: Schools organized, 19,904; officers and teachers, 212,442; scholars, 1,743,735; total, 1,956,178.

With the latest corrections applied, the report of the Statistical Secretary presents the Sunday-school army of the United States and Canada thus: Total of schools, 83,188; teachers and officers, 894,793; scholars, 6,843,997; total of teachers and scholars, 7,738,790. Of the above, the United States have: Schools, 77,793; teachers and officers, 853,100; scholars, 6,504,054; total of teachers and scholars, 7,357,154. And as many more in Great Britain and other countries.

CHAPTER XVI.
METHODISM AND REVIVALS.

The grand feature of Methodism is a revival of scriptural Christianity. "Revivals are no mere incident of Methodism. It is itself a revival. The entire significance of it is given in that word. Methodism was not a revolution against existing ecclesiastical authority, nor against established doctrines, but a *revival of religion.*"—*Bishop Marvin.*

I. What is a Revival?

It is a deep spiritual interest pervading a town or a neighborhood. It is an active, stirring excitement on the question of personal salvation. There are three states of men. There is the state of lukewarmness; the state of serious attention; then an anxious state, saying, "What shall I do to be saved?" When this state pervades a congregation, it is a revival of religion. The history of the Church is marked with periods of revivals—great divine freshets, when the rains from heaven filled the ordinary channels fuller than they could hold, and they overflowed their banks and spread spiritual beauty and fertility on both sides clear down to the day of Pentecost, which was one of the grandest revivals on record. The genuineness of revivals is so clear and marked as to set aside the necessity of argument. "I believe in the existence of revivals of religion as much as I believe in any other fact, either physical or moral."—*Dr. Wayland*. While the Methodist Church is preëminently the Church of revivals, yet nearly all the Protestant Churches have more or less adopted the principle. The revival Churches are the growing and spreading Churches in our land.

II. BENEFITS OF REVIVALS.

1. *To Promote the Piety of the Christians.*—It is a great work to elevate the Christian character of the members of the Church to a higher plane, a nobler form of development. "Even if there were to be no ingathering from the world, it is oftentimes that a 'refreshing grace' (as it is called in the old-fashioned language) in the Church is preëminently desirable, preëminently a blessing from God, though it may stop with the members of the Church; for our power is not numerical, but moral it is not so much how

many members we have in the Church that determines its power as it is the quality of that which we have. A church of twenty men who are eminent in grace and goodness is a larger church, if you measure size by power, than a church of two thousand that are living a very low, worldly form of life. So that when men in the Church have been living in routine Christianity without any very active development of personal faith and the sweetness of the Christian graces, it may oftentimes be the case that a revival of religion will be the divine work in the Church; and though many are not added to the Church, the Church itself is immensely strengthened, its power is augmented; so that while sometimes you shall find men ambitious of a large roll of members gathered in the community, this is not the most important part, important as it is. It is still more important that in gathering in these men those that gather shall themselves be built up, shall themselves be developed and made more powerful."

"A revival is the spring of religion, the renovation of life and gladness. It is the season in which young converts burst into existence and beautiful activity. The Church resumes her toil and labor and care with freshness and energy. The air all around is balmy, and diffusing the sweetest odors. The whole landscape teems with living promises of abundant harvest of righteousness and peace. It is the jubilee of holiness. A genial warmth pervades and refreshens the whole Church. Showers of 'vernal delight and joy' descend gently and copiously. Delightful influences are wafted by every breeze."

2. *The Reclaiming of Backsliders.*—One of the blessed

results of a revival is to awaken and reclaim backsliders. There are hundreds and thousands in the Church who are sunk down into a deep and fearful state of religious declension. They are too far gone to be recovered by the ordinary means of grace. The only chance to lift them up from this gulf of declension is a flood of revival grace. Nothing less than the thunder of a religious storm will wake them up and bring them to repentance and renewed obedience. A powerful revival will open their blind eyes and melt their hard, marble hearts, and break the spell of sin, and save them.

3. *The Conversion of Sinners.*—The immediate conversion of sinners is the leading idea of a revival. One of the most extraordinary elements of the gospel is its power of suddenly transforming the souls of men. It is the power of God unto salvation to every one that believeth.

"A gambler may in a moment cease to gamble, and never again touch the instrument of deceit. A drunkard may in one single moment come to a purpose by which he shall never again touch the fatal cup. The effects of his past misconduct will not pass away at once, but the man has made a stand that will affect his whole character."

"A man may be pursuing lewd courses, he may be pursuing a dissolute life, and in one single hour he may set the rudder so that his whole track after that will be upon a different line. The beginnings may be sudden, and it is the knowledge of this fact that there is a power by which men may be changed—not in single instances alone, but in multitudes—that inspires us to work in revivals of religion. We do not, therefore, get up a religious enthusiasm in a social form simply to enjoy ourselves and to exalt the feeling of the Church, but we do it because in that heat which is generated you can develop in wicked men a newness of life which it would seem very difficult to develop under any other circumstances. This is the language of experience and observation, and not of theory."

Look at the first great revival that occurred on the day of Pentecost. Three thousand hard-hearted sinners were converted in one day. Who were they? "Strangers" who had come from a distance to Jerusalem. No doubt but that they were men of spiritual ignorance and wicked lives. Paul, the blood-red persecutor, is struck down beneath the outbursting splendor of Christ's manifested presence, and transformed into a flaming apostle. The Ethiopian eunuch, riding in his chariot, is changed suddenly, and "went on his way rejoicing." The publican sunk down beneath the mountain-load of guilt, and cried, "God be merciful to me a sinner!" The burden rolled off, light flashed into his darkened mind, peace welled up in his heart, and "he went down to his house justified." The Philippian jailer is suddenly awakened to see his sinfulness and awful danger, and then in a few moments he emerges from heathen darkness into the glorious light and liberty of the sons of God.

"Name any specific sin in the catalogue of heinous crimes, the forgiveness of which God has not illustrated in Biblical history: Noah, the inebriate; Abraham, the falsifier; Moses, the son of ambition; Aaron, the idolater; Solomon, the libertine; Manasseh, the murderer; Peter, the swearer; David, the adulterer;

the nameless robber of Calvaria; Paul, the persecutor, and fallen women, but represent tens of thousands who have sung triumphantly: 'O God! I will praise thee; for, though thou wast angry with me, thine anger is turned away, and thou comfortest me!'

"Infidels, such as Newton, Rochester, and Charney; veteran sinners, such as Marcus Caius Victorius; savage chieftains, such as Africana; pagan monarchs, such as Clovis and Constantine, have found Christ's atonement ample for their salvation. Read Paul's array of sinful classes saved from among the Corinthians, as he enumerates them in the sixth chapter of his first letter to the Corinthians. What a rich freight of cheer comes to unsaved men on the opening words of our text: 'All manner of sin and blasphemy shall be forgiven unto men!'"

4. *The Conversion of Children.*--Revivals are precious seasons for bringing in the children and young persons; and special pains should be taken to lead them to Christ. The young are the hope of the Church. They will be its strong pillars when the fathers have passed away. They are soon to fill the pulpits and pews of the Church. The glory of the future Church will depend upon them. As the beauty of spring, the glory of summer, and the fruitfulness of the autumn depend upon the healthy buds and germs of the spring, so the power, excellency, efficiency, and fruitfulness of the future Church will depend upon the early conversion and thorough training of the children. And the Church that takes the best care of the lambs will have the grandest flock feeding in the green pasture of gospel grace. The Church that transplants the most of these immortal

scions will have the largest, most fragrant and fruitful orchard. The Church that gets the most youthful recruits, and trains and drills them well, will have the grandest, most aggressive and effective army to conquer the world for Christ. It requires no prophetic vision to see which denomination will be the greatest Church of the future in America. It will be that Church which is instrumental in converting the most children, and developing them into fruitful Christians. Then, work for the conversion of the children. Let there be no mock fear about them being too young to be converted. There are very early conversions.

5. *Early Conversions.*—Dr. Talmage says: "It is sometimes said that during revivals of religion great multitudes of children and young people are brought into the Church, and they do not know what they are about. It has been my observation that the earlier people come into the kingdom of God the more useful they are."

Robert Hall, the prince of Baptist preachers, was converted at twelve years of age. It is supposed he knew what he was about. Matthew Henry, the commentator, who did more than any man of his century for increasing the interest in the study of the Scriptures, was converted at eleven years of age; Isabella Graham, immortal in the Christian Church, was converted at ten years of age; Dr. Watts, whose hymns will be sung all down the ages, was converted at nine years of age; Jonathan Edwards, perhaps the mightiest intellect that the American pulpit ever produced, was converted at seven years of age. And that father and mother take an awful responsibility when they tell their child at seven years of age, "You are too young to be a Christian," or, "You are too young to connect yourself with the Church." That is *a mistake as long as eternity.*

If during a revival two persons present themselves as candidates for the Church, and the one is ten years of age and the other is forty years of age, I will have more confidence in the profession of religion of the one ten years of age than the one forty years of age. Why? The one who professes at forty years of age has forty years of impulse in the wrong direction to correct; the child has only ten years in the wrong direction to correct. Four times ten are forty. Four times more the religious prospect for the lad that comes into the kingdom of God and into the Church at ten years of age than for the man at forty.

We may add that it is stated that Bishop Asbury was converted at thirteen, Bishop Roberts at ten, Dr. Benson at sixteen, while Richard Baxter and Bishop Andrew were so taught that they never knew the exact time of their conversion.

Children are converted just as adults are converted. The child is the father of the man. The nearer we are to the birth, the nearer we are to the new birth. The oldest, the wisest, has to enter the kingdom of Christ as a child. Every child old enough to sin is old enough to repent and believe. Then, again, how much easier it is to get children converted than old, hard-hearted sinners? It is easy to turn the lamb while gentle into the pasture, but when it grows up to be an old sheep and wanders far away upon the bleak mountains of sin, becomes wild and shy, how difficult the work of hunting it up and driving it back to the gate where it stood when a little lamb! And when put into the fold, its bad habits render it liable to leave the fold and go back to its old haunts. The application is easy. The child is the gentle lamb, that can be easily turned in through the gate of conversion into the green pastures of the Church. The wild sheep is the child neglected till it wanders off, contracts the bad habits of drinking, swearing, unbelief, and other sins which render his conversion difficult.

Two men have nurseries. The wise man takes up a hundred scions while small, transplants them into a fertile and well-prepared soil. They take root and grow up into symmetrical trees, which flourish and bear much fruit. He has a beautiful, fragrant, fruitful orchard. The foolish man lets his scions alone. They grow up into scraggy trees. They must be transplanted or be destroyed. Now, he commences the work of transplanting. They have grown old, heavy, deeply rooted in the soil. What labor to dig around and around, to prize and heave, in order to get them up! Then he must work almost as hard in digging deep holes where they are to be planted. He must lop off many limbs and plant carefully, fertilize well, and then probably half of them will wither and die after all of his hard labor. The wise man represents the preacher laboring for the conversion of the children. The foolish man represents the preacher who neglects the children till they grow up into habits of sinfulness, and then works for their conversion. This whole country is full of old sinners who stand as old scrubby oaks in the forest of wickedness. Will they ever be transplanted into the garden of the Lord and become "trees of righteousness?" Will the millions of heathen rooted in the soil of superstition ever be transplanted by a handful of missionaries? This world cannot be converted by the old process of transplanting grown trees. No, never. The Church must begin at the cradle—must transplant the millions of the world while they are tender, growing plants.

III. THE AGENCIES TO BE USED IN SECURING A REVIVAL.

1. One of the most effective and reliable means is the faithful preaching of the divine truth. It should be adapted to produce the result desired.

(1) *Such Preaching as will Convince the Judgment.*— "Knowing the terror of the Lord," said Paul, "we persuade men." It was the compulsion of persuasion which the Saviour enjoined upon his disciples as a means of inducing men to come in, that his Father's house might be filled. Hence the control of attention and the impartation of instruction, however important of themselves, are nevertheless to be regarded as means to the higher end of convincing men of spiritual truth and religious duty. As God has implanted reasoning faculties in every mind, it is the preacher's duty to bring Christian truth within the action of those faculties, so that they may be enlisted in its reception and study. To this end he must be a lover of truth, and must illustrate its influence not only in his life, but in his modes of reasoning. No mental reservations must be allowed to underlie his statements, no covert sophistries to impeach his candor, and no evasions to betray his lack of confidence in the truths he assumes to utter. His

motto must be, "Having believed, therefore do I speak;" and in showing forth the reasons for the faith that is in him, he will not fail to persuade others also.

(2) *The Preaching should Arouse the Conscience.*—It was especially designed to reach and quicken that silent and often silenced monitor of every breast, which, however averse its possessor may be, seldom fails to respond to earnest reasoning in "temperance, righteousness, and a judgment to come." Powerless and valueless for true religious effect are those sermons which awaken no echoes in the chambers of conscience; whereas the faithful word which startles into action a dormant consciousness of guilt before God, and confronts a careless soul with its own shortcomings and their consequences, is of priceless value in the moral history of that soul. When the conscience is properly aroused, it becomes an auxiliary of untold power to aid the preacher in his further work. It supplies the listening ear, the tender heart, and the consenting will. Thus it is that through the office of preaching God works within men "to will and to do of his own good pleasure," and yet in perfect harmony with their individual freedom of choice and action.

(3) *The Preaching should Melt the Sensibilities.*—As man embraces in his nature the most varied powers and susceptibilities, so preaching was designed to address and influence every faculty of his being. Intensely fallacious, therefore, is the theory of some that preaching should only address the judgment. That, indeed, is to be done in a manly and faithful manner; but the more delicate task of warming the

heart and kindling the emotions is not to be left undone. For this there is no power equal to a right exercise and an unaffected expression of the religious affections. How true is the classic precept of Horace, "Weep yourself if you would see others weep," compared with the heart-utterances of the Hebrew prophets and psalmist. Listen to Jeremiah as he exclaims, "O that my head were waters and mine eyes a fountain of tears, that I might weep day and night for the slain of the daughter of my people!" Also, David, when he said: "They that sow in tears shall reap in joy. He that goeth forth and weepeth, bearing precious seed, shall doubtless come again with rejoicing, bringing his sheaves with him." The preacher who cherishes or illustrates a cold, unsympathetic nature, or whose ideas of propriety would repress every emotion that does not freeze in its utterance, is a poor representative of Him who shed tears over Jerusalem, and who wept at the grave of Lazarus. If "love is the fulfilling of the law," and if "Christian faith works by love and purifies the heart," then let no preacher of the gospel fear or fail to cherish a consuming love for his fellow-men, and to imbue his messages with a warmth of sentiment which will soften frigid hearts and melt down the obduracy of impenitence. Well has it been said that he who loves most will preach best.

(4) *The Great End, Aim, and Result of the Preaching should be to Lead Sinners to the Saviour.*—All other elements focalize in this. Hence, whether by instruction, persuasion, conviction, or entreaty, or by all combined, the preacher must by all means strive to save men. Hence, also, that method, or combination

of methods, which will save most is, without question, the best. At this point the controlling purpose of the preacher will greatly influence the character of his preaching. Moral and spiritual results rarely ensue by accident. The laws of intellectual and spiritual influence are not less positive than those which govern matter. He that would preach the gospel for the glory of God and the salvation of men must study those laws and avail himself of their power. Of all the good gifts which it is permitted men to covet, that of winning souls is the greatest. For the attainment of this it is the privilege of every minister of the Lord Jesus to toil with a holy ambition and to pray with an unwavering faith, relying upon the promised aid of the Holy Ghost. For this he should account no labor irksome, no study hard, no experiment profitless. For this even failures may become to him lessons of help, and sacrifices the source of glorious rewards. A ministry that is not crowned with the result of soul-saving, however it may win human applause or snuff the incense of admiration, is poor indeed; whereas he that is blessed of God, in using the appointed means of converting sinners from the errors of their ways, enjoys a privilege that angels might covet.

2. *Praying for the Unction of the Holy Ghost.*—"All revivals are the work of the Holy Spirit. They are never manipulated into existence. When religion is revived, God does it. Nothing can substitute the divine presence and power. The 'times of refreshing' are 'from the presence of the Lord.' But God always works among men through human *media*, so that while 'the power is of God,' 'it worketh mightily

in' his people."—*Bishop Marvin*. And as the power of developing and carrying on a revival is the Holy Spirit, the disciples were commanded to tarry at Jerusalem till that power came. "Ye shall receive power after that the Holy Ghost is come upon you." The power that leads men to Christ is not the power of eloquence. The power of eloquence may move and burn, but it cannot regenerate the soul of man. The cold moonlight of human eloquence can never melt down the icebergs of sin. It will take the summer beams of the Holy Spirit to do that.

Neither is it the power of logic. Mere argument cannot convert a soul. You have seen *sheet-lightning* how it flashes and dazzles, but it never wields the bolt that smites and kills. Cold logic is the mere sheet-lightning. It is the fire of the Holy Ghost that smites sinners and converts their souls.

"Now, it was just exactly that mood of the higher faculties which came to the apostles after Christ's ascension, when the Holy Ghost descended upon them. It is precisely that faith which is produced upon God's people now when the Holy Ghost descends into their hearts. There is not an explainable personality, there is not an explicable influence, but there is the witness, from age to age, of thrice ten thousand in every generation, that it is best for men so to hold their souls that they shall be filled with the divine enthusiasm— that it is a divine enthusiasm which in the main manifests itself by giving tone and electric, or magic, power to the higher moral and spiritual sentiments in the human soul; and it is exactly that part of the mind which is ordinarily capable of being the most efficacious upon others. No man inspires faith in his fellow-man who has not faith himself; no man inspires warmth in them who has not warmth himself; no man inspires enthusiasm in them who does not generate enthusiasm in his own soul. And to do this transcends nature. In order to do this, we need to have the divine influence exerted upon our souls. And it is for this that the truth of the Divine Spirit is revealed. It is distinctively peculiar. It was known among the prophets under the old dispensation; it became the possession or right of the whole brotherhood of men under the new dispensation; and it is possible for men to live in such a light, in such a warmth, and so under the stimulating influence of the Spirit of God, that the higher part of their nature shall be constantly in an innocuous state, warming, and lighting, and blessing men. Now, in this higher condition of the nobler faculties, more than in any other condition, we lose the fear of men, and escape from that bias and damaging influence which comes in through the love of approbation. We love the praise of God more than the praise of men, therefore we are lifted up above a thousand temptations and infelicities; above the currents which blow close down to the earth—the 'land currents,' as they are called."

In laboring for a revival, nothing is so important as earnest, persevering, and believing prayer. There must be private and public prayer. The preachers and the people must pray mightily for the outpouring of the Spirit. For our encouragement, we are told by the Master "that God loves to give good gifts to his children that ask him," more than parents love to give bread to their children. He challenges us. He says: "If ye, being *evil*, know how to give good gifts unto your children, how *much more* shall your Father which is in heaven?" That is, how much more shall One who is not evil, who is not narrow, who is not ignorant, who is not imperfect—how much more shall the wisdom and goodness of the Father in heaven do for men than the erring affection and limited wisdom of earthly parents do for their children! God's bounty is universal, unquestionable; and nothing pleases God so much as that we should draw upon him. "It is more blessed to give than to receive," said Christ. He said so because he felt it. He said so because it was true of the Eternal Father. The happiness of God comes from this, that he is eternally pouring out from himself. He loves to give, and rejoices to give.

If, then, you need consolation, enlightenment, power, enthusiasm, joy in the Holy Ghost, it is to be sought. It is not to be purchased by labor-pains, by penalties, or by tasks; it is to be received. It comes as the dew comes; it falls as the rain falls; it streams abroad as the light streams abroad; it is that which God loves to give, that which you need to receive, and that which every man should seek and should take. When the preacher is baptized with the Holy Ghost, his sermon will move the people.

> He will preach as though he ne'er should preach again,
> And as a dying man to dying men.

IV THE COÖPERATION OF THE PEOPLE WITH THE PREACHERS.

On this point, Mr. Moody has some very practical and useful remarks. He says: "There are three classes in the Church. First, the *formalists*, who criticise.

They say, We can have nothing to do with these evangelists; we must maintain dignity and order in our services. These are the same class of people who cried out, 'Crucify him! crucify him!' They resented the preaching of the Nazarene, and they objected to his unorthodox sermons, and the crowds who followed him about, and his ignorant disciples who were not of the scribes and Pharisees.

"Then there are the *sponges*. They take all the comfort they can get, but give out nothing. They are going to meetings all the time, listening to sermons; but you can never get them to work. They do not teach in our Sunday-schools; they will not visit the sick.

"The third is the class we want—the Christian *workers*. All the while the minister is preaching they are praying for the Spirit of God to carry the truth to the hearts of sinners. After the service they are looking out for some one to speak to and to make a personal appeal. A minister who has a hundred such workers in his congregation will revolutionize the part of the city he works in. The trouble is not so much in getting men to hear the gospel as in getting men to work.

"We hear much of those who show zeal without knowledge, but I had a thousand times rather have zeal without knowledge than knowledge without zeal. We must learn never to despise the weakest workers in the Master's service. God chooses the weak things; God uses the foolish things. *We want* to have the wise and the strong, and we are not content to follow God's plan, for God often passes over the wise. If you had asked the men of other days who were the great men of the time, they would not have pointed you to John Bunyan, or to Luther, to Abraham, to Enoch, or to Noah. John Bunyan got shut up in Bedford jail, but the devil found his match when he laid John Bunyan up there. We never should have had the Pilgrim's Progress if it had not been that John Bunyan had leisure in his cell to write his wonderful dream. The millionaires are not the workers in the Church; God passes them by. If they are converted, they are not used. God passes them by, and takes up some *poor tramp*. Even Paul said his strength lay in his great weakness.

"To arouse the Christian Church to a sense of its duty, and to induce Christian men to go out and work for their Master, is one of the highest missions open to man. An anxious Church is sure to bring anxious inquirers, but a cold and dead Church is dead for the work of the Lord. Very few men are *converted* under sermons; I have hardly ever met *one* who was. Men are awakened under a sermon, and then is the time for the Christian to speak, to plead, and to pray until the anxious soul finds peace. Do not forget that the precious, the useful work often begins when the sermon is just over. I believe the usefulness of many a sermon has been lost altogether by the congregation getting up directly it was over and beginning to talk about worldly matters. There has not been that support, that holding up of the hands of the ministry by the Church that there ought to be and used to be."

V The Transcendent Importance of Revivals.

"God calls us to the work of leading sinners to Christ. Inspiration tells us that 'he who converteth a sinner from the error of his way shall save a soul from death and hide a multitude of sins.' God saves men through human agency. Men perish through human neglect of duty. See the apostles as they toil for souls! Over Syrian deserts, through the storms of the sea, in pestilential climes, amid hunger and thirst and persecution, they hurried to tell dying men of Jesus. And multitudes, yearning for souls, have trodden in their footsteps. Brainerd and Eliot, Latimer and Baxter, Berridge and Venn, Whitefield and Wesley—how these have talked with seraph tongues, and labored with apostolic zeal for Christ! Were the whole Church thus consecrated to the salvation of men, the coming century would inaugurate that colossal concert of angels at which John represents them as leading and universal humanity thundering the chorus: 'Worthy is the Lamb that was slain to receive honor, and glory, and blessing; and every creature which is in heaven and on earth heard I saying, Blessing and honor and glory and power be unto him that sitteth upon the throne, and unto the Lamb, forever and ever!'"

VI. HINDERANCES TO A REVIVAL.

The following conclusions are the result of the experience and observation of a very eminent revivalist:

1. A revival will stop when the Church believes it is going to stop.
2. A revival will cease when Christians consent that it should cease.
3. A revival will cease whenever Christians become mechanical in their attempts to promote it.
4. It will cease whenever Christians get the idea that the work will go on without their aid.

5. When Christians get proud of their great revival, it will cease.

6. It will stop, when the Church gets exhausted by labor.

7. When the Church begins to speculate about abstract doctrines.

8. When Christians begin to proselyte.

9. When Christians refuse to render unto the Lord according to the benefits received.

10. When Christians grieve the Holy Spirit by ceasing to depend upon it.

11. When Christians lose the spirit of brotherly love.

12. A revival will decline and cease unless Christians are frequently *reconverted.*

13. It will cease when the Church ceases to denounce and oppose public evils.

CHAPTER XVII.
METHODISM AND MISSIONS.

I. THE GENIUS OF METHODISM IS MISSIONARY.

"THE Methodist Episcopal Church is most thoroughly committed to the cause of Christian missions. Begotten herself of a most important missionary enterprise, born and nurtured in the spirit of an intense evangelism, her course for the century has been one of unceasing evangelistic aggression. The records of her earliest history bear testimony to the self-sacrificing zeal of her preachers in pushing themselves out to the very borders of civilization, keeping themselves quite abreast of the most advanced tide of population as it flowed onward, sharing joyfully the hardships of the pioneer people, if by all means they might save some, and plant among them the institutions of the gospel. The missionary work thus begun and carried forward, under the personal supervision of Bishop Asbury, soon grew to such proportions as to suggest, and indeed to require, a special and formal organization for this sort of Church work; and so, following the clearest dictates of duty, the Missionary Society of the Methodist Episcopal Church was formed. This Society, in the scope of its spirit and purpose, proposes to be nothing more, and surely it ought to be nothing less, than the whole Church in missionary action. Since its organization the Church, through her missionary operations, has spread herself all over this land, and, overleaping its limits, has gone to Mexico, to South America, to Africa, to Europe, to Asia; and to-day her mission-fields girdle the globe, and her morning doxologies to Father, Son, and Holy Ghost keep pace with the hours and the journeys of the sun."

II. FACTS THAT SHOULD STIR OUR MISSIONARY ZEAL AND FIRE OUR HEARTS IN THE GREAT WORK.

1. "The first fact that confronts us in connection with this theme is, *Christianity is in the minority.* After eighteen centuries of evangelizing, it is outvoted by heathenism almost three to one. There are vast regions yet untouched by the gospel plowshare. On this continent, where we boast the best civilization, away to the north, natives sit in their ice caves wrapped in furs and feeding on oil, into whose huts not one ray from the Sun of righteousness has penetrated. A few villages have been turned into mission-stations, but the great tribes are uncalled. Swing down through the

north-west belt, and through the great valley, and by the coast—the mass of the people are in deep paganism. The painted warrior follows the bloody trail, and measures his greatness by the number of his scalps. Drop down through the vast regions of the gulf, cross the isthmus, plunge on into the kingdoms and republics of South America, and over this great stretch you find a kind of religion that has lost out of it every thing but its heathenism, and that now stands as the mortal enemy of civilization and a bar against the kingdom of Christ. What do we find in Africa? Here and there a mission-house, now and then a weary evangelist; but the millions sit in a darkness by which their own complexion pales. Pass over into Asia, crowd through the millions that follow the False Prophet, ascend the Ural Mountains, look down upon half the human race in idolatry and lust; then you will understand that the work is not all done."

2. "Another fact arresting attention is this, *there is universal need of salvation.* The heathen, like ourselves, *need* to be saved. They are lost, and need a Saviour. We are wont to look at the physical condition of the heathen, and to exhaust our sympathies over their low-grade comforts. This state is bad enough to stir every heart. Think of a land like China, where there has not been a bridge or a road made for twenty centuries, where there is not a spring wagon, nor a mile of railroad, nor a yard of telegraph in the whole empire! think of this people living in their cities with the streets six feet wide and the avenues twelve! The sewer in the streets is piled up against the one-story buildings (they have no other, except the government buildings), on one side of the street,

to the very eaves; in the avenues it is ricked up in the middle of the street ten or twelve feet high. This rick is the accumulated filth of ten or fifteen centuries. At night they water their streets with the filthy water from their filthy homes. The stench is beyond description. A glue-factory would be a deodorizer in a heathen city. The terrors and torments of their minds far exceed the perils or exposures of their bodies. They are plagued by superstitions, and robbed by priests, and murdered by magistrates, and enslaved by rulers. In China they have vast, healthful, productive regions almost unoccupied, while the people swarm in about the ancient centers, not daring to move away lest they offend the spirits of their ancestors. They have great deposits of coal and mines of the precious metals, but they dare not touch them lest they offend the spirits of the mighty dead. This fear has filled China with portions of stone walls, from the Great Wall of the empire to the fragments just long enough to enable a man to cower behind them. These walls are theological, not political or military. The people believe that the spirits of the dead are blind, and that when enraged they dash at a mortal; if he can hide behind a wall, the spirit dashes its head against the wall and falls down senseless; when it recovers, it has forgotten its wrath. Thus China is filled with walls, and the people are pursued and tormented with perpetual fears. In India their case is no better. Their cruel deities demand blood as the price of peace. Infants and women and self-sentenced men are sacrificed. The natural affections of the heart are perverted."

3. "*The great law of Divine action makes human in-*

strumentality a necessary part of the redemptive plan. He works with us, not without us. I cannot say what God could have done; I do not know, but I can tell some of the things he has done. He has ordained human agency as the way of carrying forward his work. He never advances an inch without our coöperation. This is a universal law. All results in society and life require both human and divine factors. God loves us infinitely. I cannot think of him as out of love. He seeks necessarily, all the time, by all possible means, to bring men out of their sins. Any letting up, even for a moment, would come short of the dictates of infinite love. The remitted effort might have achieved success and salvation. If God could have his way, every poor sinner on earth would be saved before to-morrow's sun shall rise. If God could have his way, every prison-pen in the universe would be thrown open, and every sorrowing sinner would be loved up into purity and peace. But in the way of these results stand the order of human agencies and the power of the human will. Thus God waits upon our slow movement. He is estopped from remitting his experiments with remedial agencies by the love that caused our creation, and he is estopped from the use of his omnipotence by the freedom he has vouchsafed to every moral agent. Thus the world's salvation awaits our action.

"The salvation of the world is now reduced to a question of money. If Christian people will so wind the parchment of their creed about the cross as to make a divine dollar-mark ($), God's kingdom will be upon us in the next decade. Talk about ability! We have money enough, if we only had *availability*. The interest on what we spent in our war would put a missionary in the field for every eight hundred heathen, and this interest would keep them there forever. God lacks no love; Christ has died; the Holy Ghost has been shed forth upon us. All lands are open, all peoples are inviting, all languages are mastered. The Church has all necessary experience of personal pardon and free grace. The old errors of fatalism are sifted out of the faith of the Church; the gospel is restored to its early purity; all things are now ready. Over the gate of the future it blazes the dollar-mark, while God says, 'By this conquer.'

"Brothers, *with our treasure consecrated, the world is our easy prize.* I want to see all the kingdoms of the earth given to our God, and to his Christ; and I expect to see it done in my day, if I am permitted to work as long in the vineyard as I desire to. If the Methodist Church would take hold of this with the old battle-cry, 'No matter what it costs in men and money, this must be done!' the world would be startled from the sleep of the age, and nations would be born in a day."

III. STATISTICS—GENERAL CREEDS OF THE WORLD.

The population of the world is religiously distributed in the following proportions:

Professors of Christianity	418,000,000
Buddhism	400,000,000
Mohammedanism	215,000,000
Brahmanism	175,000,000
Judaism	7,000,000
All other forms of religious belief	174,000,000

The results of missionary labors among all the Churches:

	Communicants.		Communicants.
India	87,854	Madagascar	68,317
China	16,287	West Africa	25,636
Ceylon	7,490	South Sea Islands	55,378
Burmah	20,811	Sandwich Islands	14,976
Persia	1,221	Australia and N. Zealand	2,512
Japan	2,006	American Indians	17,142
Sumatra	2,420	The New Hebrides	1,820
Turkish Empire	9,132	South Africa	57,840

The above figures were taken from Bishop Hurst's "Outline of Church History."

CHAPTER XVIII.
METHODISM AND EDUCATION.

METHODISM has not neglected the important work of educating her followers. The charge that the Methodist Church was founded in ignorance, that uncultivated people only joined her Communion, that illiterate ministers preached in her pulpits, has no foundation in truth.

John Wesley, her founder, was educated at one of the most famous institutions of learning known in the world. He was a man of superior mental culture. Charles Wesley, whose heaven-inspired hymns are sung in all the Churches; John Fletcher, whose ponderous battle-ax of logic well-nigh demolished the iron system of Calvinism; Adam Clarke, who was called a walking encyclopedia; Richard Watson, whose intellectual greatness is seen in his "Theological Institutes," are all shining monuments of educated mind. In America, the Methodist Church can show as many well-cultured intellects as any other denomination. Mr. Wesley early began to organize schools among his people. These schools have expanded and multiplied into colleges, theological schools, and academic institutions of every grade. Every Methodist body in England and America recognizes the duty of providing schools for the education of the people. "Edward Everett, in his day, said that there was no Church in the United States so successfully engaged in the cause of education as the Methodist Church." The Methodist Church, North, "can point to her twenty-seven colleges and theological seminaries erected and endowed at a cost of three million one hundred thousand dollars; her eighty-four academies, seminaries, and female colleges, with her regiment of eight hundred professors and teachers, and her army corps of twenty-five thousand five hundred students, marching up the highway of intelligence and virtue, and erelong to occupy the posts of influence and power."

The Southern Methodist Almanac says: "The interests of education have been greatly promoted of late in the Methodist Episcopal Church, South. The General Conference of 1878 was not able to present a complete list of the institutions of learning under the care of the Church; but in the Journal of the General Conference is published a tabular statement of ninety-five institutions—with their grade, location, when founded, by whom chartered, names of presidents, number and names of instructors, number of students, value of property, volumes in library, endowment, and times of commencement. The Conference resolved 'that we recognize the hand of a gracious Providence in the magnificent gift which established and endowed Vanderbilt University, and

254 *The Methodist Armor.*

rejoice to hear that it has already entered upon its field of extensive and rapidly increasing usefulness.'"

GENERAL EDUCATIONAL STATISTICS.

Number of instructors and students in universities and colleges of the United States by religious denominations, as reported by United States Commissioner of Education for 1878:

Denominations.	Institutions.	Instructors.	Students.
Roman Catholic..	49	733	7,851
Methodist.	50	499	8,930
Baptist.	40	299	5,085
Presbyterian.	35	325	5,088
Congregational.	20	239	3,878
Lutheran.	16	127	2,073
Christian.	14	112	2,043
Protestant Episcopal.	11	127	911
Reformed.	7	68	764
United Brethren.	7	46	1,040
Friends.	6	50	780
Universalist.	5	62	394
Seventh Day Advent.	1	15	281
Jewish.	1	4	24
New Church.	1	6	41
Non-sectarian.	78	1,021	16,302
Not reporting.	10	36	514
Additional, but not reporting.	27	...	.....
Grand total.	378	3,759	56,035

Of the 351 colleges and universities reported the average number of instructors for each was 10.7, and the average number of students was 169.6.

Most of the number of non-sectarian colleges and universities were founded under religious influence, and include religious teachers in their board of instruction.

Over nine-tenths of all the colleges and universities in the United States are under positive Christian supervision.

Infidelity has not sustained a single college or university in the United States.

There is not a single flourishing State university not under the supervision of religious instructors.

CHAPTER XIX.

Acts of the General Conference to 1844.

(*Methodist Year-book.*)

1784. The "Methodist Episcopal Church" was formally organized at a Conference of the Methodist ministers called by Thomas Coke, LL.D., an assistant of Mr. Wesley in England, and sent over by the latter for the purpose of consummating such organization. The first Bishops, Coke and Asbury, were elected. This Conference (called the "Christmas Conference") met in Baltimore, December 25, and continued its session until January 2, 1785.

1787 A General Conference was called at Baltimore in May, by Dr. Coke, at the request of Mr. Wesley; but as the Annual Conferences had not been consulted, and hence had not authorized it, many of the ministers did not attend, and no official record of its doings was preserved. Some additions, however, were made to the Discipline, and the word "Bishop" was substituted for "Superintendent," as applied to Bishops Coke and Asbury. It is believed also that the term "presiding elder" was then first applied to superintendents of districts.

1789. In order to supply a central authority long

felt to be needed, the several Annual Conferences concurred in the formation of a "Council," to be composed of the Bishops and presiding elders, who should recommend such changes as they should unanimously agree upon, but which, before becoming binding upon the Church, should be adopted by the several Annual Conferences.

1790. The "Council," referred to in the preceding paragraph, was composed of the Bishop and of elders elected from each district. This had been done in order to meet objections made to their appointment to the Council by the Bishops. The Council, however, being without power except as advisory, was unpopular, and was substituted by a General Conference of the preachers of all the Conferences.

1792. First General Conference, held in Baltimore, November 1. This Conference directed that the next General Conference should meet after an interval of four years. Though embodying, as its members believed, the full ecclesiastical authority of the Church, the Conference bound itself by special enactment not to change any recognized rule of Methodism except by a two-thirds vote. The presiding elder's term of office in any one district was limited to four years. The Book Concern (previously opened at Philadelphia by authority of the "Council") was formally established by General Conference action.

1796. Second General Conference, held in Baltimore, commencing October 20, composed of one hundred and twenty members. Bishop Asbury presided. "Chartered Fund" instituted and incorporated by Legislature of Pennsylvania. The Annual Conference boundaries first determined by General Conference action. Number then designated, six, but the Bishops were authorized to add a seventh.

1800. Third General Conference, held in Baltimore, May 6–20. The previous one had been held in the fall, but owing to the prevalence of yellow fever in 1799, the Annual Conferences had authorized Bishop Asbury to change the time to May. Richard Whatcoat was elected Bishop. His competitor for the office was Jesse Lee. The second ballot was a tie, but on the next Whatcoat was elected. The Book Concern was removed to New York. [John Dickins, the Book Agent, had died of yellow fever the year previous.] Bishop Asbury, in consequence of physical debility, sought to resign his episcopal office, but was induced by the earnest request of the Conference to continue in the office. The Bishops were authorized to ordain colored preachers. [Richard Allen, of Philadelphia, was the first colored preacher ordained under this rule.]

1804. Fourth General Conference, held in Baltimore, May 7–23. Members, one hundred and seven. The pastoral term was limited to two consecutive years on any one charge. Previously there had been no limit to the episcopal prerogative, except in the case of presiding elders. A motion to change the General Conference into a delegated body was voted down, but the matter was left for the Bishops to consult the Annual Conferences during the *quadrennium.*

1808. Fifth General Conference, held in Baltimore, May 6–26. Members, one hundred and twenty-nine. William McKendree elected Bishop. Bishop Coke was granted permission to reside in England, but not

17

to exercise while there his episcopal functions. Delegated General Conference first provided for, the ratio of representation to be one member for each five of the traveling ministers. The "Restrictive Rules" first adopted. No one of these Rules was to be changed without the concurrence of a majority of all the members of the Annual Conferences (present and voting at the Annual Conference sessions) with a two-thirds vote of the General Conference. This requirement continued until 1828, when the word "majority" was substituted by the word "three-fourths."

1812. Sixth General Conference, held in New York City, May 1–22. This was the first delegated Conference. Members, eighty-eight. Bishop McKendree presented a written Episcopal Address, the first presented to the General Conference. Local deacons made eligible to elder's orders. Ordered that stewards' nominations be referred by preachers to Quarterly Conference for confirmation or rejection; preachers had hitherto appointed the stewards.

1816. Seventh General Conference, held in Baltimore, May 1–24. One hundred and three members. Rev. Messrs. Black and Bennett were present as fraternal delegates from British Conference. "Course of Study" for ministers provided for. Enoch George and Robert Richford Roberts elected Bishops. Number of Conferences increased to eleven, and Bishops authorized to organize another. Monthly *Methodist Magazine.* Ratio of Annual Conference representation changed from "five" to "seven."

1820. Eighth General Conference, held at Baltimore, May 1–27. Members, eighty-nine. John Emory appointed delegate to British Conference. Improved edition of Hymn-book ordered. Missionary Society, previously organized in New York City, was approved. Bishop McKendree was relieved from effective labor. Bishop Soule was elected Bishop, but declined to be ordained, and resigned the office because the Conference had adopted, as a compromise measure, a resolution authorizing the Annual Conferences to elect presiding elders. The application of the resolution was suspended for four years, until the question should be submitted to the Annual Conferences.

1824. Ninth General Conference, held at Baltimore, May 1-29. Members, one hundred and twenty-six. Joshua Soule and Elijah Hedding elected Bishops. Revs. Richard Reece and John Hannah delegates from England. The Annual Conferences having voted against the change of rule so as to permit the election of presiding elders, the provision for such election, previously adopted, was declared null and void.

1828. Tenth General Conference, held at Pittsburg, May 1-24. Members, one hundred and seventy-six. Connection with the Canada Conference substantially dissolved. William Capers elected delegate to England.

1832. Eleventh General Conference, held in Philadelphia, May 1-24. James O. Andrew and John Emory elected Bishops.

1836. Twelfth General Conference, held at Cincinnati, May 1-27. Members, one hundred and fifty-eight. Bishops Roberts, Soule, Hedding, and Andrew presided (Bishops McKendree and Emory had died). Dr. Wilbur Fisk appointed fraternal delegate to British Conference. Separate Bible Society dissolved, and a resolution of coöperation with American Bible Society adopted. Liberia Conference organized. A "resident Corresponding Secretaryship" established. Beverly Waugh, Wilbur Fisk, and Thomas A. Morris elected Bishops. Dr. Fisk, who was absent in Europe at the time, declined the office in order to remain at the Wesleyan University, of which he was President. Authority given to Annual Conferences to locate ministers for unacceptability.

1840. Thirteenth General Conference, held at Baltimore, May 1 to June 3. Members, one hundred and forty-two. Rev. Robert Newton fraternal representative from British Conference. Bishop Soule appointed representative to British Conference, with Rev. Thomas B. Sargent as traveling companion. Bishop Hedding requested to attend Canada Wesleyan Conference. Sunday-school Union reörganized.

THE ORGANIZATION OF THE METHODIST EPISCOPAL CHURCH, SOUTH.

1844. "The Plan of Separation" between the Northern and Southern Methodists was agreed upon. The General Conference met in New York on the first of May. The feelings on the slavery question quite stormy. Bishop Andrew having become connected with slavery by marriage, was censured by a resolution requiring him to "desist from the exercise of his office so long as this impediment remains." Passed by majority of 110 to 68. There being no possibility of reconciliation, "The Plan of Separation" was adopted by a large majority.

1845. The Convention composed of delegates from

fourteen Southern Conferences, met in Louisville, Ky., on the first of May. It was presided over by Bishops Soule and Andrew. The Convention proceeded to organize "The Methodist Episcopal Church, South," as an independent branch of Christ's Church. The doctrines of Arminianism, the peculiar usages and Discipline of Methodism, and ecclesiastical polity, remain about the same in both Churches.

1846. The first General Conference of the Methodist Episcopal Church, South, met in Petersburg, Va., in May. William Capers and Robert Paine elected Bishops. From this time on our General Conference has met quadrennially. The Northern Church refusing to divide the property of the Book Concern in *pro rata* proportion, a suit was commenced in the United States Court, which was finally decided in favor of the Church, South. The Court decided that the ministers of the South had vested rights in the profits of the book establishment, and by this decision the Church, South, held the printing establishments of Richmond, Charleston, and Nashville. The debts due from persons residing within the limits of the Southern Conferences, and two hundred and seventy thousand dollars in cash, were paid to the Methodist Episcopal Church, South.

1866. The General Conference adopted a system of lay delegation, both in the General and Annual Conferences. The probationary period of members was abolished, and the rule on class-meetings made voluntary instead of being compulsory. The Methodist Episcopal Church, South, has prosecuted its work vigorously throughout its bounds, and its statistical tables show a rapid and steady increase in all the departments of Church work.

BISHOPS OF THE M. E. CHURCH, SOUTH.

The following admirable sketches of our living Bishops were published in *Harper's Weekly*, June 3, 1882:

Bishop GEORGE FOSTER PIERCE, D.D., son of the late venerable and distinguished Dr. Lovick Pierce, is the senior Bishop in order of election. He was born in Greene county, Georgia, February 3, 1811, and resides near Sparta in that State. He designed in his youth to enter the profession of law, but turned from his studies, and in his twentieth year was admitted into the Georgia Conference. Possessed of superior pulpit abilities, as well as scholarly attainments, he commanded prominence in South Carolina and Georgia. He was prominent in the General Conference of the Methodist Episcopal Church in 1844, although a young man, in sustaining the Southern view of the question at issue. He was also a member of the Louisville Convention in 1845, and of the General Conference of the Church, South, in 1846. In 1848 he was elected President of Emory College, and held the position until 1854, when he was elevated to the episcopacy. He is still a royal preacher, but unable from throat trouble to preach often. Very refined and courtly in his manners, scholarly, and of aristocratic carriage; tall, without being portly; gentlemanly in dress; with piercing eyes, and a benign countenance. The principal work from his pen is entitled "Incidents of Western Travel." He has written much and well on education and Church topics for the Church press.

Bishop HUBBARD HINDE KAVANAUGH, D.D., was born in Clark county, Kentucky, in 1802, and in his boyhood received his first training as a printer. Converted in his sixteenth year, five years afterward he was received into the Kentucky Conference, and from that time to the present, fifty-nine years, he has been effective. Possessing great physical endurance and superior pulpit talents, his ministry has been one of wonderful success both in the pastorate and episcopate. He has recently returned from California and Oregon, where he spent a year, preaching with the same power as in his younger years. In 1854 he was elected Bishop, and was among the first to cultivate fraternal feelings toward the Methodist Episcopal Church. His visit to Round Lake, Sea Cliff, and other points in the North, in the interest of fraternity, was a source of satisfaction in the wide domain of Methodism. Though eighty years of age, he is still an untiring and successful worker, not only in the local Church work in and near Louisville, Kentucky, his residence, but in the Church generally. He gives but little evidence of his great age. He has a heavy suit of black hair, silvered a little with gray; is stalwart in frame, with a patriarchal bearing, full habit, small, piercing eyes, and pleasant countenance.

Bishop HOLLAND NIMMONS McTYEIRE, D.D., was born in Barnwell county, South Carolina, July 28, 1824, and entered the ministry of the Virginia Conference in 1845; but his fine talents brought early promotion, and he was transferred to the extreme South, and filled important appointments in Mobile and New Orleans. While in the latter city, the *New Orleans Christian Advocate* was started by a committee in 1851—Rev. H. N. McTyeire, editor—and brought out the first number February 10. At the General Conference in 1854 the paper was received by that body as one of the official Church organs, and Dr. McTyeire was elected editor, thus making seven years at that post. In 1858 he was elected editor of the *Christian Advocate* of Nashville, Tenn. In 1866 Dr. McTyeire was elected Bishop, and has always been devoted and prominent in that position. He received the title of D.D. from Emory College, Georgia, and La Grange College and other institutions have since honored him similarly. He was chiefly instrumental in securing the gift of one million dollars from the late Cornelius Vanderbilt, to found Vanderbilt University, and the subsequent munificent gifts from Mr. W H. Vanderbilt. Commodore Cornelius Vanderbilt placed it in his hands as President of the Trust, with an elegant and permanent residence upon the spacious grounds. The Bishop's wife is a cousin of Mr. Vanderbilt's widow. He is naturally a leader, quick in his movements, firm and judicious. He possesses much of the *hauteur* of Bishop Soule, without his Andrew Jackson stern manners. He is the author of the "Manual of the Discipline," and "The Duties of Masters;" "Catechism on Bible History," prepared for the Colored Methodist Episcopal Church in America, but used extensively by the Church, South; also "Catechism on Church Government," which is now in the Course of Study for young ministers. Bishop McTyeire was Vice-president of the Western Section of American Methodism of the Ecumenical Conference, and made one of the speeches of welcome at City Road Chapel, London, September, 1881. In person he is always courtly-looking, with bright eyes and dark complexion; he has a tall and well-knit frame, without being stout.

Bishop JOHN CHRISTIAN KEENER, D.D., the youngest in the order of election, is a native of Baltimore, Maryland, born February 7, 1819. Through the influence of Rev. Dr. Wilbur Fisk, who was visiting his father, the widely-known late Christian Keener, he spent three years at Wilbraham Academy, Massachusetts, under his care; and when Dr. Fisk became President of Wesleyan University, Middletown, Connecticut, he became a member of the first class, and graduated in 1835. Shortly after his graduation he was converted, and entered mercantile life, but, abandoning his bright secular prospects, he went South and entered the ministry, and was admitted into the Alabama Conference in 1843. In a few years he was sent to New Orleans, then especially a post of danger, and yet of honor because of its importance. He spent a score of years in the pastorate of chief churches and presiding eldership. In 1866 he was elected editor of the *New Orleans Christian Advocate*, and in 1870 was elevated to the episcopacy. Bishop Keener is known, but not published, as author of the "Post-oak Circuit," written as a prize essay on the support of the ministry, which appeared in 1855, and has gone beyond the twelfth edition, and is still going; it is humorous, pathetic, and argumentative by turns, and has done much to aid in the support of the ministry. In person Bishop Keener is large and measurably stalwart, with a genial countenance. He is a pulpit orator of the magnetic type. He has been largely identified with the Mexican mission-work of the Church.

Five new Bishops were elected by the General Conference of the Methodist Episcopal Church, South, lately in session at Nashville, Tennessee. Of this number, one, the Rev. Dr. Haygood, declined to be ordained. The College of Bishops is, therefore, at present nine in number.

Bishop ALPHEUS WATERS WILSON, D.D., is the son of the late Rev. Norval Wilson, a prominent minister of the Methodist Episcopal Church, and widely known in Maryland and Virginia. He was born in Baltimore, Maryland, in 1834, converted in early life, and was educated at Columbia College, Washington City, and afterward studied with the intention of practicing medicine, but abandoned the idea, and entered the ministry in the Baltimore Conference of the Methodist Episcopal Church in 1853. He soon took high rank, and commanded some of the best appointments in Baltimore and elsewhere. His health failed, and he read and practiced law; and when restored, he reentered the active ministry. He was identified with the Baltimore Conference organized in the Methodist Episcopal Church, South, and became prominent in that body, and was elected a delegate to the first General Conference thereafter, and has been reelected three times to this highest court, which meets quadrennially He was at this time honored with the degree of Doctor of Divinity. At the General Conference held at Atlanta, Georgia, in 1878, he was elected Secretary of the Board of Missions, which, through his thorough canvass of the churches and fervid appeals, has resulted in large contributions to the cause, and the enlargement of the foreign mission work. His able pulpit and platform ministrations in behalf of this cause, and rare executive abilities, have led to his elevation to the higher work of the episcopacy. He was a delegate to the great Ecumenical Conference at London, England, in September, 1881, and read an able paper on "The Influence of Methodism on Other Denominations." He is the author of a new work (just issued) on "Missions," which is highly spoken of. He has the elements of a leader, and will make his impression in the councils of the Church and in shaping her aggressive movements. He is of almost medium height, compactly built without being fleshy, and with admirable poise—a vigorous mind in a vigorous body; his face is heavily bearded; he is sociable, yet dignified, and neat in person. He was the only one elected Bishop on the first ballot.

Bishop LINUS PARKER, D.D., is a native of Rome, New York, born in 1829, but removed to New Orleans, Louisiana, in his boyhood. While engaged as a clerk in a dry goods store, he supplemented a meager education by rising in the mornings at four o'clock to study Latin and Greek before entering upon the duties of business. Converted young, he entered the ministry in the Louisiana Conference in his twenty-first year (1849), and after spending four years at two appointments in that State, he was sent to New Orleans, where he has labored ever since as pastor, presiding elder, and editor. A considerable portion of the past quarter of a century he has been presiding elder, and editor of the *New Orleans Christian Advocate*, successor to Bishops McTyeire and Keener in the editorship of that paper. He was honored by Centenary College with the degree of Doctor of Divinity. The *Advocate* under his editorship has risen to Connectional fame; his polished editorials have won him journalistic renown among cultivated people outside of the pale of the Church. He has been elected a delegate to the General Conference five times, the first in 1858, when he was quite young in the ministry. As a writer he is clear, smooth, and forcible; as a preacher, he is elegant and profound, and remarkable for bringing out the hidden meaning of difficult texts; he is regarded in the front rank of preachers in the South. By his culture and scholarly attainments, deep piety, sound judgment, modest demeanor, meekness of spirit, amiability and simplicity of manners, he has won great popularity among people and preachers. He is regarded as eminently fitted to fill any position in the gift of the Church. A man of fine presence, tall and large frame, well filled without being unduly stout; rather tawny skinned, with black, piercing eyes, and dignified and courtly manners—the picture of vigorous health. He was elected Bishop on the second ballot, and ranks second in the order of election.

Bishop JOHN COOPER GRANBERY, D.D., the scholarly Professor in Vanderbilt University, is a native of Norfolk, Va., born December 5, 1829. He was noted in his boyhood and youth for his exemplary character, and in his fifteenth year was converted. He entered Randolph-Macon College, and graduated with the first honor in 1848. The same year (his twentieth) he was received on trial in the Virginia Conference, and has been identified with that body ever since. He soon rose to be one of the foremost ministers in that body, and commanded appointments to churches at Washington City, Richmond, and Petersburg. He was also chaplain of both Randolph-Macon College and the

University of Virginia, the former honoring him with M.A. and D.D. When the war began, he entered the Confederate Army as a chaplain, and continued to serve the army until the close of the struggle—a service in which he fearlessly discharged his duties, and was severely wounded in the temple, which injured the sight of one eye, and he was taken prisoner. He held for a time the position of superintendent of chaplains from the Virginia Conference. In 1875 he was elected Professor in the Theological Department of Vanderbilt University, which position he has adorned, and if he had not been elected to the episcopacy, he would have been chosen Dean, to fill the vacancy caused by the death of Dr. Summers, because of his varied talents and scholarly culture. He is the author of a "Bible Dictionary," and has written much and well for the Church press. He has been a member of four General Conferences, and though honored so often, he rarely speaks, but has the reputation of being an elegant, chaste, scholarly, and eloquent preacher. He possesses a clear, analytical mind of a judicial cast, and is an able theologian. He is a man of the purest character, humble in his walk, retiring, sweet-spirited. He is of medium height, with high forehead; good habit without being stout; well bearded; eyes shaded with glasses. He was elected on the second ballot, and is fourth in the order of election.

Bishop ROBERT KENNON HARGROVE, D.D., very unexpectedly was elected, as he was not a member of the General Conference, which is the only instance except one in the history of the Church. At the first ballot he developed strength, and at the second he only lacked two votes of an election. There being only one to elect, he was chosen by an overwhelming majority. He was born in Pickens county, Alabama, September 17, 1829. Converted when but eleven years old, he soon after became a student in the University of Alabama, and graduated with honor. He was admitted on trial into the Alabama Conference in 1857, and was sent to some of the best appointments at Mobile, Summerfield, and Greensboro, Alabama. He was transferred, and appointed to Lexington, Ky., and thence to the Tennessee Conference, and was appointed pastor of the McKendree Church, the seat of this General Conference, and also presiding elder of the Nashville and Franklin districts. At the time of his election he was presiding elder of the Clarksville District. For some time he was adjunct professor in the University of Alabama, which had honored him with A.B. and A.M. Emory College gave him D.D. Then he was elected President of the Centenary Institute, and afterward became President of the Nashville Female College. He was one of the famous Cape May Commissioners who drew up a compact between the Methodist Episcopal Church and the Methodist Episcopal Church, South, to regulate certain disputed Church questions, which has given him fame in American Methodism. His name had been prominently mentioned in regard to certain Connectional offices, had he not been elected to the episcopacy. He has been a member of three General Conferences previous to this one, and was a member of the Book Committee and Board of Missions the past four years. He is a man of broad culture and progressive views, and, though not widely known in authorship, is a fine writer. He is regarded as a strong preacher and an able theologian. It is believed that he has all the elements of character to make a successful and useful Bishop. He is of good height, large frame well filled, pleasant countenance, with slight beard, quite gray hair for his years, very genial, and courtly in appearance.

DECEASED BISHOPS OF THE M. E. CHURCH, SOUTH.

Bishop JOSHUA SOULE, D.D., was born in Maine, 1781; elected Bishop, 1824; died in Tennessee, 1867. A grand man, whose sermons were distinguished for great breadth of view and majesty of style, oftentimes bearing down upon the audience like an irresistible storm. With a masterly hand he scattered the vital seeds of the gospel from Maine to Texas, sowing beside all waters.

Bishop JAMES O. ANDREW, D.D., born in Georgia, 1794; entered the South Carolina Conference, 1812; elected Bishop, 1832; died in Mobile, Ala., March 2, 1871. "As a man he was spotless in reputation, social and genial in intercourse, and as a preacher he was earnest, strong, and useful, grasping his subject firmly, and often presenting his thoughts with peculiar force and effect."—*Bishop Paine*.

Bishop WILLIAM CAPERS, D.D., born in South Carolina, 1790; elected Bishop, 1846; died in South Carolina, 1855. "He was one of the master spirits of the second generation of Southern Methodists; a worthy successor of Asbury, Hull, Humphreys, and Daugherty; intrepid, whole-hearted, well poised, strong in influence that had been nobly won by great labors. A very special fluency in utterance, ease of movement, refinement and elegance of manner, and a chaste and finished delivery, characterized his preaching."—*Bishop Wightman.*

Bishop HENRY B. BASCOM, D.D., born in New York, 1796; joined the Ohio Conference, 1813; elected Bishop, 1850; and died in September of the same year. He presided over only one Conference before he died. He rose from an obscure birth, and "attained to an eminence never before reached by any preacher in America, and was regarded as the first pulpit orator of the world." In personal appearance he was a Daniel Webster, in magnificence of oratory a Cicero, in learning a walking cyclopedia.

Bishop JOHN EARLY, D.D., born in Virginia, 1786; entered the ministry, 1807; elected Bishop, 1854; died in Virginia, November, 1873. He was a man famous for business tact, for stirring energy, and fruitful work. For over half a century he served his Church with great fidelity.

Bishop W M. WIGHTMAN, D.D., born in South Carolina, 1808; joined the Conference of South Carolina, 1828; elected Bishop, 1854. Bishop Wightman was one of the most scholarly men in the Southern Methodist Church. He was a most excellent writer, a magnificent preacher, and a fine presiding officer. He died February 15, 1882.

Bishop ENOCH M. MARVIN, D.D., a native of Missouri; born, 1823; entered the Conference of Missouri, 1841; elected Bishop, 1866; died in St. Louis, Mo., November, 1877. A man of rare purity, richly gifted as a writer, and of extraordinary power as a preacher.

Bishop DAVID S. DOGGETT, D.D., born in Virginia, 1810; joined the Conference of Virginia, 1829; elected Bishop, 1866; died in Richmond, Va., 1880. A polished and scholarly writer, and the "golden-mouthed" orator of the Southern pulpit.

Bishop ROBERT PAINE, D.D., died October 20, 1882, in his eighty-third year. He was born in North Carolina, November 12, 1799, but settled in his youth in Tennessee. In 1818 he was admitted into the Tennessee Conference, and soon took rank, filling prominent appointments until 1830, when he was elected President of La Grange College, Alabama. There he remained seventeen years, until the first General Conference of the new Church, South, in 1846, when he was elevated to the episcopacy. He had been a member of the General Conferences of the Methodist Episcopal Church five times, until the separation in 1844 owing to the action against Bishop Andrew. He was chairman of the Committee of Nine, whose report forms a memorable chapter in Methodist history. He was a member of the Louisville Convention in 1845, and at the first General Conference in 1846. He was elected Bishop, and became the colleague of Bishops Soule and Andrew, formerly of the Methodist Episcopal Church. His "Life and Times of Bishop McKendree" has proved a valuable contribution to Methodist history.

STATISTICS OF THE METHODIST EPISCOPAL CHURCH, SOUTH, 1883.

CONFERENCES.	Traveling Preachers.	Superannuated Preachers.	Local Preachers.	White Members.	Colored Members.	Indian Members.	Total Preachers and Memb'rs.	Sunday-school Teachers.	Sunday-school Scholars.
Alabama	135	14	203	33,366	631	...	34,349	2,454	18,089
Arkansas	97	2	211	17,084	...	...	17,394	1,281	10,972
Baltimore	171	17	117	31,918	52	...	32,275	4,597	28,427
Columbia	20	1	26	1,446	...	...	1,493	76	316
Denver	24	1	10	758	...	...	793	226	1,116
East Texas	65	6	142	16,370	...	...	16,583	915	6,655
Florida	83	3	128	10,994	16	...	11,224	948	5,974
German Mission	22	...	16	1,322	...	...	1,360	156	803
Holston	157	15	303	43,591	53	...	44,119	2,649	30,289
Illinois	41	3	49	5,294	...	...	5,387	694	5,305
Indian Mission	40	...	105	1,284	20	4,774	6,223	310	2,465
Kentucky	112	7	95	23,600	38	...	23,852	1,279	9,267
Little Rock	96	9	169	18,670	...	...	18,944	1,449	10,966
Los Angeles	22	2	16	1,161	1	1	1,203	155	1,242
Louisiana	81	7	88	14,820	29	...	15,025	1,033	6,917
Louisville	139	17	203	33,196	15	...	33,570	1,725	13,787
Memphis	132	7	238	35,334	...	...	35,711	2,695	20,268
Mississippi	109	6	136	25,686	...	...	25,956	1,596	10,735
Missouri	125	10	135	26,837	...	...	27,107	1,978	15,178
Montana	7	...	6	222	...	...	235	24	138
North Alabama	133	9	381	38,321	...	...	38,844	2,210	20,465
North Carolina	203	13	239	72,256	158	...	72,870	5,145	45,167
North Georgia	209	17	423	67,982	29	...	68,660	4,468	40,137

Acts of the General Conference.   275

North Mississippi	118	10	165	30,479	...	...	30,772	1,571	12,837
North Texas	126	9	257	27,654	...	...	28,046	1,332	11,602
North-west Texas	134	12	276	24,741	...	...	25,163	1,358	10,855
Pacific	66	4	47	4,480	8	7	4,612	501	3,572
South Carolina	158	20	148	50,575	...	...	51,000	3,685	28,382
South Georgia	122	13	205	34,425	108	...	34,765	2,563	18,718
South-west Missouri	103	13	157	19,550	...	...	19,823	1,350	10,590
St. Louis	68	8	93	11,747	...	...	11,921	921	7,695
Tennessee	184	11	322	47,900	2	...	48,419	2,765	24,587
Texas	76	8	111	11,377	...	...	11,572	807	6,120
Virginia	187	22	155	60,549	86	1	60,999	7,421	45,195
Western	31	1	33	2,727	...	...	2,793	148	1,073
Western Virginia	65	6	119	15,045	9	...	15,244	1,505	9,358
West Texas	86	8	98	8,842	...	...	9,034	665	5,376
White River	74	2	158	13,695	...	...	13,929	919	7,196
China Mission	16	...	17	131	...	...	164	...	311
Brazilian Mission	5	...	5	113	...	...	123	...	121
Mexican Mission	13	...	82	2,552	...	...	2,653	...	1,668
Bishops	8	...	...	...	...	...	8	...	...
Total in 1883	3,863	313	5,892	838,094	1,255	4,783	904,243	65,574	509,934
Total in 1882	3,736	309	5,869	861,244	1,030	5,111	877,299	65,198	483,426
Increase	127	4	23	...	225	...	26,949	376	26,508
Decrease	...	...	...	26,850	...	328	...	...	...

CHAPTER XX.

GENERAL SUMMARY OF METHODISTS.

(Methodist Year-book.)

THE following summaries have been compiled from the latest official statistics reported by the several branches of the great Wesleyan Methodist family. Those of the Methodist Episcopal Church are to January 1, 1883, and include the official numerical returns of the fall Conferences of 1882 and the spring Conferences of 1883; those of the Methodist Episcopal Church, South, are for 1882; those of the Canadian, British, and affiliating Conferences are for 1883. In two or three of the Churches the number of local preachers is "estimated," but in each of those by distinguished members of large observation in the respective denominations:

I. EPISCOPAL METHODISTS IN UNITED STATES.

	Itinerant Ministers.	Local Preachers.	Lay Members.
Methodist Episcopal Church	12,654	12,337	1,799,593
Methodist Episcopal Church, South	3,963	5,892	904,248
African Methodist Episcopal Church	1,832	9,760	391,044
African Methodist Episcopal Zion Church	2,000	2,750	300,000
Colored Methodist Episcopal Church	1,046	683	155,000
Evangelical Association	963	599	119,758
Union American Methodist Episcopal Church	112	40	3,500
United Brethren	1,257	963	159,547
Total Episcopal Methodists in United States	24,026	33,024	3,832,690

II. NON-EPISCOPAL METHODISTS IN UNITED STATES.

	Itinerant Ministers.	Local Preachers.	Lay Members.
Methodist Protestant Church	1,358	1,010	123,054
American Wesleyan Church	267	215	23,590
Free Methodist Church	263	326	12,719
Primitive Methodist Church	27	162	3,716
Independent Methodist Church	25	27	5,000
Congregational Methodists	....	23	20,000
Total Non-Episcopal Methodists in United States	1,940	1,763	188,079

General Summary of Methodists.

III. METHODISTS IN CANADA.

	Itinerant Ministers.	Local Preachers.	Lay Members.
The Methodist Church of Canada	1,216	1,261	128,644
Methodist Episcopal Church of Canada	259	255	25,671
Primitive Methodist Church	89	246	8,090
Bible Christian Church	79	197	7,398
British Methodist Episcopal Church (colored)	45	20	2,100
Total Methodists in Canada	1,688	1,979	171,903

IV. METHODISTS IN GREAT BRITAIN AND MISSIONS.

British Wesleyan Methodists in Great Britain	1,917	14,183	441,484
British Wesleyan Methodists in Missions	385	....	70,747
Primitive Methodists	1,147	16,982	196,480
New Connection Methodists	188	1,271	29,299
Wesleyan Reform Union	551	....	8,663
United Free Methodists	391	3,417	84,152
Bible Christians (including Australia)	228	1,009	28,624
Total Methodists in Great Britain and Missions	4,807	36,762	859,449

V. WESLEYAN AFFILIATING CONFERENCES.

Irish Wesleyan Conference	239	....	25,050
French Wesleyan Conference	196	....	2,024
Australasian Conferences	449	4,480	69,392
South African	167	....	26,038
Total in Wesleyan Affiliating Conferences	1,051	4,480	126,504

GRAND TOTAL OF MINISTERS AND LAY MEMBERS.

Methodists in Churches of United States	25,966	34,737	4,020,672
Methodists in the Dominion of Canada	1,688	1,979	171,903
Methodists in Great Britain and Missions	4,807	36,762	859,449
Methodists in Affiliating Conferences	1,051	4,480	126,504
Grand total of Methodists and Missions in 1883	33,512	77,958	5,178,528

NOTE.—Total Methodist *population* (estimated), 25,472,370.

COMPARATIVE STATISTICS—UNITED STATES, 1879.

Denominations.	Ministers.	Members.
Methodists	23,888	3,506,891
Baptists	20,292	2,656,221
Presbyterians	8,301	897,598
Lutherans	2,976	808,428
Congregationalists	3,496	375,654
Protestant Episcopalians	3,147	321,367
Universalists	711	37,500

NOTE.—In the number of Methodist ministers here given the local Methodist preachers are not included. The number of local preachers in the United States is 25,498. The total number of Methodist preachers—traveling and local—in the United States is 48,526.

DENOMINATIONAL STATISTICS FROM THE UNITED STATES CENSUS, 1870.

Denominations.	Congregations.	Church Edifices.	Church Sittings.	Church Property.
Methodist	25,278	21,837	6,528,209	$69,854,121
Baptist	15,829	14,032	4,365,135	41,607,198
Episcopal	2,835	2,601	991,051	36,514,549
Presbyterian	7,824	6,071	2,697,244	43,365,306
Lutheran	3,032	2,776	977,332	14,917,747
Roman Catholic	4,127	3,806	1,990,514	60,985,566
Congregationalist	2,887	2,715	1,117,212	25,069,698

THE PRE-EMINENT SUCCESS OF METHODISM.

The Methodists began to preach in this country in 1773. The Baptists began in 1639. The Presbyterians began in 1703. The Congregationalists in 1648. The Catholics, Lutherans, and Episcopalians began with the settlement of the country. It will be seen that the Methodist is the youngest of the Churches mentioned. She is one hundred and seventy-seven years younger than the Baptists, one hundred and eighteen years younger than the Congregationalists, sixty-three years younger than the Presbyterians; while the Catholics, Episcopalians, and Lutherans are as old as immigration to the American shores. Notwithstanding this, the Methodist Church is by far the largest in numbers. The census table shows that she has one-third of all the Church organizations in the United States; one-third of all the Church edifices; preachers to one-fourth of all the Church-going population; and has built, on an average, nearly two churches per day for the last twenty years. The Methodist population in the United States is estimated to be 23,440,465. "In twenty-two of the thirty-seven States in the Union, the Methodist Church is first in numbers; in eleven others she is second; in three others she is third. The Roman Catholic Church is first in five States; the Baptist is first in six States; and the Congregationalist is first in four States."

It will be seen from the above tables that the Methodist Church stands far in advance of all other denominations in this country. She ranks first in the number of her communicants, in the number and capacity of her Church buildings, and in the value of Church property, and in the amount of money collected and expended for Church purposes. Let it be understood once for all:

1. The success of Methodism did not arise from any government aid. Methodism received no special favors from human government. It is well known that the Episcopalians in England, the Presbyterians in Scotland, and the Lutherans in Germany, are supported largely by State taxes. Methodist people there are forced to pay the ministers of these Churches. In America, the Episcopalians and Presbyterians have occupied largely the leading offices in the gift of the civil government.

2. Methodism has not grown to its enormous proportions by immigration. It is well known that the growth of the Roman Catholic Church in this country has been mainly by immigrants. The other Churches have swelled their ranks by immigration, while Methodism had to grow by the conversion of native Americans.

3. Methodism has not succeeded through superior educational facilities. The first colleges built in this country were run in the interest of other Churches. The education of the Methodist ministers, especially in early times, was not equal to that of other denominations. The success of Methodism, then, is not found in superior intellectual culture.

4. The success of Methodism did not arise from the possession of great wealth and social advantages. The early Methodists were generally poor people. One of the glories of Methodism was the fact that it preached the gospel to the poor, obscure, neglected people. It sought out the "uncombed million" living in the highways and hedges.

5. Nor did it grow to greatness because the times were propitious. The time of its origin was one of darkness—one of infidelity—rampant immoralities. The world was sunk in moral degradation when Methodism began.

We must, then, find the causes of Methodist success to be (1) the superiority of its doctrines; (2) the efficiency of its ecclesiastical organization; (3) the piety, earnestness, and activity of its ministers and members; (4) and above all, the baptism of the Holy Spirit—firing the hearts and enlightening the minds of the preachers and people. "It is not by power, nor by might, but by my Spirit, saith the Lord." As the life and fruitfulness of the vine depend on the vitalizing sap circulating through it, so does the fruitfulness of a Church depend upon the Holy Spirit. "The fruit of the Spirit is love, joy, peace." As the earth is dependent on the sun for its beauty and fruitfulness, so is the Church dependent on the light and warmth of the Holy Ghost to make it rejoice and blossom as a rose.

CHAPTER XXI.

THE APOSTOLIC FEATURES OF THE METHODIST CHURCH.

1. THE apostolic Church was a voluntary company or society. Men attached themselves to this by choice, and not under force. It is said of the early disciples, "They went to their own company." This apostolic society soon grew to a company of thousands. Like the apostolic Church, Methodism began by forming a society for religious culture, and soon grew to thousands.

2. The apostolic Church was a separated company—a society to promote holiness. Its members were called out from among the people of the world and consecrated to the service of God. Like the apostolic Church, the Methodists consecrated themselves to the service of the Lord. The leading design of Mr. Wesley's societies was to get good and spread holiness over the land. "The king's daughter is glorious within." "As the Lord is holy, be ye also holy."

3. The apostolic Church had its rules of government. These were very few and simple. When any member of this Church became wicked, "such were delivered unto Satan." Mr. Wesley selected these apostolic rules of moral conduct, and formed a code known as "The General Rules," by the observance of which the people were required to live.

4. The members of the apostolic Church had experimental religion. They were converted by the Holy Ghost on the day of Pentecost. They lived in the enjoyment of religion. "Then had the churches rest throughout all Judea, and Galilee, and Samaria, and were edified; and walking in the fear of the Lord, and in the comfort of the Holy Ghost, were multiplied." (Acts ix. 31.) Like these churches, the Methodist Church from the beginning preached and enjoyed experimental religion. This is a peculiar and distinctive feature of Methodism.

5. The apostolic Church grew and "multiplied." And has not Methodism grown from a handful to an army of millions? And while Methodism has grown so extensively, its doctrinal unity has not been broken. Among all its many branches its doctrinal unity is the great trunk of these branches.

"I saw in Natal," says James Anthony Froude, "a colossal fig-tree. It had a central stem, but I knew not where the center was, for the branches bent to the ground, and struck root there; and at each joint a fresh trunk shot up erect, and threw out new branches in turn which again arched and planted themselves, till the single tree had become a forest; and overhead was spread a vast dome of leaves and fruit, which was supported on innumerable columns, like the roof of some vast cathedral." Mr. Froude applies this to England and her colonies; but I apply it to Methodism. We know well enough where the parent stem is, and the remotest branches are proud of their ancestral roots; but the secondary growths are enormous, and are so many that they become a forest, and the branches have taken root in every soil and have sprung up again, till they extend over continents and reach across seas, and the leaves of the tree are for the healing of the nations, and millions find refreshment beneath its shade and are feasted on its golden fruits; and, whether in the frozen north or underneath the fiery sun of the tropics, every stem and branch and leaf has a common life and draws its strength and vigor from the same indestructible root.

Looking at these points of spiritual resemblance, all fair-minded men must see the apostolic features of the Methodist Church, and that their claim of being evangelical is well founded. She bears stamped upon her brow the mark of divine approval. It is impossible to account for her spiritual success upon any other theory. We are now prepared to see the absurdity of those Church claims which are founded on any thing else except the piety of its members. Fruit is the one decisive test. Christ said, "By their fruits ye shall know them." And this test is just as true of Churches as it is of individuals. The scriptural soundness of a Church is to be known by its spiritual fruits. High-sounding names are of very little value. Not what Churches pretend to be, but what they are, in reforming the world, must be the standard of excellency. . . ("That orchard may claim superiority over every other which sends the best apples to market, the most uniformly, no matter whether they have a name or not. Apples are apples, good apples are good apples, the best are the best, and no thanks to anybody, scientific or unscientific. The center of the universe is God, and the noblest creature which he has created on this globe is man, and the highest thing which man has attained is Christian manhood, and he that is best developed in manhood has priority everywhere and in every thing. And any Church that has the power of genius in it, or the power of art in it, or the power of eloquence in it, or any other mark of superiority in it, though it has had an existence coextensive with the globe, and though it has a lineage running through all time, if it turns out a poor article of Christian manhood, is a sham—a bogus concern. But a Church without a lineage, though it has been ever so obscure, and though its pretensions are the humblest, if it has achieved the reputation of turning out the noblest and the best men, has priority over every other Church. And therefore men should be careful how they claim superiority on the abstract ground that there are links which carry them back to the times of the apostles. What a shame it would be for a Church to have the links all just right, and to turn out the poorest members! What a shame it is that such a Church should not turn out members as good as a Church that has not a single link, and does not know who its Church-father or Church-grandfather is! A Church that has great radiant natures in it; a Church in which there are men who are willing to sacrifice themselves for others; a Church whose members grow larger and larger by works of benevolence; a Church filled with great, generous souls; a Church like the Methodist Church; a Church that has in its membership good men, and makes good men, and keeps making them all the time, and many of them. What else do you want but that? What more authenticity do you want than it has?")

What is the end of Church organization? Why, of course, to turn sinners into saints. To lead men to repentance, to faith in Christ, to obedience to God's law; to make bad men good men—to turn men from the vanities of earth to serve the true and living God; to lead men to holiness of heart and life, and thence to a glorious heaven. And a Church that is doing such a glorious work is God's Church. If there be but one Church doing so, then there is but one Church, but if there be a hundred Churches doing such work, then there are a hundred gospel Churches in the world, and the more of them the better it will be for the world. Methodism does not claim to be the only Church, but a Church among the many. It claims to be one of the "seven stars in His righthand" to enlighten the world. It claims to be one of the fruitful branches growing out of Christ, "the Vine." And "herein is my Father glorified, that ye bear much fruit; so shall ye be my disciples."

The general Church is one. It is the entire body of all justified persons, adults or infants, in every period of time, in earth or in heaven. A gospel Church is a company of believers organized into a society, believing a Bible creed, having its own ritual and ecclesiastical machinery, claiming for its head Christ, for its object the diffusion of the gospel, and for its destiny a glorious triumph. And such is the Methodist Episcopal Church, South.

THE EXTERNAL FORM OF CHURCH GOVERNMENT.

We do not claim that the external form of our Church government is divinely prescribed. Neither is the form of other Churches prescribed. Mr. Wesley said: "It is unanswerably proved that neither Christ nor his apostles prescribe any particular form of Church government." The Jewish Church evidently with certain modification became the Christian Church. Christ did not command his disciples to form a new Church. No such command can be found. "It is true that there is not on record one single line or word from him which prescribes a new Church as distinct from the Jewish Church. He lived in the Jewish Church himself. He died a member and communicant of that Church. Nor did his disciples understand that they were to step out of it and fashion another one. They, all of them, for more than twenty-five years, lived in communion with the Jewish Church. Forty years after the ascension of their Master, they still sacrificed in the temple, and were a Christian brotherhood only as a party in the original Jewish Church. It would seem to be the height of historical phantasy, therefore, to declare that the Christian Church was outlined and prescribed by the Lord Jesus Christ, understood to be so by his apostles, and taught by them to be so. A greater mistake can scarce be imagined."

We have almost an exact analogy of this in Methodism. When Wesley undertook to reform the Church of England, he did not separate his disciples from the Established Church. They remained in it and observed its ordinances and rules, at the same time holding separate meetings of their own, over and above those of their own Church. Finally, it became necessary for them to draw out and set up a new and independent organization. And so the early disciples still adhered to the temple services, though they had social and spiritual meetings of their own besides, till the Roman army destroyed the city and the temple with it. Then they were forced to organize some other form, and they modeled their future organization mainly after the pattern of the synagogue. There is no specific form of Church government to be found anywhere in the New Testament.

"Nevertheless, there was a Church. There were religious institutions. They were accepted. They were implied. And the moment the apostles began to preach outside of Judea, where there was no temple, and where there were no synagogues, they were organized, they were officered; and there came to be laws and methods and usages, and the apostles commanded them, interpreted them, and ranked them.

"Therefore, if any man say that there is no warrant in the word of God for any Church organization, I think he misses the mark on one extreme as much as the hierarch misses it on the other when he declares that there was a specific form of organization prescribed for the Christian Church. These are the extremists on the one side and on the other."

Secondly, it is recognized that there is perfect freedom in taking up and laying down the rites, the usages, the forms, the customs, and the instructing methods of the New Testament. You can make your election among them. You can avail yourselves of them, not according to any prescribed divinely appointed scheme, but according to the exigences and necessities of the work which you yourselves have in hand; for the liberty of man, by virtue of his adhesion to the Lord Jesus Christ, is the axis of the teaching of the New Testament.

All men have the inalienable right to worship, love, and serve God. There can be no question on this point. This right carries with it another right—the right of men to form themselves into an association to improve and protect their spiritual interests. The right to civil liberty implies the right to organize a government to secure, perpetuate, and defend it; so the right to worship God carries the right, on the part of men, to organize a Church to promote that divine service. A company, then, of godly men have the inalienable and inherent right to organize a Church as a means of cultivating and propagating holiness. As Luther and his followers had a right to organize the Lutheran Church, as John Calvin and Knox had a right to organize the Presbyterian Church, as Bishop Cranmer and Henry VIII. had a right to organize the Episcopal Church in England, and Roger Williams and his brethren had a right to organize the Baptist Church, so had Mr. Wesley, Coke, and Asbury a right to organize the Methodist Church. They all stand precisely upon the same ground. The whole Protestant world stands or falls together.

Thirdly, in organizing the externals of a Church where there is no divine prescription given, men are left free to choose that form which promises the most good.

"Methodism, then, had a great advantage in its beginning, in that it was extremely modern. Episcopalians on the one hand and Congregationalists on the other alike claimed to find the warrant for their characteristic outer forms in those of the apostolic Church. Presbyterians and other people between the two extremes also anchored themselves in deductions from the

Acts of the Apostles and the Epistles of Paul. It was the good fortune of Methodism to be a system based only on expediency, not claiming a "divine right" for its circuits, its annual removals, its clock-work system of wheels within wheels, its class-leaders, and stewards, and exhorters, and local preachers. It did not go further for authority for its agencies than this, namely, that they were needed, and that they were useful. It was the divine right, not of precedent, but of common sense. The whole superstructure of the canon law went down before the military necessity of a missionary Church. It was not asked what Paul thought best to do in founding a Church at Philippi or at Ephesus, but straightforwardly it was demanded what was best for Philadelphia, and what was wisest for Charleston; not what the elders thought best in conference at Jerusalem, but what the delegates thought wise in General Conference in Baltimore. Hence the immense flexibility and mobility of this aggressive ecclesiastical system, which thus unloaded itself, not only of the lumber of the mediæval centuries, but of the out-of-date expedients of the apostolic age as well."

THE CLAIMS OF METHODISM.

While we do not claim to be *the only* Church, we do claim to be superior to some others in many important particulars.

1. We claim superiority in the scriptural soundness of our leading doctrines. There are four great doctrinal systems in the world—the Roman Catholic, the Calvinistic, the Lutheran, and the Wesleyan. The Catholic creed teaches that salvation comes through the

Papal Church alone. The Calvinistic creed makes the salvation or non-salvation of every soul to depend on the unchangeable decree of God. The Lutheran creed lodges the salvation of the soul too much in the sacraments. The Methodist creed makes the salvation or non-salvation of every soul depend on his *willingness to receive and appropriate the free grace of the gospel offered to all men.* This creed presents a doctrine high as the love of God and wide as the deep wants of the human race. This ground view of Methodism appeals to the common sense of mankind for its truth, has driven Calvinism practically out of the pulpit of Christendom, and is rapidly ascending to the throne of universal acceptance. It preaches a free and full salvation, justification by faith alone, carefulness to maintain good works, the witness of the Spirit to the believer's present acceptance, holiness of life, a burning love for the salvation of souls, an entire reliance upon the Holy Spirit as the source of spiritual power; it has an open communion-table, contends for a pure and spiritual worship, a deep and heartfelt experience of vital religion, encourages and promotes revivals as vital to the health and growth of a Church. The vast army of Methodism has been recruited mainly through its system of revivals. While other Churches have been gathering a few members, through family training and catechetical instruction, Methodism has swept them in by hundreds and thousands. The first method is the slow way of fishing with hook and line, the revival method is fishing with a net that goes far out into the waters and sweeps in thousands at one haul.

2. Methodism claims superiority in adapting itself

to the circumstances of human life. "Methodism," says the celebrated Dr. Talmage, "in England preaches in a gown; in our Eastern cities, in broadcloth; in the West, in shirt-sleeves, if the season be appropriate—preaching in the house or in the fields, anywhere, it makes no difference where—preaching just as well in one place as in another. It takes the express train and goes across the continent, or a horse and rides with saddle-bags across the prairie; it is at home in the magnificent St. Paul's, New York, and is not at all inconvenienced in a log-cabin. . Here is a man fallen down in the ditch of sin and crime. How are we going to get him out? We come up elegantly appareled, and we look at him, and we say, 'What a pity it is to see a man so deep in the mud! We wish we could get him out. Is it not awful to see that man suffering there? Get a pry, somebody, and help now! I wish I had on my other clothes.' While we stand there looking at the poor man, the Methodist comes along, and says, 'Brother, give me your hand,' pulls him up, and sets him on the Rock of Ages." We are told in one of the Arabian stories of a fairy tent which a young prince brought, hidden in a walnut-shell, to his father. Placed in a council chamber, it grew till it encanopied the king and his ministry; taken into the court-yard, it filled the space till all the household stood beneath its shade; brought into the midst of the great plain without the city, where the army was encamped, it spread its expansive shade all abroad till it gave shelter to a mighty host of people. It had wonderful flexibility and expansiveness And such is the expansive flexibility and adaptedness of Methodism. It has this power of easy adaptation to the most diversified conditions of life; it reaches out its arms to embrace the negro in his hut, the backwoodsman in his forest home, the scholar in his study, and the prince in his gilded palace.

3. Methodism, more than any other denomination, has exercised a watch-care over individual members. To visit, from time to time, every house where there is a Methodist member, though it may be but a servant-girl, and to talk and pray with them, is the old ideal of a Methodist preacher's duty, and it is yet held and acted on in most places. The class-leader is also to watch over the members in his charge, and "to see every member of his class once a week" was formerly exacted of him. This constant watchfulness checked incipient backslidings, recovered those who had gone astray, and was a powerful engine for the enforcement of discipline. The class-leaders are appointees of the pastor, and are his deputies. Attendance upon the class-meeting is no longer compulsory, but the watchfulness of the leader over his flock and his accountability to the pastor in the regular meetings of the official board are yet great powers for the conservation of the membership. A system of intelligence is thus established by which the pastor is enabled to consider every member, even the most obscure, in his individual circumstances and qualities. Methodism is not so much an organization, but an organism in which every part, even the remotest, is vitalized by its connection with the whole. Of late years an effort has been made to supply the lack of the old efficiency of the class-meeting system by organizing the ladies of the city congregations into societies for the purpose of assisting the pastor in visitation and supervision.

Methodism has always been intensely social. Its class-meetings were family gatherings; its love-feasts, and prayer-meetings, and "general class-meetings," were so many ever-recurring expressions of its social life. More powerful than any oratory is the influence of fellowship upon the masses of the people, and this fellowship Methodism furnished and still furnishes. In the older and less conventional days I have seen class-meetings and love-feasts break up with what the enthusiastic Western people called "a good old-fashioned Methodist shake hands all round." No social distinctions were tolerated then. The title of "brother" and "sister," in all but universal use between Methodists as substitutes for "Mr." and "Mrs." was a symbol of the entire equality of brethren in the Church.

4. Methodism claims superiority in her methods of diffusing the gospel over the world, through the itinerant ministry. It is this grand agency that has enabled Methodism to keep up with the march of frontier settlements, cross the Alleghanies, follow the Indian trail beyond the Mississippi, and at length fill the far West with the sound of its victories. In the wake of its luminous progress have sprung up all kinds of improvements. It has been a popular educator, civilizer, and refiner to the rude masses of the West. A distinguished outsider has "recognized in the Methodist economy, as well as in the zeal, the devoted piety, and efficiency of its ministry, one of the most powerful elements in the religious prosperity of the United States, as well as one of the firmest pillars of their civil and political institutions." Bancroft, the historian, acknowledges the Methodists as "the pioneers

of religion" in this country, and says that they have "carried their consolations, songs, and prayers to the farthest cabins in the wilderness." Another talented writer has said: "Their voice went through the land as a trumpet-call. It sounded over the heights and depths, and filled the country with its echoes." Not only have the banners of Methodism been planted in all the States and Territories of the Union, from sea to sea, but it has spread rapidly over Great Britain, its native home, into Scotland, Ireland, to Nova Scotia the West Indies, France, Africa, India, Germany, and is achieving remarkable success in the Cannibal Islands of the Southern Sea. "The world is my parish," said Mr. Wesley. And it seems that this prophecy is about to be realized, for the bright eye of the sun sees no longitude on the rolling earth where Methodism is not working for the salvation of men. May her future history realize the noble anticipations of the poet Montgomery, who said: "Century expanding after century, like circle beyond circle in broad water, shall carry farther and farther the blessings of the Methodist dispensation, till they have tracked every sea and touched every shore!"

CHAPTER XXII.

THE TRAINING OF CHILDREN IN CHRISTIAN HOMES, SO AS TO BRING THEM TO CHRIST AND ATTACH THEM TO METHODISM.

(Address of Rev. Joseph Wood, in the Ecumenical Methodist Book.)

THE subject limits us to the consideration of one institution for leading our children "to Christ and attaching them to Methodism," viz., their "training in

Christian homes." It is obligatory upon parents to bring up their families "in the nurture and admonition of the Lord." The lessons imparted at the fireside, the spirit of Christianity pervading the house, and the gentle courtesies and sweet attachments of home, ought to engrave the words of God and the gospel of his Son upon the heart and mind of every child and every member of the household. We shall lay down and briefly discuss several propositions:

1. THE RELIGION OF METHODISTS OUGHT TO BE TRANSMITTED TO, AND REPRODUCED IN, THEIR CHILDREN.

What is the religion of Methodists? Has it any peculiarities—any distinctive features? It is not simply a creed or a profession; it is life and energy, a power in the heart controlling the center of our being. John Wesley had to insist on a religious life. He found the profession without the power of godliness, and his great object was to revive vital Christianity. We want to see Methodism, in its true import, handed down from generation to generation. We do not desire to alter its form or principles, but to diffuse its living spirit and power. It will profit our children but little to have the name of Methodists and to cling to the traditions of their fathers, if they be destitute of the great reality—the inward and spiritual change. The kingdom of God is not "in word only, but also in power, and in the Holy Ghost, and in much assurance."

Our subject speaks of "bringing children to Christ," and "attaching them to Methodism;" that is the order—"to Christ," and then "to Methodism." It would not be desirable to retain such as are alienated from

Christ Our churches have but few attractions for the unrenewed. They lack those external elements which are the great charm and fascination of worldly minds. The world will love its own. Then to abide with us, our sons and daughters must be born again, partake of our faith, and repeat our life. If they have no saving relation to Christ, their relation to the Church cannot profit either them or us; to hold in connection with it ungodly persons would diminish the power and tarnish the glory of any Church. A worldly and impure element is an element of weakness and decay. To be satisfied with any thing less than the new birth for our members, we should lower the standard which our fathers set up, and surrender the object for which Methodism, by the providence of God, was called into existence. If we cannot persuade our young people to fulfill the conditions of such change, and thereby pass from death unto life, we shall not have power, and, it is hoped, shall not desire to retain them in our Communion.

Then follows the prodigiously important question, How far are parents responsible for the regeneration of their children? We do not believe any more in a spiritual "birthright membership" in the Church than we do in baptismal regeneration. All are born in sin. Every child must be won to Christ personally, and be renewed by the Holy Ghost, or that child remains under the condemnation due to sin, even though its parents are as godly as Elkanah and Hannah of old. Is there any ground for the general belief that, whatever be the training, it is wholly uncertain what our sons and daughters, in character, will become, as uncertain as if it were a case of lottery? The best is hoped for them; but there is no fixed law on which a confident expectation may be entertained. When we know the character of the fountain, we can judge of the streams. By virtue of a like sequence, may we not determine the character of children when we have ascertained that of parents? There is as real a connection between means and ends in the spiritual economy as in the natural economy. We reap what we sow; the harvest answereth to the seed.

In its doctrines and precepts the Bible sees the religious character of the child in that of the parent. (Gen. xviii. 19; Deut. iv. 40; Isa. xliv. 3, 5; Ezek. xx. 5, 6; Ps. cxlvii. 13; Jer. xxxii. 39; Acts ii. 30, xvi. 31; 1 Cor. vii. 14.) The divine purpose evidently is that from godly parents there should be a godly seed—walking in all the ordinances and commandments of the Lord blameless; that as the race is a body under Adam, the Church should be a body under Christ, grafting its children into the living Vine, and teaching all to know the Lord, from the least unto the greatest. The home teaching of the Hebrews was intended to produce regeneration of character in the children, to make them Jews inwardly as well as outwardly, that they might not be "a stubborn and rebellious generation," but might "set their hope in God" and "keep his commandments." When Paul directed Christian parents to bring up their children "in the nurture and admonition of the Lord," the intention was not that they should be trained to be merely Christian formalists, but that they should have that kingdom of God in the heart which is "righteousness, and peace, and joy in the Holy Ghost."

The practicability of this work belongs exclusively to God. Our business is to obey his commands. Since it is his method to regenerate children by means of Christian nurture, it is our duty to assume that what he contemplates can be done, and to adapt our machinery to the work. There is no scriptural foundation for the theory that all children must grow into sin before they can grow into Christ; that all education will produce a crop of iniquity before it can produce a crop of holiness. So far as human instrumentality is concerned, it is easier to persuade the young to decide for Christ than it is those who are hardened in sin. The work must be attempted on a large scale, and if Methodists can solve the problem of transmitting vital religion from generation to generation, the ultimate triumph of Christianity will become a matter of course.

The theory of the Church of England in relation to children is no idle dream. That Church takes it for granted that infants ought to be formally dedicated to God by being baptized in the name of the adorable Trinity, that this solemn rite should be followed by careful and ample evangelical instruction—that the instruction will, at an early age, result in personal conversion to God; hence, at thirteen or fourteen, children are to be examined and urged to take upon themselves the vows made at their baptism, one of which is that they will "keep God's holy will and commandments, and walk in the same all the days of their life." The order is baptism, evangelical instruction, and official examination. Methodists ought to take hold of this theory and turn it into a living reality. We do not require all the details of it, but the general principle. We have the baptism; that is the beginning of the plan. Instead of the godfathers and the godmothers, the real parents are obligated to undertake the religious instruction of the child. In place of the confirmation and the laying on of the bishop's hands, there must be examination, an individual appeal to the conscience, to gain the personal consent and formal promise of each youth to submit to Christ, and, as a present guarantee that this promise will be fulfilled, now, at once, to join the Church by going to some class.

In our ministry and pastoral work we must make this duty clear to heads of households, and render them all the assistance we can in the performance of it. For the ignorance and neglect which prevail in regard to it, ministers are largely responsible. In our sermons we have assumed, if we have not directly taught, that young people are to live several years to the world, and then be converted. We have looked for our increases more from revival meetings and the penitents' form than from the family altar; and been more hopeful of converts from the ranks of those who are well bronzed in iniquity, and have passed through a kind of tragical experience in turning to God, than of those who have been trained in the way they should go from earliest infancy; and to whom the Christian spirit of their home has been a process of domestic conversion, leading them into the path of life before they had wandered in the way of sin and death. Let the great design of baptism, and especially its covenanting character, be duly impressed upon parents, showing that the ordinance is part of a great plan; that it is to be followed by suitable treatment in order that the baptized may become true and living Christians as soon as moral existence begins; then shall we realize what Methodism most needs, and what is enforced in the Scriptures, viz., an adult Church which transmits vital religion to "the generation to come."

II. THE FAMILY LIFE AND HABITS OF METHODISTS SHOULD BE REGULATED WITH A VIEW TO THAT END.

What are the elements of a truly Christian and Methodist training?

1. *High-toned piety in the house and in the daily life of the parents.* In the family more than anywhere else is it true that example is better than precept. It is what parents are, rather than what they say, that will take effect. They are the child's first gospel. He reads them before he can tell a letter in his primer. He imbibes the spirit of the house before he is able to judge of the moral character of it. The atmosphere of many a Christian professor's house is very unfavorable to the salvation of the young. The malaria of worldliness infects the whole family. Commands to be good are made a substitute for goodness. There may be the morning and evening devotion, strict attention to the public means of grace, wise counsels frequently given; but a defective example will neutralize the whole. Religion should not be a separate subsistence occasionally introduced to serve a purpose as masks are worn; but the very life and soul of the family, ever-present, pervading, regulating, and sanctifying all events. Not simply summoned to soothe and cheer in times of affliction and

adversity, but its voice blending with the merriest moods, and shedding "sweet glories" on those moments when the loved ones meet, and affection gushing from warm and full hearts sparkles in the gleams of pleasant wit and humor. The homes of Methodists ought to be the brightest and happiest out of heaven. We have all the essential elements to make them such; the literature, the hymns, the tunes, the devotion, the social enjoyments—in fact, every thing to render them cheerful and attractive with a living piety.

Such homes would be nurseries for our churches— a perpetual means of grace to the children. There the young would grow up, like Samuel and Timothy, a seed to serve God in their generation. The rule would be for them to be saved at home, and not in a preaching service or a revival meeting. Baxter says: "I do verily believe that if parents did their duty as they ought the word publicly preached would not be the ordinary means of regeneration in the Church, but only without the Church, among practical heathens and infidels." He was greatly troubled about his own salvation, because he could not call to mind any distinct time when he was saved, until, tracing his experience as far back as he could, he found that he had been saved too soon to recollect the time of it. The particular moment, if there was one, was lost in the dim memories of childhood. The love of God had mingled with blessings of infancy, and the way of sin he had not known. John Wesley was awakened to a sense of religion when a child at home, and was so remarkable "for the seriousness of his spirit and the general propriety of his behavior," that "at the age of eight years he was admitted to the sacrament of of the Lord's Supper." Methodism, traced up to its fountain-head, must be regarded as the outcome of all domestic piety, rather than of any special evangelistic enterprise. We are more indebted to Susannah Wesley than to Peter Bohler. To be like our founder our members must begin to serve the Lord in childhood, under the influence of parental training and example, and continue to walk before God in holiness and righteousness to the very end of life.

2. *The institution of suitable means in the house for the spiritual enlightenment and regeneration of children.* All must not be left to the involuntary influence of the life. The reading of the Scriptures with veneration and prayer is of supreme importance, and cannot in any house be omitted without immense loss. To read with profit, it is necessary to have a system, and to accompany the reading with explanatory remarks and occasional questions. When this cannot be done twice a day, nor even once, as is often the case in this busy, bustling age, in most houses if proper efforts were made one hour a week could be set apart for it, and something like a regular service be held. It was the custom in Puritan households to spend the Sunday evening in giving Bible-lessons and catechetical instruction to the children and the servants. This cannot be done in Methodists' homes, because we have our most important public service at that hour, when we should have the whole family with us in the house of God. But if there be a will to have it done, time will no doubt be found for teaching the family the way of salvation, and building them up in the most holy faith.

Should not all Methodists be urged to use their

Connectional catechisms in home training? Every child and servant might have a copy, and a question or two be asked and answers required daily, and the whole reviewed at the weekly service. This would furnish the young with distinctions and definitions of doctrine and Christian evidences, and thus fortify them against the errors and sophistries of the age. If such duties were faithfully attended to in all our homes, we should have no fear respecting the next generation of Methodists. We might defy either popery or infidelity to lead our youth astray.

The prayers of the family should be short and simple, and refer to incidents which are occurring. Singing adds much to the interest of the service, and prepares the family to join more freely in the praises of the sanctuary. No house is as it ought to be which has not stated times not only for worship, but for conversation with the children, to ascertain their mind in relation to divine things and persuade them to decide for Christ. Should not Methodists have a family class-meeting weekly, when all would feel perfectly free to ask any question relative to their circumstances, trials, and temptations, and all be encouraged to pray a few words, even down to the lisping little one, who asks, "Pleathe, God, bleth little mammy—bleth uth all for Jethuth' thake?" Besides this, it is well to take the children apart occasionally and converse with them in the presence of God about the soul, Jesus Christ, the judgment to come, the glorious provision of the gospel to make them happy forever. What constitutes real worth of character, what are the elements of true happiness, and what are the objects which life has been given to accomplish, should be solemnly and frequently explained to them, and the interview always end in prayer. The great point for parents to realize is that, as a sphere of divine influence, the family is equal to the Church. They may regard the place of their abode as no less holy than the sanctuary, the little gathering at the fireside as no less sacred than the assembly in the church or chapel, the instruction and service on the domestic hearth as no less efficacious for spiritual ends than the rites and observances in the great congregation.

To train the children in regular attendance on public worship is also a powerful means of bringing them to Christ and attaching them to his cause. A little fellow asked his parents to take him to church with them, and they told him he must wait till he was older. "Well," was his shrewd reply, "you'd better take me now, for when I get bigger I may not want to go." If parents regard the worship of the sanctuary as a pleasure, and not merely a duty, their children will generally wish to attend, and it will not be necessary to enforce it by an act of compulsion. But care must be taken not to make the Sabbath-day one of irksome restraint and burdensome requisitions—not one that will be regarded as an unwelcome interruption to the amusements and pursuits of the week, but anticipated as a day of rest and peaceful enjoyment. We much like the idea of catechising the children on the sermons they hear, as well as on the doctrines, duties, facts, and privileges of Christianity, as taught in our forms of catechism. We cannot but think that these means would prevent at least the majority of young people from forsaking the altars of God and the courts of Zion.

3. *The exclusion from the family circle, so far as practicable, of all pernicious and dangerous influences.* We scarcely need indicate the channels through which these influences come. The books that are brought into the house, the persons who visit it, the social entertainments provided, and the companionships formed, are sources of good or bad influences which enter into the mental and moral being, and become interwoven with the very life of children. We cannot but regard the superabundant supply of light literature as more or less dangerous. Young people feed upon it until they have no appetite for any thing solid and substantial. Books which deal with unreal persons and things—with scenes, events, and characters far removed from the facts of existence—unfit and incapacitate the mind for the stern realities of life. It is a grievous mistake for those who desire to attach their families to Methodism not to supply them with an attractive and wholesome literature, and especially with the magazines and various works issued by our Connectional Book-rooms.

We should not, more than is absolutely necessary, expose our children to influences hostile to Methodism in school, business, and social life. Too often there is but little care as to what teachings and surroundings they come under at school or business. If there be some anxiety not to endanger their morals, there is not much thought whether their Methodism or religion will be safe. At the most critical time of their life they are placed in the midst of conditions which can hardly fail to deaden their moral sense, and alienate them from the Churches of their fathers. We were pleased to read the earnest words spoken at the

Wesleyan Conference on this point. One gentleman stated that he knew three county magistrates, one a Congregationalist, one a Baptist, and another a Methodist; the two former sent their children to Church schools, and all had forsaken Nonconformity. The Methodist took care that his children were guarded in youth, that they were kept under godly Methodist influences, and five out of his seven children had become members of the Methodist Society. Mr. Holden said it had cost him much to educate his family in Methodist schools, but the result was worth far more than the expense, for his children were members of the Church, and engaged in God's work. The sphere of Methodism is now large and comprehends a sufficient variety of rank and of profitable and honorable employment, and our young people, as far as practicable, should be kept within it, with the best examples ever before them.

Is there not reason to fear that some are not well instructed in regard to their friendships, and particularly the marriage union? They may set their affections on persons of doubtful religious character, and even doubtful morality, providing those persons are equal to them, or a degree above them, in the social scale. There is always going to be a good match if there is worldly respectability. This infraction of the divine law, which allows believers to marry "only in the Lord," is the cause of many of the sons and daughters of our members being lost to Methodism. In primitive times the sanction of the Church was required for the marriage of any of its members. In the Conference of 1763, Mr. Wesley said: "Many of our members have lately married unbelievers, even such as were wholly unawakened; and this has been attended with fatal consequences. Few have gained the unbelieving wife or husband; generally they have themselves either had a heavy cross for life or entirely fallen back into the world. To put a stop to this, let every preacher publicly enforce the apostle's caution, 'Be ye not unequally yoked with unbelievers.' Let it be also openly declared in every place that he who acts contrary to this will be expelled the Society. When any such is expelled, let an exhortation be subjoined dissuading others from following that bad example." Had not we better have some of these good old rules reprinted in our Conference Minutes?

4. *An intelligent and conscientious attachment on the part of parents themselves to Methodism.* Is not the want of this the cause of many failing to connect their families permanently with our churches? It is not enough to be Christians; we must be Methodists, and let our children see that we regard the system so called and distinguished as the highest form of Christian and Church life. Seeing the value of Methodism, not simply in our declared opinions, but in its lovely effects upon our lives and conversation, they will learn to regard it not as a human institution, to which our partialities or our prejudices have attached us, but as a divinely appointed system of religion and happiness.

That they may profit by the exercise of the Christian ministry among us, we must ourselves respect the minister's holy vocation, and be painstaking to make them understand it and respect it too. If they but lightly esteem the messengers of God's mer cy, they will be in danger also of rejecting the message itself. Let parents be careful not to offend against the ministers of the word, against the commands of God, against their own souls, and against the highest interests of their families, by uncharitable or unguarded remarks about the men who hold the most sacred and important office ever intrusted to human beings.

Methodist parents ought to make known to their children the distinctive principles of the several denominations, that an intelligent choice may be made. But we need not attach so much importance to those little barriers which divide the various branches of the great Methodist family, and which we rejoice to see are becoming beautifully less, as to the broad and general features of Methodism, and the advantages which we are proud enough to think we have over all other Christian denominations. Let us often address to our children the words of the prophet: "Mark well, and behold with thine eyes, and hear with thine ears, all that I say unto thee concerning all the ordinances of the house of the Lord, and all the laws thereof." (Ezek. xliv. 5.) Parents who train their children on the principle that they may go to any Church where they can feel most comfortable, need not wonder when it seems to be most comfortable for them to go nowhere. If Methodism is the best for us, is it not likely to be the best for our children?

To say nothing of the unseemliness of families being divided in their Church connections, is it not most ungrateful to be careless whether or not our sons and daughters be permanently attached to Methodism? Under its influence, with God's blessing, we have obtained our spiritual illumination, our Christian peace, our gracious transformation, and the immortal hope of a heavenly inheritance—indeed, all that we hold dear. When we look at lower things, under its shadow many have acquired manifold temporal advantages. In all respects it claims their attachment as an availing form of godliness, which has the promise of the life that now is and of that which is to come. To be indifferent to its preservation and continued efficiency in the world, or its influence in and upon the future character, relations, and circumstances of our children, would be the utmost inconsistency and the deepest ingratitude.

Then, how to transmit inward religion—true Methodism—to "the generation to come" is the great problem we have to solve; how to find, as Dr. Osborn a few years ago so admirably put it, "the connecting link between the baptismal font and the Lord's table." For this we are persuaded we shall have to look more to the family than we have done. We must teach our people how to realize God's saving grace in domestic worship and Christian nurture; and not only in the Sunday-school and the sanctuary, but parents and teachers, ministers and leaders, will have to combine, that the great end may be gained. As the late Rev. S. Jackson said, "We must be at the children, or the millennium is a long way off." Those who rock the cradle have the Church's, as well as the nation's, destiny in their hands. Daniel Webster said to Thomas Jefferson, the great statesman of America who wrote the Declaration of Independence, "What is to be the salvation of our nation?" After a few moments' thought, Jefferson replied: "This nation will be saved, if saved at all, by teaching the children to love the Saviour." Methodist churches cannot always live solely by conquest, by conversions from without, by a kind of gospel campaigning. While they continue to make sallies and excursions into the kingdom of darkness, they will have to learn how to grow, and populate, and become powerful from within. "As arrows in the hand of a mighty man, so are children of youth." To neglect them is to commit a great military blunder. It is to leave our arrows to rust and become blunt and totally unfit for use, when they ought to be collected, polished, and sharpened for the day of battle. God says to his faithful people, "Thou shalt see thy children's children and peace upon Israel." The results of a system which, by God's blessing, transmits our principles and practices from generation to generation will be general peace and prosperity to the end of time. It is recorded that Cyrus, when besieging Babylon, perceived the importance of the river on the banks of which the city stood, as being at once the cause of its security, by shutting out its enemies, and the source of its internal prosperity. He therefore devised the plan of cutting channels for the purpose of turning the stream of the river out of its natural and proper course. By this means he obtained an easy entrance for his troops, and doomed the city to slow but certain decay. That illustrates the stratagems of the devil to prevent the universal triumphs of Christianity. It is high time to interrupt his proceedings and frustrate his plans by repairing and keeping up the banks of the river from which our great stores of supply come, and that our youth may glide onward to the city of God, at once its defense and glory, and the source of its increase and perpetuity.

CHAPTER XXIII.
A MODEL CHRISTIAN AND A LOYAL METHODIST.

To be a model Christian and a loyal Methodist is the high standard set before every member of our Church. Such a standard is possible to all. A Methodist and a good Christian should mean one and the same thing. A good Methodist is one who has been soundly converted, one who has "the love of God shed abroad in his heart by the Holy Ghost given unto him," one who "loves the Lord his God with all his heart, and with all his soul, and with all his mind, and with all his strength, and his neighbor as himself." To be deeply pious, holy, consecrated, is the duty and the privilege of all our members. We say that the highest standard of Christian purity, of moral power, and dignity lies within the reach of the lowest and poorest. The highest type of manhood is a full-hearted Christian. The great mass of mankind cannot wear the golden crown of wealth, nor the laurels of high worldly honors, nor carry diplomas of a finished education; but they can wear the crown of Christian love, they can have the wealth of spirituality, they can rise to dignity in the kingdom of God. There is nobody so ignorant, or poor, or obscure, that cannot love his God supremely and serve his fellow-men. It does not require genius, nor education, nor wealth, nor high position. Spiritual goodness is within the reach of all classes and conditions of men. To get good and do good are the privilege and duty of all. Such religion is the royalty of mankind, the crown, the beauty, and glory of human life. "The fruit of the Spirit is love, joy, peace, long-suffering, gentleness, goodness, temperance." Such is the blessed fruit which the tree of the gospel bears.

Be useful; and in order to be useful, be really and truly good. A beautiful disposition will make your manners lovely and attractive. A heart sweetened with Christian love will diffuse its fragrancy all around, like a garden full of sweet-smelling flowers. Keep the oil of the Holy Spirit in your heart, then your life will be "a burning and a shining light." A profession of religion without the Holy Spirit is a lantern without a candle. A Church full of members without the fire and the power of the Holy Ghost is nothing more than a box of unlit candles, having the latent capacity but not the power of warming and illuminating those around them.

The man who walks close with God, as Enoch, who obeys his laws, who opens his heart to divine influences as the flower to the sun, who lives in communion with Christ, will be ready to every good work, and coöperate with all laboring to spread the gospel.

CHRISTIAN ACTIVITY.

Be a model in Christian work. This is a world of work. God, Christ, the Holy Spirit, are all active workers. The angels work. "They are ministering spirits sent forth to minister for them who shall be heirs of salvation." The natural world works. The trees pump up the sap, bloom, and bear fruit. The rivers speed on in their courses, watering fruitful fields, turning mill-wheels, and floating ships. The winds are the great water-carriers of earth. The stars move on in their orbits. The moon catches the radiance of the set sun, and throws it back upon the dark hills of night. The sun is a grand worker. He illuminates, warms, and fructifies the world. And the command of the great Teacher rings over the earth, "Go, work to-day in my vineyard!" We must work for others, if we would save ourselves.

Little Talents to be Worked

Do not evade this duty, this blessedness, by arguing with yourself that you have no talent for any important usefulness. The ambition to do only signal things may be the veriest pride of the depraved heart. If you have only small talents—even the one talent of the parable—use it with your might; remember it is all your divine Master will hold you accountable for; but remember also that it was the man who, in the parable, neglected his one talent that was lost in the day of reckoning. That one talent of yours, if used aright, may place you as high in heaven as any monarch who may go thither from any earthly throne.

Man of God, if thou hast but one talent, where is it? Is it hid away in a napkin? Is it buried? Remember that the final judgment will ferret it out. Canst thou not speak for thy Master? Canst thou not go from house to house among thy neighbors, in his name, teach his little ones in a Sunday-school, testify for him in a prayer-meeting, give a pittance of thy earnings for him? Remember him, in the parable, who buried his talent, and beware of his fate.

"Why stand ye here all the day idle?" Begin

something good, though it be small. The mightiest oak in the forest grew from a small acorn. Two grains of wheat would suffice, with proper care and labor, to cover, in time, all the grain-bearing soil of this planet, and transferred to other orbs, could cover in like manner all the worlds of the heavens. "Despise not the day of small things. Thou art but a small soul if thou doest so."

Personal Effort.

Whenever a man, an individual Christian, finds that he has both time and capacity, it is his duty to follow the Master in seeking and saving his fellow-men; and let me say to you that the beginning of revivals of religion is like the beginning of a fire, in which you take a single coal, it may be, and lay a little fuel on it, and blow it a moment; at first it blazes a little bit, and then blazes a little bit more, every additional stick you put on making it more certain that the next one will catch. Do not wait until the whole Church is waked up before you move. If you can find any member of it that is in sympathy with you, put your heart and his together, and they will make a sympathetic influence which may bring another in. Draw in individuals. Look around for them; do not look around for the Church; the Church will take care of itself, and you should take care of yourself. Collect two, three, four people; and the moment you thus form a center of feeling, it begins to whirl and sweep in others. It is not difficult for three or four persons in a community to form a center that will begin to draw in those that are around about them. Next, let me say that I think there is nothing in this world that is so sure to be successful as personal adhesion to your fellow-men. Preaching, at best, is like artillery firing; but when you come into close personal relations with men and talk to them, not once or twice, not when you happen to meet them, but often, seeking suitable times and opportunities, and press upon them the duty of entering absolutely upon a Christian life, and follow it up gently and quietly, I believe that even the most difficult cases will eventually be won over to the higher life. I think there is no influence so powerful in bringing men from darkness to light, and from death to life, as that of man upon man, heart upon heart.

If every one of those in the Church who are able, in the providence of God, to do this kind of work would bring a single person into the Christian life, there would be hundreds brought in. There are many in the community who are so thoroughly interested in religion that all they need to induce them to enter the Christian life is the opportunity. It would require but very little to carry them over distinctly to a knowledge of Christ. They know what the dispositions of Christ are, they know what the walk and conversation of a Christian ought to be; and all they need is to be led to say, "By the help of God, I will enter upon a spiritual course." Nobody does more than that in the beginning. All the rest of one's life is the filling up, of which this is the commencement. So it is in the power of men to carry their fellow-men over from animalism to spirituality, and those that are strong can take those that are weak, and, by the impulse of their souls, lift them above matter and the flesh. On the other hand, it is oftentimes the case that men who are feeble are a very great help to those who are strong. William Wirt owed his conversion to a negro nurse. This old servant prayed for him, and he knew it. In his pride he resisted the influence that he was conscious was acting upon him; but by and by the power of God through her prayer was too strong for him to withstand, and he humbled himself, and went and asked her what he should do to be saved. He would not go to the minister, but he would go to the poor old negro nurse for advice. When a ship is a little too heavily freighted, they sometimes put under her empty casks, that buoy her up and carry her over sand-bars; and sometimes God blesses empty men to the buoying up of other men who are too heavily freighted with worldly elements, and to carrying them over the sand-bar of Christian experience. There is use for slenderly endowed men. Great strength, great wisdom, and great experience all have their place; and so small endowments have their place. Every man can do something.

WORK TO-DAY.

"Go, work *to-day* in my vineyard." The Christian worker should not wait to be appointed to some special office, and do nothing and feel no duty unless appointed to some official position. Plan your own work and do it. The doing good is a question of TO-DAY. "Behold, now is the accepted time." "Whatever thy hand findeth to do, do it with thy might." Improve present opportunities. The *Christian Union* says: "A tired mother who had been occupied all day with an active and very troublesome boy, as she sat down in the evening and thought of the numberless details into which her strength had gone, said: 'After all, it is a day toward the making of a man.' There was a world of truth in this brief and pointed summing up of a day's work. Nothing is so hard to overcome as the illusion of time and distance. Thousands of lives are wasted because they are never freed from it, and thousands of other and faithful lives are saddened because they too are under its spell. The woman under the pressure of daily and nightly cares who feels no inspiration from them, but continually dreams of greater services and nobler occupations in some other place and at some other time, is surely missing the secret of the deepest living, and is thirsting with the water of life flowing freshly about her. The man who chafes under his present burden, and scorns his place and work as small and mean compared with the thing he would do, is every day widening the breach between his ideal and his possible achievements. Every great work grows out of endless and toilsome details. The historian is years in the dim seclusion of libraries before he gives the world a new chapter in its life; the great orator works far into sleepless nights before he stands on the platform, with his fingers on the keys of human passion and sentiment; the writer denies himself even rational pleasures through laborious years, that he may enrich his thought by contact with the world's thought and put the eloquence of simplicity into his style. Grappling with small difficulties is the only training which fits one for dealing with great problems; faithful performance of small duties the only preparation for grand services; patience, fidelity, and steadfastness to-day the only seed that will make tomorrow golden with harvests of fame or usefulness. The boy who to-day is doing his 'chores' well and cheerfully is in training for the cares of empire; the mother who is to-day giving strength, time, and wealth of affection to her children, in the seclusion of her home, is making the whole world richer by her obscure ministry—is very possibly shaping the characters that are to shape the destiny of the age, and is surely building in the only material which defies decay, survives death, and declares its architecture in the fadeless light of eternity. After all has been said about the work of the artist, the poet, and the thinker, it is the mother who stands nearest God in creative power."

RESULTS.

"Work, O man, while the day lasteth! The ancient painter said that he painted for eternity. The humblest worker in this world is working for eternity, whether he thinketh of it or not. There is something grand in the heroism of the great worker. No mind but that of God can tell the full result of his agency in the universe. It may go on in its unforeseen consequences forever and forever. Good men, martyred ages ago for their good works on the earth, are still extant, leading on the human race. *Omnia vincit labor*—'Labor overcomes all things.' St. Paul was never more alive and powerful on the earth than he is at this hour. Galileo, Newton, Bacon, are still living an ever-widening life. Luther, Calvin, and Wesley have only begun their lives. Death has not power over them: they still live and labor in the spirit among men, are still exerting influence upon the interests of the world. But these are great examples; let them not discourage humble workers. Do what thy hand findeth to do, and thou shalt do well, and the divine

Master will see that thy labor shall not be in vain. If you turn one soul to righteousness you shall achieve a greater deed than the creation of a world—than the creation of a material universe. You, the anxious mother, training your little household flock, may be preparing a choir for heaven; you, the plodding, ill-paid school-teacher, may be preparing constellations for the eternal skies; you, the village pastor, may be leading up a circle to encompass the throne of God; you, the sufferer, apparently laid aside from all activity to languish on a sick-bed, even you may be ministering by patient endurance the highest lessons to all around you; and you who know not what to do, who sometimes think that God has not found you to be worthy or fitted for any good activity, even you may bear in mind Milton's wise saying, 'They also serve who only stand and wait.' The humblest lot in life may thus be consecrated. Every life should have an aim, and it should be as high as heaven."—*Christian Labor, by Dr. Abel Stevens.*

CHAPTER XXIV.
LOYALTY TO YOUR OWN CHURCH.

THE fact that you are a member of the Methodist Church implies that you *prefer* her doctrines, government, and usages to those of any other Church. In the bosom of this Church you get your spiritual food, and within her borders lies the field of your usefulness; she is your spiritual mother, and claims you as a loyal and dutiful son. By voluntary vows you have obligated yourself to be faithful to all her interests. In her communion your family and kindred live; in her communion perhaps a mother or father died, and passed away to the better world. Your Church has a splendid history in the past, a present influential prominence among other gospel Churches, and golden prospects for future usefulness. Let the following beautiful lines express your love and devotion:

> Beyond my highest joys
>   I prize her heavenly ways;
> Her sweet communion, solemn vows,
>   Her hymns of love and praise.
> For her my tears shall fall,
>   For her my prayers ascend,
> To her my cares and toils be given,
>   Till toils and cares shall end.

This membership entitles you to the sacred ordinances of Christ's Church, to the spiritual benefits of pastoral care, and all the means of grace to fit and prepare you for heaven. You see, then, that it is an exalted privilege to be associated with the people of God. You are hereby introduced into the royal family of God—a family composed of patriarchs and prophets, "all of whom resemble the children of a king." Being a member of this royal family, it is expected that you walk and be worthy of this high vocation, that you seek in all laudable ways to promote the prosperity of the Church, cheerfully sharing her burdens, and coöperating harmoniously with all her movements.

If a Church has the right to live at all, it has the right of living on the highest plane of prosperity. The faith that carries us into a Church ought to lead us to consecrate ourselves to promote its welfare. The highest stamp of Christianity, therefore, is altogether consistent with the warmest denominational zeal and activity. If "Methodism is Christianity in earnest," then to be devoted to Methodism is to be consecrated to Christianity. Supreme loyalty to one's Church does not imply, by any means, sectarian narrowness. A decided preference for your own home is not to be construed into any dislike toward your neighbor's home. The consecration of a man to his store, farm, trade, or profession is not to be taken as any hostility toward anybody else's business. The fact is, the hope of evangelizing the world lies in the Methodist being devoted to his Church, the Baptist to his Church, the Presbyterian to his Church, and so with others. Good-will toward all others, but supreme loyalty to your own Church, is the true principle. A fault of too many Methodists is that false kind of liberalism which patronizes the interests of others, to the neglect and pecuniary damage of its own. Let us now proceed to show:

1. Loyalty to the Methodist Church requires her members to send their children to her schools. Mr. Wesley emphasized "the duty of the Church to maintain schools which are Christian in their character and influence." This implies the duty of the Church to project, organize, and establish academies, colleges, and universities. But if it is the duty of the Methodist Church to establish such schools at the expense of heavy outlays of money and men as teachers, then a corresponding duty rests upon Methodist people to patronize these schools. This is perfectly clear. The obligation is mutual; because the establishment of the schools is a complete failure without the patronage of the people. And when Methodists

turn aside from the educational institutions of their own Church, and send their children to the schools of other Churches, they plainly betray disloyalty to the Church of their own adoption.

2. Loyalty requires you to worship in the Methodist Church in preference to others. There may be another Church nearer than yours, more attractive—with better singing and preaching—yet loyalty requires you to attend the services of your own Church. You have joined this Church, taken the vow to attend her ordinances—her doctrines, songs, prayers, all are best calculated to edify, to bless, and to nourish the spiritual life of your soul. Your seat should always be filled in your own church. Your duty requires it, and your pastor expects it. It is all right and proper to attend services in other churches when your own is closed. But to divide up your attendance, running to this or that church while yours is open, breaks the force of your denominational loyalty, mars the beauty of your example, diminishes the influence of your own Church in that community. What would you think of a man who neglects his own family and runs around to attend to the business of other people? The soldier that is worth any thing stands at his own post of duty, marches under his own flag, and fights in his own company; but the soldier who deserts his company, and spends his time running around hither and thither, is a dead failure. The application is easy.

3. Loyalty requires you to send your children to the Sunday-school of your own Church. It is a lamentable fact that many Methodists are sending their children to Sunday-schools of other Churches; that too while schools are open in their own Church. The

result is that Methodism loses many of her children. Owing to this neglect, many children have left the Methodist persuasion—the sons of Methodist parents are seen in other pulpits, their daughters forming centers of influence in other Churches. And so thousands of our children slip out of our hands into other communions. But if all Methodist parents would send their children to our schools, where they could be properly taught the soundness of our doctrines, the wisdom of our discipline, and utility of our government, their attachment to Methodism would remain strong and unbroken. The children of our members belong to us as rightfully as the lambs of a flock to the shepherd who owns and feeds the flock. Take the children away from any Church and its hope of future prosperity is gone. That orchard, however fruitful it may be now, is doomed to utter extinction whose scions are plucked and planted in another. That farm is doomed to barrenness whose seed-corn is borne away. And what seed-corn is to the harvest of the field, children are to the future prosperity of your Church. To send your children, then, to other Sunday-schools is to sap the very foundation of your Church.

4. A loyal Methodist will patronize Methodist literature. Every member of the Church should avail himself of whatever makes him wise and useful. Every good Methodist ought to have the Discipline of his Church. It contains not only a brief statement of the doctrine, but the General Rules, the Ritual, the temporal economy, and much other matter necessary for Methodists to know. A knowledge of the Discipline is indispensable to a member of the Meth-

odist Church. The Methodist Hymn-book is also a necessity. A Bible, a Discipline, and a Hymn-book are to be possessed and well used by every Methodist. And hundreds of other valuable books, such as Clarke's Commentary, Watson's Theological Institutes, Wesley's Sermons, Fletcher's Checks, etc., should be found in the libraries of Methodists. Nothing costing no more is so valuable as good books. Franklin says: "When a boy I read a little book entitled 'Essays to Do Good,' by Cotton Mather. It was tattered and torn, and several leaves were missing, but the remainder gave me such a turn of thinking as to have an influence on my conduct through life; and if I have been a useful citizen, the public owes all the advantage to that little book." Books suggest ideas and produce thoughts, and living thoughts revolutionize nations. Buy good books and read them. One half hour devoted each day to reading will conduct you through the Bible—the largest and best book—in less than a year; it will acquaint you with one good work on theology, one on philosophy, one on geology, and others on history, biography, and travels, besides much miscellaneous reading, in the same brief period; if continued from year to year, it will secure to you all the requisite qualifications for all the ordinary requirements of business, religious, and social life.

Every Methodist should take a religious journal representing the views of his Church. It is the poor man's library, the rich man's monitor, the honest counselor of the young, the companion of the aged, the consoler of the troubled, the comforter of the sorrowing, the recorder of blessed spiritual births, and still more blessed spiritual deaths. It is the defender of the doctrines of the Church, and of the Holy Bible as God's word, the preacher of glad tidings, and the encyclopedia of vital and saving truth.

The Glory of Methodism

Methodism as Seen by Others.
(From the Christian Union, 1873.)

When that eccentric Pennsylvania-Dutch Methodist preacher, Jacob Gruber, was once badgering a Catholic priest, the latter twitted him with the youthfulness of Methodism. "Your Church," he said, "is not yet a hundred years old, while ours, according to Protestant count, is at least fifteen hundred years old." "Fifteen hundred years old!" exclaimed the other, in broken English. "Why, that's the reason she's so blind!" The retort was worth as much perhaps as the argument, but we have revived the story to say that Methodism can no longer be accused of lacking the age of a century. The Methodist Church has now three times kept a hundredth anniversary. In 1839 there was the famous centenary in England and America of Wesley's first Conference; in 1866, the hundreth year after the founding of Methodism in New York was made the occasion of liberal contributions to Church objects; and now we have just had in Philadelphia the celebration of the hundreth anniversary of the meeting of the first Conference in this country — the starting-point of organized Methodism in America.

Considering what Methodism has come to be in one century of growth, we are not surprised that the denomination should indulge in self-gratulation. A hundred years is a short period in the life of a great religious movement. A centennial is like the first return of a baby's birthday—it is the beginning of reckonings. And when the youngest of religious denominations finds that in its first hundred years it has outstripped all its fellows with the odds against it, a little bit of rejoicing, and even of exultation, is natural enough. It will be strange indeed if Methodists do not yet find another hundreth anniversary to celebrate.

Numerical increase is by no means the only criterion by which the success of a religious movement is to be judged, nor is it the chief; but it is one element of success, and in the order of time it is the first element. In religious work, as in every thing else, the hare must be caught before it can possibly be cooked. And in this light we may see what an opportunity the Methodist Church has made for its second century. With more communicants than any other religious body in America, the influence which it may exert upon the religious life and intellectual progress of the nation is simply incalculable.

But the true glory of the first century of Methodism in America lies not in the three million of adherents attracted to its standard so much as in what it has done for them. Early Methodism, with its zealous preachers, its vehement oratory, its pathetic melodies, its unconventional services, its democratic social meetings, boldly laid hold upon the working masses of the country. It hesitated not to go to those who were at the bottom of society as regards wealth, culture, and morals. It is the glory of Methodism that her early converts were largely from the poor and the illiterate, and not rarely from the wicked. Out of this material the earnest type of Christianity propagated by Methodism has made intelligent Christian citizens. Let the magnificent educational enterprises of the denomination and the general culture of its members bear witness to the zeal and success with which Methodism has lifted up the crude masses of people converted by the preaching of her tireless evangelists. It is the bad taste of some Methodist people to try to hide the illiteracy and poverty of the first generation of those reached by Methodist preaching. But the Church has no such laurels on her head as the glory of having labored for the lowly in the first instance, and the glory of having elevated them by her labors.

The secrets of the success of early Methodist preaching are open secrets, albeit there is little likelihood that any other body will practice the arts by which this denomination won its commanding position. A ministry that was sent and not called, that had no abiding-place, that literally left houses and homes and lands, that in most cases sacrificed even the ties of family, was a ministry to conquer the world with. Ambitions they could hardly have; there was nothing to choose. In every age of the world the successful propagandists have been noted for singleness of purpose, and entire singleness of purpose was the prominent characteristic of the itinerants whom Asbury annually redistributed throughout the country. The oratory of such men could not but have the highest elements of effectiveness—intense earnestness and perfect sincerity. Their disinterested lives commended them to every man's conscience, their isolation and separation from local entanglements gave them authority. Their chivalrous devotion to their work was contagious. They were the knights-errant of our modern days, seeking, like those who sat by Arthur's table round, to bring in the "rude beginnings of a better time." Doing battle against every sort of moral wrong, living in poverty and celibacy, and carrying with them everywhere a noble religious psalmody, they were the knights-errant, the mendicant friars, and the minne-singers of Protestantism.

It is vain to regret that the Methodism of to-day is different. It could not but be different. A mature man cannot have the elasticity of youth. The Methodist Church of to-day has set before her a task very different from that which was laid upon that little Conference in Philadelphia in 1773. They had only to throw themselves upon the enemy at every point. There were no complications. They had no baggage-train to protect, no communications to keep open. The Methodist Church is now in possession. She must guard as well as attack, develop as well as plant. To every religious movement there comes the blade, the stalk, the ear. The development of each period is different from that of all others. It is not for the Methodist Church of the future to attempt to do over again the work of the past, but to build wisely upon the foundations already laid.

Such a past ought to be an inspiration. To have furnished the world the most fearless, self-denying, and devoted ministry of modern times, to have produced the most compact organization of Protestantism, to have developed the finest congregational singing in the world, to have won the poor, the unlearned, and the wicked to the gospel, to have set the noblest example of fervor and freedom in worship and of zeal and self-denial in life, and to have grown to be the largest of American Protestant bodies, is enough to make one century glorious. But if the higher and more difficult work set before the Methodist Church of our day shall be performed in the same spirit, and with like success, the second century of Methodism in America may outshine the first.

APPENDIX.

World-wide View of Methodism.

METHODISM IN THE UNITED STATES.
(*Methodist Year-book.*)

STATISTICAL SUMMARIES OF THE METHODIST EPISCOPAL CHURCH (NORTH).
July 1, 1882.

	1882.	1881.	Increase.
Number of Annual Conferences	99	96	3
Number of missions (not included in Conf's).	13	16	d.3
Number of bishops	11	12	d.1
Number of itinerant preachers	12,552	12,142	410
Number of local preachers	12,106	12,323	d.217
Total number of preachers	24,658	24,465	193
Lay members on probation	172,468	164,538	7,930
Lay members in full connection	1,551,952	1,553,029	d.1,077
Total lay members	1,724,420	1,717,567	6,853
Total ministers and members	1,736,983	1,729,722	7,261
Number of churches	17,935	17,656	279
Number of parsonages	6,150	5,877	273
Value of churches	$66,405,568	$63,700,774	$2,704,794
Value of parsonages	$ 9,021,034	$ 8,710,297	$ 310,737
Total value of churches and parsonages	$75,426,602	$72,411,071	$3,015,531
Number of Sunday-schools	20,894	21,100	d.206
Number of S. S. officers and teachers	222,803	219,262	3,001
Number of Sunday-school scholars	1,608,836	1,592,062	16,774
Number of officers, teachers, and scholars	1,831,699	1,811,324	20,375
Deaths of ministers during the year	174	147	27
Deaths of lay members during the year	22,970	21,671	1,299
Total deaths during the year	23,144	21,818	1,326
Number of presiding elders	446	445	1
Number of mission superintendents	13	16	d.3
Number of pastoral charges left to be suppl'd.	1,602		
Number of local preachers stat'n'd as pastors	1,593		
Average number of deaths per week			445
Average number of deaths per day			63
Average weekly net increase of ministers			8
Number of adult baptisms during the year ending July 1, 1881			51,067
Number of infant baptisms during the year			55,703
Total number of baptisms			106,770

Average number of baptisms per week 2,053
Average number of new Sunday-schools organized per week 4
Average number of new churches dedicated each week 5
Average number of new parsonages per week 5

ANNUAL CONFERENCE COLLECTIONS.
For Year Ending July 1, 1882.

	Collected.	Increase.
For Conference claimants	$161,280	$16,202 47
For Parent Missionary Society	594,452	72,658 30
For Woman's Foreign Missionary Society	99,012	13,921 87
For Board of Church Extension	101,266	13,273 35
For Tract Society	14,763	1,604 24
For Sunday-school Union	16,272	d.2,673 33
For Freedmen's Aid Society	49,051	4,126 39
For Educational Fund	40,254	d.4,843 31
For American Bible Society	27,507	506 93
Total	$1,103,857	$214,777 91

The above sums embrace only the Connectional collections reported at the Annual Conference sessions, and *not the totals contributed by the whole Church* for the several causes during the year. Four of the societies named above (Parent Missionary Society, Woman's Foreign Missionary Society, Board of Church Extension, and Board of Education) report for the year ending in 1881, receipts, *additional to the above*, amounting to $201,493.41. Adding this to the total sum reported to the Conference sessions gives a grand total of $1,305,350.41.

METHODIST EPISCOPAL CHURCH, SOUTH.
(*General Minutes, 1883.*)

SUMMARY OF STATISTICS.

	1883.	1882.	Increase.
Traveling preachers	3,863	3,736	127
Superannuated preachers	313	309	4
Local preachers	3,736	5,869	23
White members	888,094	861,244	26,850
Colored members	1,255	1,030	225
Indian members	4,783	5,111	28
Total preachers and members	904,248	877,299	26,949
Infants baptized	29,232	27,205	2,027

	1883.	1882.	Increase.
Adults baptized	43,994	38,832	5,161
Sunday-schools	9,875	9,649	226
Sunday-school teachers	65,574	65,198	376
Sunday-school scholars	509,934	483,426	26,508
Collections for Conference claimants	$ 87,146 07	$ 81,432 82	$ 5,713 25
Collections for Missions	227,640 38	207,759 06	19,881 32

CONNECTIONAL OFFICERS OF THE METHODIST EPISCOPAL CHURCH, SOUTH.

BISHOPS.

H. H. KAVANAUGH, residence, Louisville, Ky.
GEORGE F. PIERCE, residence, Sparta, Ga.
H. N. McTYEIRE, residence, Nashville, Tenn.
JOHN C. KEENER, residence, New Orleans, La.
A. W. WILSON, residence, Baltimore, Md.
LINUS PARKER, residence, New Orleans, La.
J. C. GRANBERY, residence, Richmond, Va.
R. K. HARGROVE, residence, Nashville, Tenn.

Missionary Secretary, R. A. YOUNG, D.D., Nashville, Tenn.
Treasurer of Board of Missions, D. C. KELLEY, D.D., Nashville, Tenn.
Book Agent, J. B. McFERRIN, D.D., Nashville, Tenn.
Editor of Sunday-school Publications, W. G. E. CUNNYNGHAM, D.D.; Assistant, J. A. LYONS, Nashville, Tenn.
Editor of Nashville Christian Advocate, O. P. FITZGERALD, D.D., Nashville, Tenn.
Book Editor, W. P. HARRISON, D.D., Nashville, Tenn.
Secretary of Church Extension, D. MORTON, D.D., Louisville, Ky.

AMERICAN BRANCHES OF METHODISM.

While the growth of Methodism has been rapid and constant, yet there has been internal dissatisfaction enough to produce several secessions and separations. The first secession took place in 1792. The leader was James O'Kelly; the Church was called the "Republican Methodist Church," afterward called the "Christian Church." The cause of the secession was dissatisfaction with the appointments of the Bishop. It reduced the ministry to an equality of authority, and elected all of its officers by the popular vote. It was largely a failure.

AFRICAN M. E. BETHEL CHURCH.—It began in 1792, but was not fully organized till 1816. The cause of its organization was to get rid of a mixed congregation in public worship. It is Methodist Episcopal in every thing, except it rejects the office of presiding elder. It reports 9 bishops, and 321,004 members. They have a publishing house in Philadelphia, publish a weekly paper, and support a college in Ohio.

UNITED BRETHREN CHURCH.—It was founded by P W Otterbein, a useful preacher, at Baltimore. The first Conference, composed of 13 ministers and laymen, was held in 1800. In 1882 it had 5 bishops, 47 Annual Conferences, 2,196 ministers, 159,547 lay members, and 150,141 Sunday-school scholars.

THE EVANGELICAL ASSOCIATION. — Organized by Rev. Jacob Albright in 1800, in Eastern Pennsylvania. This Church reports 21 Annual Conferences, 893 itinerant ministers, 585 local preachers, 112,197 lay members.

UNION METHODIST EPISCOPAL CHURCH.—Founded in Wilmington, Delaware, in 1813. It was composed of colored members who seceded from the Methodist Episcopal Church. Its present strength is 5 Conferences, 121 preachers, and about 2,600 lay members.

AFRICAN M. E. ZION CHURCH.—Organized in New York in 1819, by colored members who withdrew from the Methodist Episcopal Church. It reports 7 bishops, 1,500 itinerant preachers, 2,600 local preachers, and about 300,000 lay members.

METHODIST PROTESTANT CHURCH. — Organized in

Baltimore, 1830. Its doctrines and usages same as Episcopal Methodists, the difference being in Church government. They reject presiding elders and bishops. Each Annual Conference elects its president for the year, who, together with a chosen committee, makes the appointments of the preachers. It reports 1,314 traveling ministers, 925 local preachers, 121,716 lay members.

FREE METHODISTS.—Chiefly in Western New York, Illinois, and Michigan. They report about 90 preachers and 14,000 members.

COLORED METHODIST EPISCOPAL CHURCH.—Organized since the late war, under the direction of the M. E. Church, South. It reports 125,000 members.

AMERICAN WESLEYANS.—Organized in the State of New York in 1842. They took high ground against slavery. They discard all bishops and presiding elders, supplying their places by presidents of Conferences, stationary committees, and chairmen of districts. Doctrinally they are Methodistic. Number about 26,000.

CONGREGATIONAL METHODISTS.—They are Methodist in doctrine and usage, but are Congregational in Church government; number only about 20,000 members.

INDEPENDENT METHODISTS.—Organized 1819 by a Mr. Stilwell, who became dissatisfied with the Church order and appointments. It reports 2,574 members.

DENOMINATIONAL STATISTICS OF UNITED STATES.

Total Methodists in United States	4,020,672
Methodist population in United States	18,345,000
Methodist members in the world	5,178,528
Methodist population in the world	25,345,545

Regular Baptists	2,102,085
Free-will Baptists	75,685
Anti-Mission Baptists	40,000
Six Principles Baptists	2,000
The German Baptists	100,000
The Seventh-day Baptists	7,446
Total Baptists in United States	2,394,742
Baptists in the world	2,914.214
Presbyterian Church	600,605
Southern Presbyterians	127,017
United Presbyterians	84,573
Cumberland Presbyterians	111,855
Reformed Synod Presbyterians	10,093
General Synod Presbyterians	5,750
Associated Reformed Presbyterians	6,740
Total Presbyterians in United States	916,489
Protestant Episcopal Church	344,888
Reformed Episcopal Church	10,000
Dutch Reformed Church	80,156
German Reformed Church	147,788
Church of the United Brethren	155,437
Shakers	6,000
Unitarians	30,905
Universalists	37,965
Christian Connection	57,000
Church of God	30,000
Congregationalists	387,619
Campbellites	563,923
Evangelical Association	107,732
Evangelical Synod of the West	40,000
Friends, or Quakers	70,000
Lutherans	800,189
Menonites	50,000
Moravians	16,223
Swedenborgians	19,000
Roman Catholic population	6,143,000
Total Mormon population	110,377
Total population of the Jews	500,000

THE PRESENT STATUS OF ENGLISH METHODISM.

The original tree of Methodism, the seed of which was planted by Mr. Wesley in 1739, has grown up to be a wide-spreading and life-giving and fruitful tree of living Christianity. This original Church is called the "Wesleyan Methodist Church."

STATISTICS OF WESLEYAN METHODISM.
(*Methodist Year-book*, 1880.)

	Districts.	Circuits.	Ministers.	Lay Members.	Probationers.	Ministers and Members.
Great Britain	34	721	1,914	376,678	25,824	404,416
France	1	7	8	131		
Germany	1	25	30	2,117		
Italy	2	38	28	1,374		
Spain and Portugal	1	5	8	336		
Malta	1	1	2	100		
South Ceylon	1	44	40	2,154		
North Ceylon	1	27	27	857		
Madras District, India	1	31	22	582	10,636	97,903
Mysore District	1	16	15	560		
Calcutta District	1	6	8	143		
Lucknow and Benares District	1	5	6	64		
Canton District, China	1	4	10	179		
Wuchang District, China	1	3	8	174		
South Africa	7	111	114	18,288		
Western Africa	3	53	45	13,047		
West Indies	7	72	108	46,082		
Total	65	1,169	2,393	463,466	36,460	502,319

Sunday-schools in Great Britain	6,376
Sunday-school teachers and officers	119,911
Sunday-school scholars	787,143
Volumes in libraries	744,293
Expenses of Sunday-schools	$332,870
Wesleyan day-schools	851
Scholars in day-schools	179,900
Expenses of Wesleyan day-schools	$1,088,645

The British Conference collections in 1879 for Connectional Funds reached the following totals:

For Foreign Missions	$ 675,701
For Home Missions and Contingent Fund	172,724
For Theological Institutions	49,921
For School Fund	45,946
For General Education	42,292
For Children's Fund	132,500
For Worn-out Ministers' Fund	116,194
For General Chapel Fund	49,007
Total in 1879 for Connectional Fund	$1,284,285
Raised in 1879 to relieve Church debts	$ 213,275
Paid in 1879 for new church-edifices	$1,916,220

The above is exclusive of the sum raised directly for pastors' salaries and for Thanksgiving Fund.

Thanksgiving Fund.—This great special Connectional offering was planned in 1878, and duly reported to the Conference in 1879. At first it was proposed to raise the sum of $1,000,000. This was soon raised to $1,200,000; later, to $1,500,000; and still later, fixed by the Conference at $1,575,000! On November 17, 1880, the subscriptions to the Fund had already reached the magnificent sum of $1,465,096!

THE ENGLISH BRANCHES—OFFSHOOTS FROM THE PARENT METHODIST STOCK.

WELSH CALVINISTIC METHODIST.—This branch first originated in Wales, about the time the Wesleys began to attract attention in England. Among all the secessions in the history of Methodism, this is the only one that ever occurred on *doctrinal grounds*. Their Church government is Wesleyan. They number about 119,809 members.

METHODIST NEW CONNECTION.—Organized in 1797. The cause of its organization was to give more freedom to ministers in administering the sacraments. A few brethren had previously been selected by Mr. Wesley, who were authorized to administer the sacraments. The same right was claimed by others, and Alexander Kilhom became the leader of a party which culminated in a new organization. They retain all the doctrines and usages of the Wesleyan Church, and its general polity. They have not grown very much, having only about 30,853 members.

THE PRIMITIVE METHODIST CHURCH.—This was organized in 1810. The immediate cause of its organization was the expulsion of some preachers for insubordination in their mode of conducting meetings While very earnest Christians, they refused to submit to the prescribed order of the Wesleyan Church. They preserve all the outlines of Methodist doctrine, and, like the early Methodists, they labor successfully among the poorer classes. Present membership is 182,691, and over 300,000 Sunday-school scholars.

THE BIBLE CHRISTIANS.—Organized in 1815, under the leadership of William O'Brien. Having been rebuked for various extravagances in his methods of holding religious meetings, he withdrew and organized a new Church. Its membership is 53,450.

WESLEYAN PROTESTANT METHODISTS.—This body separated from the British Conference in 1827, protesting against organs in churches, and what they called too much ministerial power. Their success is small.

THE UNITED METHODIST CHURCHES OF ENGLAND.—Organized in 1857. Present membership is 79,477

A GENERAL VIEW OF METHODISM IN OTHER LANDS.

METHODISM IN AUSTRALASIA.—The first Methodist mission was opened in Australasia in 1815. A General Conference was organized in 1875. Methodism has in that country now 423 traveling ministers, 3,763 local preachers, 65,905 lay members, an adherent population of 331,882 persons. Sunday-school scholars, 134,183.

METHODISM IN FRANCE.—Societies first formed in 1790. A French Conference organized in 1852. The working force of Methodism in that country now is 29 traveling ministers, 92 local preachers, 16 evangelists, Sunday-school scholars 2,552, adherents 10,622.

METHODISM IN SWEDEN.—The Methodist Episcopal Church began its work in that country in 1854. It has there 61 native traveling preachers, 75 local preachers, 7,824 lay members, 6,436 Sunday-school scholars.

METHODISM IN NORWAY.—The Methodist Episcopal Church began to organize in this country in 1876. It reports now 27 circuits, 32 preachers, 2,997 lay members, 2,285 Sunday-school scholars.

METHODISM IN GERMANY.—The first Methodist society organized in 1830. The Methodist Episcopal Church commenced its work there in 1849. That Church reports as having in that country 69 traveling ministers, 59 local preachers, 11,812 lay members, 18,716 Sunday-school scholars. The English Wesleyans have in Germany 25 pastoral charges, and 2,117 lay members.

METHODISM IN DENMARK.—The first mission established in 1858. There are now in that country 4 ministers, 712 lay members, 696 Sunday-school scholars.

METHODISM IN ITALY.—Methodism first introduced in 1852. Methodist Episcopal Church began there in 1872; the Wesleyans in 1879. There were in Italy in 1879 48 Methodist preachers, 2,932 lay members, 44 churches, two of which are in Rome, and three in Naples.

METHODISM IN INDIA.— The British Wesleyans opened a mission in Ceylon in 1813, and in India proper in 1817. Wesleyan statistics are, 112 preachers, 10,636 lay members. The Methodist Episcopal Church planted missions in India 1856. That Church has now 2 Annual Conferences, 6 districts, 46 preachers, 4,687 lay members, 38 churches, 7,097 Sunday-school scholars.

METHODISM IN JAPAN.—The Methodist Episcopal Church organized a mission in Japan in 1873. Statistics: 8 missionaries, 5 assistant missionaries, 40 native helpers, 5 lady missionaries, with 5 native assistants, 620 lay members, 773 Sunday-school scholars. The Methodist Church in Canada has also a prosperous mission in Japan.

METHODISM IN CHINA.—The Methodist Episcopal Church began missionary work in China in 1847 The Methodist Episcopal Church, South, opened missions here in 1848, the British Wesleyans in 1852, the Methodist New Connection in 1872. Statistics: In 1879 the Methodist Episcopal Church reported 3 missions (viz., Foochow, Central China, and North China), with 25 American missionaries and 12 assistants, 86 native preachers, 12 Bible-women, 2,370 lay members and probationers, 266 baptized children, 25 day-schools with 370 pupils, 53 Sunday-schools with 907 pupils, 59 chapels and 18 parsonages valued at $54,901. In

1880 the British Wesleyan Church reported 2 districts (Canton and Wuchang) and 6 circuits with 19 preachers and 353 full members. The Methodist Episcopal Church, South, reports 24 preachers, 126 members, 383 Sunday-school scholars, and 33 teachers.

METHODISM IN AFRICA.—The British Wesleyans sent their first missionaries to Sierra Leone in 1811, and to South Africa in 1814. In 1880 the Minutes of that Church reported a total of 7 districts, 111 circuits, 114 preachers, and 31,935 full members. The Methodist Episcopal Church organized its work in Liberia in 1833. The Liberia Conference returns of 1879 show 4 districts, 18 preachers, 47 local preachers, 2,110 lay members, 29 churches and 3 parsonages valued at $22,925, 30 Sunday-schools with 221 teachers and 1,560 scholars. The United Methodist Free Churches have also a flourishing mission work in Africa, but the recent statistics are not in hand.

METHODISM IN MEXICO.—Under the appointment of the Methodist Episcopal Church, the Rev. Dr. William Butler organized the mission work in the City of Mexico in the spring of 1873. In the same year the Methodist Episcopal Church, South, entered the same field, the early work being supervised by Bishop Keener. In 1879 the Methodist Episcopal statistical summaries were as follows: 6 missionaries, 6 assistant missionaries, 4 missionaries of Women's Foreign Missionary Society assisted by 4 Bible-women, 12 missionary teachers, 13 Mexican preachers, 544 lay members, 70 pupils of orphan school, 24 day-school teachers, with 473 scholars, 33 Sunday-school teachers with 479 scholars, 7 theological students, 5 churches owned by the mission, 14 other preaching-halls, 5 parsonages, value of Church-property $94,400, collections during the year $4,253. The Methodist Episcopal Church, South, reports 65 preachers, 1,419 members, 830 Sunday-school scholars.

METHODISM IN SOUTH AMERICA.—The first Methodist Church was planted in Buenos Ayres, in 1835, by Rev. F. E. Pitts. There are now three principal missions, viz.: at Buenos Ayres, Montevideo, and Rosario. The latest summaries show 3 missionaries and 3 assistants, 6 missionaries sent by the Women's Foreign Missionary Society. There were also 3 native preachers and 6 local preachers, 693 lay members, 3 churches and 1 parsonage valued at $61,000, 12 Sunday-schools with 58 officers and teachers and 770 scholars. In 1879 the Rev. William Taylor visited the western coast of South America, and opened schools and missions in several of the principal towns in Peru and Chili, and a year later repeated this work in Brazil. The Methodist Episcopal Church, South, has 8 preachers, 113 members, 120 Sunday-school scholars, 20 teachers.

METHODISM IN CANADA.—In 1828 the Methodist Episcopal Church in Canada organized in a separate jurisdiction from the Church in the United States. The Canada Wesleyan Conference in 1833 changed its polity and became affiliated with the British Wesleyan Conference. In 1874, by a union of the Wesleyan and New Connection Conferences with the Wesleyan Conference of Eastern British America, the Methodist Church of Canada was organized. The statistics of 1880 show 6 Annual Conferences with a total of 1,182 traveling ministers, 861 circuits, 122,627 lay members, 3,486 preaching-places.

www.ingramcontent.com/pod-product-compliance
Lightning Source LLC
Chambersburg PA
CBHW031853220426
43663CB00006B/609